The management of change

The management of change

Douglas C. Basil
Graduate School of Business, University of Southern California

Curtis W. Cook
School of Business, Southern Illinois University, Edwardsville

London · New York · St Louis · San Francisco · Auckland · Düssel-
dorf · Johannesburg · Kuala Lumpur · Mexico · Montreal · New
Delhi · Panama · Paris · São Paulo · Singapore · Sydney · Tokyo ·
Toronto

Published by

McGraw-Hill Book Company (UK) Limited
MAIDENHEAD · BERKSHIRE · ENGLAND

Library of Congress Cataloging in Publication Data

Basil, Douglas Constantine, 1923-
The management of change.

(McGraw-Hill European series in management)
Bibliography : p.
1. Organizational change.   2. Social change.
3. Technological innovations—Social aspects.
4. Management. I. Cook, Curtis W., joint author.
II. Title.

HD31.B3694348   658.4'06   73-10929

ISBN 0-07-084440-2

PRINTED IN GREAT BRITAIN

Contents

Part 3 STRATEGIES FOR CHANGE RESPONSIVENESS

Preface

Change is readily apparent but its magnitude and consequences are relatively unknown. The worker in a Volkswagen plant in Germany finds himself a victim of Japan's drive for greater exports of Toyotas and Datsuns, of the success of the Ford Pinto in the United States, and of his own country's revaluation of its currency. Small French shops are closed by the tens of thousands as the United States model of supermarkets and shopping centres bring more plentiful and cheaper foodstuffs to the French consumer. Containerized ships bound for the United Kingdom are offloaded in Rotterdam and Antwerp when British dockworkers demand that the containers be treated like any other cargo and therefore be packed and unpacked on the docks.

The dysfunctions of change are primarily caused by inadequate environmental scanning, the lack of change responsiveness in organizations, or utilization of a crisis-change model. Society and its institutions are faced with a need to manage change and not merely to react to change.

Management of Change consists of three parts: origins of change, transitional responses to change, and strategies for change responsiveness. Origins of change—structural–institutional, technological, and social–behavioural—once identified, allow the prediction of the rate, direction, and magnitude of change. Specific predictions such as the GNP of the United Kingdom or the net trade between EEC countries in 1985 are not the province of this work. Prediction failures of forecasts just a few years old point to the temporal value of such data. Instead, the accent is on the classification and categorization of change as the first step toward more effective change management.

An example is to project the effect of such a change as television, which has had such far-reaching consequences, even to changing the abilities of a pre-school child. This was categorized as a type I change which would impact widely and with great magnitude on all of society's institutions. But colour television, perhaps an even greater technological breakthrough from a scientific point of view, had little impact on society's institutions compared to its black and white predecessor.

Transitional responses to change, the second part of the book, deals with how nations, institutions, organizations, and individuals have developed change responsiveness by the 'seventies. Such transitional responses as decentralization and organization development are measured against the motivational patterns of man and the coordination needs of organizations.

The final part is prescriptive—how can society and man deal with and manage change? The requirements for a change-responsive model are built upon the diagnostic conclusions of the first two parts of the framework to develop change-responsive strategies. Since man, his institutions and society as a whole must survive in and adapt to environmental states, considerable attention is paid to the development of such concepts as environmental scanning and vector analysis. The need for creation of change agents, and the differentiation of strategies for twentieth-century and twenty-first-century man are well recognized at this point in the development of change responsiveness. The major issue is how to develop an independent man rather than a dependent man. As man becomes more adaptive, so also will his organizations and institutions become more adaptive and change responsive.

Part 1
Origins of change

The origins of change can be analysed and diagnosed in three major classifications: structural–institutional, technological, and social–behavioural. Structural–institutional change is particularly pervasive in the second half of the twentieth century with the birth of the EEC, the evolution of a Communist Bloc in Eastern Europe, the monetary crises of the 'seventies and similar world geopolitical manifestations. But perhaps even more consequential for the management of change is the altered role of government with massive tax revenues and the emergence of the welfare state and managed economies.

Technological change has proceeded at a pace totally unknown and unpredicted a few decades ago. Such major technological advances as jet aircraft and television have changed the face of the earth. But these very advances have also brought in their wake the problems of pollution and cries that technology is out of control. Future technologies may face the quantum jump which will require the infusion of vast sums of research funds by governments as well as by private corporations creating needs for new institutional forms.

Social–behavioural change is almost frightening in its manifestations and impact. Hirsute styles may be disturbing to the older generation but sabotage in a company is potentially the death knell of society. The protestant ethic may be in its last stages soon to be replaced with a social ethic. The major question for society is can its affluence and its surplus support civilization under a social ethic?

1

Institutional and structural change

Change—massive change—is impacting on all facets of society, creating new dimensions and great uncertainty. Instant television communication, jet aircraft at three times the speed of sound, rioting students, the Hippy movement, the emerging independent black nations, total government expenditures approaching 40 per cent of GNP in the United States, fringe benefits amounting to over 50 per cent of wage costs, and situations such as 20 per cent of the population of Boston, Massachusetts, on welfare—these are a few of the earth-shaking changes which have occurred in but two decades. The issue facing mankind today is how to manage such change.

Every facet of life from behavioural ethics to organizational and even national survival is undergoing change as forces external to each facet change. Three origins of change—institutional–structural, technological, and social–behavioural—are identifiable as shown in Exhibit 1.1. Each origin of change impacts on the other origins. For example, the technological breakthrough of television resulted in tremendous changes of behaviour through an extensive and immediate involvement of the average citizen in world events. The rioting of students at Berkeley in California had considerable effect in sparking the French student revolt in 1968, and the Vietnamese war deaths projected into the American family's living room resulted in a forceful citizen attempt to end the Vietnamese war.

The television technological revolution resulted not only in behavioural shifts but also in major institutional–structural changes. A new industry was created. Governments developed regulatory agencies or assumed total control of television broadcasting. New international agreements are required for satellite broadcasting, and nationally there is considerable fear that television could be used by governments or individuals for some form of brainwashing. South Africa is so apprehensive of the effect of the new media on the Afrikaans language with the potential tendency for utilizing English language programmes that it will not introduce television until 1976, over a quarter of a century after the commercial birth of television. Several reasons were advanced originally by the South African government in their suspicion of television:

> These arguments were: that communists and leftists would use television for their own purposes; that imported programs would bring about the collapse of the white man in South Africa; that television produced backward and inferior children and South Africa could not allow that to happen because its children were the leaders of the future, and it was essential that the leaders should be whites; and that television was injurious to the eyes. Basically, though, the objection to television has been that it would take Afrikaaner supporters out of their cocoons and anglicize and internationalize them. And that is why programs will be so strictly controlled. (*Los Angeles Times*, 19 November 1972, pp. 4–5)

Exhibit 1.1

Change sources and impact levels

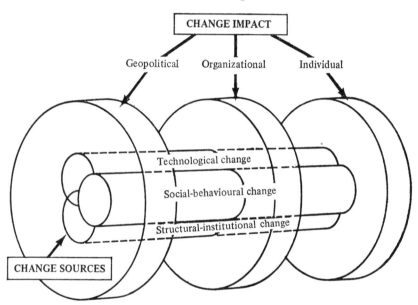

Exhibit 1.1 graphically illustrates the impact of the three change origins on the individual, on organizations, and on geopolitics. The management of change by individuals, organizations, and national and international bodies is critical to survival and health in the decades ahead. The individual who invests his most formative years in an education and his most productive years in occupational activity must build his personal competence both to survive and manage change. Organizations require flexibility in structure and appropriate strategies if they are to survive and be viable in the decades ahead. And governments, institutions, and international coordination must create the

4

appropriate environment to permit individuals and organizations to prosper and create the fruits of civilization.

An overview of change

Our emphasis is primarily on how individuals and organizations can develop appropriate strategies and structures for the effective management of change. Institutional, national and international strategies and structures impinge upon, constrain, and shape individual and organizational options and therefore must be identified. When governments directly control 30 to 40 per cent of the GNP of a highly industrialized economy such as the United Kingdom or the United States through taxation and expenditure, the impact of any

Exhibit 1.2

Average annual growth rates of real
gross domestic product expenditure

	Government (per cent)		Private (per cent)	
	1950–60	1960–9	1950–60	1960–9
All developed nations	3·0	5·0	4·0	4·9
United States	3·2	5·6	3·4	4·7
United Kingdom	0·7	2·3	2·7	2·5
France	2·5	3·3	4·6	5·7
Germany, F.R.	4·9	3·8	7·6	4·5
Sweden	4·7	5·0	2·9	4·2
Japan	1·8*	6·5	7·7*	8·8

* 1952–1960.
Source: United Nations, *Yearbook of National Accounts Statistics*, vol. II, UN, New York, 1970, 1972.

change in their policies and actions almost totally dominates society and its institutions. Any country is but the sum of its citizens and organizations, however, and therefore management of change must provide guidelines for institutional and structural change as well as for individual and organizational change.

The most pervasive change in the past few decades has been the growth of government and its changing role in society. Exhibit 1.2 notes the annual rates of growth of private versus public expenditures over the last two decades for selected countries. Since a 2·3 per cent annual growth rate accumulates to a 25 per cent total growth in 10 years, and a 7·2 per cent annual rate to 100 per cent growth for a decade, it can be seen that government expenditures generally have kept pace with or exceeded growth in the private sector. Exhibit 1.3 shows the ratio between government and private sector expenditures together with their growth over a 17-year span. For France, Germany, Sweden and

Japan, absolute government expenditures by 1969 were larger than private expenditures had been in 1953. Friedman, using the United States as an example, emphasized the scope of these changes:

> In short, active war apart, from 1789 to 1930, residents of the U.S. never spent more than about 15 per cent of their income on the expenses of government. In the past four decades, that fraction has nearly tripled and is now about 40 per cent. (Friedman, M., 1972, p. 98)

Although the arms race between the super powers, the expulsion of Asians from Uganda, and the nationalization of foreign-owned companies in Chile would seem to be evidence to the contrary, there is a growing trend toward

Exhibit 1.3

Ratio of government–private consumption expenditure

	1953	1969	17 year per cent growth* Govt.	Private
United States	32/68	32/68	154	151
United Kingdom	27/73	28/72	155	149
France	23/77	20/80	287	329
Germany, F.R.	24/76	28/72	342	472
Sweden	26/74	41/59	378	202
Japan	16/84	16/84	531	555

* Calculated on the basis of current (inflated) values.
Source: United Nations, *Yearbook of National Accounts Statistics,* vol. I, UN, New York, 1970, 1972.

internationalism in the world. The long history of animosity between Germany and France culminating in three horrendous wars in the last 100 years has been submerged and perhaps even eliminated in the European Common Market. Even a border war between El Salvador and Honduras did not terminate the embryonic Central American Common Market. The unprecedented growth of Eurodollar reserves and the declaration of the inconvertibility of the American dollar in 1971 did not end international trade. Although it may have seemed a highly nationalistic act by the United States, the result was an ever greater recognition of the importance of international cooperation and institutions.

Internationalism, and particularly the creation of the European Common Market, has created a new phenomenon in the multinational corporation. Here is an outstanding example of a symbiotic relationship where structural and institutional change created the large open market of Western Europe in which multinational corporations could prosper and grow. Interestingly enough, as Servan-Schreiber noted in *The American Challenge* (1969), it was primarily American firms which capitalized on this opportunity at first. From a management of change of view, the institutional and structural change of the creation of the European Common Market generated a major change in the business environment. The more highly competitive environment of the United States resulted in more innovative organization structures and adaptable or flexible attitudes in US-based firms than in European-based firms. This change responsiveness allowed the US-based firms to respond more quickly to the opportunities of the European Common Market.

The truly multinational firm is still more of a vision than a reality. In theory a multinational firm would (a) locate its headquarters solely in the country affording optimal taxation, stability, etc.; (b) have no national characteristics or attitudes; (c) move its manufacturing facilities to the most cost-effective sites; and (d) promote its executives without any bias as to national origin. Old traditions die hard and even multinational firms tend to have a national bias.

Managed economies exist in the majority of nations, whether highly industrialized or underdeveloped. Older economic theories of dislocations creating new opportunities over time have been replaced with Keynesian-welfare economic theories of government manipulation of the free market economy through subsidies or tax incentives. If coal mines become uneconomical in Wales, the government assumes the responsibility for relocating industry into Wales or alternatively providing subsidies to permit uneconomic coal mines to operate. The departure of the textile and shoe industry from the North-East of the United States to the South because of unsatisfactory labour practices and high wages, and the subsequent rejuvenation of the North-East by the growth of the electronics industry carries little credence in the 'seventies. Although this example proved the applicability of the older economic theories that a new equilibrium would be created and in the long run the free market system would operate, there is some question whether this temporary dislocation would be tolerated today. Drucker doubts the efficacy of governments to manage economies:

> Government has proved itself capable of doing only two things with great effectiveness. It can wage war. And it can inflate the currency. Other things it can promise but only rarely accomplish. (Drucker, 1969a, p. 217)

The welfare state is another phenomenon of the past two decades with far-reaching changes in motivation and in the attitudes of people towards work and leisure. The majority of the world is committed to the concept of full employment, and follows Keynes' advice in fiscal manipulation. But the result has been price-level instability, a country like the United States having only two budget surpluses in the last 20 years, and inflation has become a world-wide disease. Motivations have changed drastically as the incentive to work has shifted from that of survival or self-respect to indifference and apathy. Human beings are being changed from the independence of the protestant ethic to dependence on government for support of a social ethic. The welfare

B

state has modified the role of private enterprise towards more of an agency for remedying social ills than for economic production and distribution of goods and services.

Institutional rigidity to the point of a crisis-change model has crippled the ability of the private and the public sector alike to institute meaningful change and manage existing change. Outmoded legislation that airlines, railroads, and trucking firms cannot own competing modes of transportation in the United States has cost the American consumer very highly in the lack of innovation in multimodal transportation systems. The ownership of railways and airlines by governments in Europe has resulted in a cost per kilometre for air travel in Europe as much as four times the cost in the United States in the effort to force individuals to use railways. At the same time, the subsidies to French and British railways under government ownership amount to almost 1000 million dollars per year. Post offices have instituted greater price increases than private sector business, and provided less or poorer service. The United States has created innumerable new governmental agencies with resulting confusion and fantastic waste because of the institutional rigidity of existing agencies. At a time when the balance of payments is unfavourable for the United States, the American citizen abroad is prohibited from joining any form of cartel even if it is legal in another country and is taxed on the basis of citizenship rather than residence.

Organizations and individuals must operate in environments as they exist today and will exist tomorrow. Our main thrust is to identify, classify, and organize such environments. Then our task is to provide guidelines and prescriptions for organizations and individuals to manage such environments. What institutional–structural changes have taken place in the past few decades and how will they affect organizational and individual actions and strategies?

Geopolitics in a narrowing world perspective

The Swedish political economist Rudolf Kjellen coined the term *geopolitics* after the First World War to explain the dynamics of governmental politics resulting from the interaction of external economic, physical, and cultural forces with the respective internal forces. The second half of the twentieth century has been a period where no nation, small or large, is immune to the political and governmental action of other nations. The changes engendered by geopolitical pressures have resulted in cultural congruence unknown to any previous generations:

1. Television has resulted in rising aspiration levels throughout both the developed and the underdeveloped world.
2. Increasing nationalism in small, emerging nations has created turbulent environments and a return to dictatorships.

3. Small nations have far greater influence in world politics than deserved on the basis of size of country, GNP, or contribution to the world scene.

4. Any form of international war, other than civil wars, is anathema to the rest of the world, greatly limiting the options open to large powers.

5. International cooperation is increasing as common problems of pollution and depletion of the world's resources affect all mankind.

6. There is rising affluence in the developed nations and increasing poverty in the underdeveloped nations (see Exhibit 1.4).

7. Considerable action and concern by governments for the redistribution of income to level differences between economic strata is common to all industrialized nations.

Exhibit 1.4
Annual per capita national income
expressed in US dollars

	1960	*1969*
All developed market economies	1360	2480
United States	2559	4151
Europe	970	1840
France	1220	2485
Germany, F.R.	1188	2246
United Kingdom	1275	1817
Italy	644	1420
Japan	421	1396
All developing market economies	130	190
Latin America	300	460
Asia–Middle East	220	380
Africa	120	170

Source: United Nations, *Yearbook of National Accounts Statistics,* vol. II, UN, New York, 1972.

8. Massive social welfare actions are pervasive, ranging from subsidized housing to forced integration of work forces and total health care.

9. Increasing government involvement is taking place in areas normally the domain of private enterprise.

In Italy the phenomenon of the increasing impact of state intervention in the nation's economy has acquired, especially since the conclusion of World War II, a remarkable and quite special dimension. The traditional free enterprise concept that entrusted the state with the task of defence, public order maintenance and management of certain fundamental public interest services seems headed toward obsolescence to make room for a type of public enterprise that increasingly tends to enter the operational field that was once the exclusive domain of private enterprise. (*The Wall Street Journal*, 15 October 1971, p. 9)

10. Apathy and alienation of voters is characteristic of most democracies while at the same time there is a demand for ever-increasing government power and action.

11. Restrictions are placed on the freedom of action of business firms, often resulting in inefficiencies and higher costs.

12. International trade with communist nations is primarily at the whim of central government decisions and not related to actual cost–value differences.

13. Monetary crises are endemic, resulting from an over- or undervaluation of a country's currency and the lack of an effective international monetary system.

Exhibit 1.5

Geopolitical change impacts

Changes	Impacts		
Geopolitical change	*Nations (Institutions)*	*Organizations (Business firms)*	*Individuals*
International interdependence	Loss of national options to control own economies	Increasing competition and world-wide joint ventures	Loss of national independence
Population explosion and increasing poverty of have-not nations	Diversion of industrialized nations' income for have-not nation development	Opportunity for new business ventures (but with danger of nationalization)	Less affluence for richer nations
Rising aspirations and populist governments	Increasing control over all facets of society and business	Potentially hostile environment and cooperation of government and business	Loss of personal freedoms in exchange for greater security

What is the environment for the business firm and for the individual that is created by these trends and actions? Can these changes be categorized to permit firms and individuals to develop viable strategies to manage them?

Exhibit 1.5 identifies three major geopolitical change categories and their impacts on nations, organizations, and individuals. The adjustment process to geopolitical change has been less dramatic for both organizations and individuals primarily because such change has evolved slowly. It has required negotiations at the international level and considerable discussion and gestation at the national level. For example, the EEC has been slow to introduce major changes like a common currency, anti-monopoly laws, realistic agricultural policies, and political unity. The Ostpolitik accommodation of Chancellor Brandt with Eastern Europe, and the potential expansion of private-enterprise firms into the Eastern Bloc requires years of negotiation, thus permitting the opportunity for positive identification of environmental change over time.

The trend to trade between the Eastern Bloc countries and the West will increasingly result in political rather than economic decisions. An example is the United States purchase of Russian natural gas until 1985 with the Russians receiving no payment for either interest or labour in the contract:

> Politically speaking, the two powerful nations will begin to be bound together by chains of trade. The Russians presumably will be less likely to make political mischief for the U.S. in the Middle East and elsewhere. . . . That the U.S. needs gas is beyond question . . . 34·5 trillion cubic feet in the year 1980. . . . At that rate, U.S. reserves would be wiped out by the year 2000. . . . Meanwhile, the benefits to other parts of U.S. industry could be enormous. Liquefication and transportation across vast oceans will consume almost endless amounts of capital—which means a boom for U.S. capital goods industries. . . . The Soviet Union, more than Arab nations, wants and needs Western investment to develop its economy. If Arab nations cut off supplies, they lose money they are not using in the first place; if the Soviet Union cuts anybody off, it loses all hope of investment and credits from the west. (*Forbes*, 1 December 1972, pp. 25–6.)

Geopolitical change is both pervasive and difficult to manage. A simple agreement to change tariffs can mean life or death to a business firm, and perhaps unemployment or relocation to thousands of individuals.

Managed economies

The Great Depression of the 'thirties was the *coup de grâce* of free-market economies. When unemployment rates rose to 25 per cent, and the equilibrating forces of the free-market economy failed to restore even a modicum of prosperity over almost a decade, the seeds were planted for the emergence of the managed economy after the Second World War. At first governments considered that their role was to eliminate or dampen business cycles. But soon the Mezzogiorno of Southern Italy; poverty in Scotland, Wales and Northern Ireland; the death of the coal mines in the Appalachians of the United States—all seemingly regional problems—were equated with business cycles, and governments started to control the location of business. Next, concern for the control of natural monopolies or major industries took governments into ownership of means of production.

In the 'seventies, it makes little difference whether a country calls itself capitalistic, socialistic or communistic, and even whether the form of government is democratic or totalitarian from a managed-economy point of view. All have managed economies although the degree to which they are controlled and type of ownership—government or private—varies from country to country. The critical issue is not ownership of the means of production. Rather it is the extent to which economic decisions, resources, and use of income are shaped by national policies that restrict or regulate self-determination and choice. The strategies and impacts of managed change are illustrated as a continuum in Exhibit 1.6.

Concern over the environment, unemployment, price stability, distribution of income, and the ephemeral concept 'quality of life' have resulted in all nations adopting the political philosophy that individual freedom of action must be restricted to preserve the basic ideals of that society. Unfortunately, the state of the art in central planning and of the economic sciences is not sufficiently advanced to permit effective managed economies. Even in totalitarian communist countries where the power of the government can be exercised openly, central planning has been a failure. The riots in Poland over massive price increases, the total miscarriage of the great leap forward in China, and the swinging pendulum of Russian planning from centralization to decentralization are testimonies to the difficulty of total central economic planning or the totally managed economy.

The 'seventies phenomenon of unemployment coupled with fast rising price levels also testifies to the failure of managed economies in the Western democracies. But failures or not, inadequacies of current planning tools, and even attempts to reverse the process will not turn the tide against increasing government control of business and the trend toward completely managed economies. The see-saw of United Kingdom elections has merely been a matter of degree to which a managed economy is practised.

> Revolution it may well be. Heath believes that government intervention in business since World War II has eroded the discipline of the marketplace by interfering with successful companies, and, at the same time, by pampering losers. . . . By 'disengaging government from business', Heath hopes to create a tight, competitive climate, a species of industrial Darwinism that will make British companies better fit to survive—or let them die. (*Business Week*, 20 March 1971, p. 41)

Nationalization is an ultimate form of the managed economy, and has particularly plagued Britain. In some cases the motive has been that the government could operate the industry better than private enterprise, and in others to attain certain economies by the elimination of wasteful and uneconomic business practices. Transportation in the United Kingdom is a prime example with the 1933 Road and Rail Traffic Act decreeing that the government must assume control and ownership of the railways to preserve the basic concept of their use for passenger and freight movement. The Transport Act of 1947 set up the British Transport Commission (BTC) to provide 'an efficient, adequate, economical and properly integrated system of public inland transport and port facilities'.

But in reality the BTC was to protect the railways against the inroads of the trucking industry, and finally all road haulage over 40 miles was nationalized. This placed the government in the position of nationalizing some 3744

Exhibit 1.6
Strategies of managed economies and their impacts

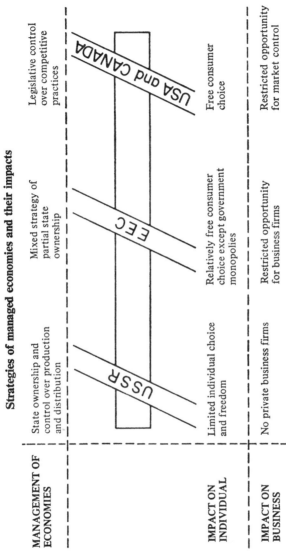

	USSR	EEC	USA and CANADA
MANAGEMENT OF ECONOMIES	State ownership and control over production and distribution	Mixed strategy of partial state ownership	Legislative control over competitive practices
IMPACT ON INDIVIDUAL	Limited individual choice and freedom	Relatively free consumer choice except government monopolies	Free consumer choice
IMPACT ON BUSINESS	No private business firms	Restricted opportunity for business firms	Restricted opportunity for market control

separate businesses with over 42 000 lorries. The end result was the doubling of private carriage freight in the next three years as the vote of dissatisfaction of private industry with the services of the nationalized railways and long-distance lorry haulage. Meanwhile the overall deficit and therefore the direct subsidy of the British railways amounted to an estimated 157 million pounds in 1968 and was trending upward.

Many arguments could be advanced in support of this particular managed economy, such as that control of trucking and diversion of freight to railways would save the United Kingdom countless millions of pounds for the building of super motorways. But unless the British government is willing to veto private car ownership (such as Denmark has done through excessive taxation), the phenomenal growth of car ownership is going to demand the construction of such super motorways, regardless of lorry transport. There are more aesthetic or ethical justifications such as air pollution, destruction of the countryside, and highway deaths. But much of the original decision was based upon economic considerations that it would be cheaper to utilize railways rather than lorries. It is in this economic realm where the private-enterprise, free-market system has proved to be the best decision maker. But even in the United States there is a strong movement among the advocates of central planning and managed economies to veto any truck transport over 500 miles.

Air transportation in Europe falls into the same category of government-managed economy actions to decide what is best for the people, not by outright interdiction but by juggling the prices or services to favour rail transport. Even the recognition by the British government in 1962 and 1968 of the failure of transportation policies and the subsequent changes to allow greater competition and fewer restrictions has not restored this casualty of a managed economy.

A similar action was taken in the United Kingdom to preserve by national-ization the coal industry in the face of declining demand and falling produc-tivity. The 1959 action to eliminate coal imports, the imposition of high tariffs on fuel oil, the forcing of the electricity generating industry in 1961 to burn six million tons of coal per year in excess of normal usage, and the order that all government agencies must use coal for heating seems more like an episode in a modern *Alice in Wonderland* than the actions of a responsible government. This might be called the Las Vegas or Monte Carlo effect since once the first bet is placed, the government is committed to backing it with continuing wagers. What has this cost the British government and the British people in resources that could have been allocated to other, more profitable enterprises? How does this forced burning of coal relate to a desire for clean air and an end to pollution?

When industrial Darwinism and free-market mechanisms are abandoned in one sector by public rather than private ownership, the floodgates are opened to all sorts of pressures by the private and public sector alike:

1. Business and labour both plead for special interest legislation to compensate them for their inefficiencies or retard the threat of competition.

2. Agriculture demands special subsidies on commodity prices, and tariffs and quotas to block the importation of cheaper foreign products.

3. The extractive industries require special depletion allowances on gravel and oil and subsidies to encourage finding more natural resources.

4. The housing industry wants subsidies for low-cost housing and the special treatment of the capital-gains tax.

5. Small businesses request subsidies to allow the retention of an outmoded way of life.

Even totally new entities like the EEC with its intricate system of subsidies to agriculture amounting to more than 6000 million dollars per year have not learned from the experience of older agencies. So-called capitalist countries are as guilty of attempting to manage economies as the most socialist and there are few success stories. Of course, government has an important role in providing the appropriate climate for the nurturing of organizations like business firms and its individual citizens. Unbridled private ownership would rape any economy and exploit individual consumers and workers. Business must be regulated and the government must protect the consumer. But the managed economies go far beyond these basic roles to manipulate resources, institutions, business firms, and the consuming public to achieve what often are badly formulated national goals.

The welfare state and institutionalized dismotivation

The old economic concept that there is no such thing as a free lunch is no longer considered as true by the general public. Government payouts in some form or other are now taken for granted and rarely is the question asked about who is going to pay for the service. Erik Brofoss, retired governor of the Bank of Norway, emphasized this point: 'It's just unbelievable what people think they can get by way of public services without paying for them.' (*Scandinavian Times*, July 1971, p. 14)

A new humanism and disenchantment with the excesses or perceived excesses of business have resulted in populist governments in democratic countries with a major thrust to equalize income distributions and end poverty and human suffering. The two strategies to achieve these new national goals have become the managed economy and its bed partner, the welfare state. In strategy formulation in the private sector, two major constraints come into immediate play: (a) the amount of resources available—or what can the organization afford; and (b) what goals can be achieved with the resources available. But governments are not subject to these constraints because they have the ability to use deficit financing and confiscate resources used for other goals; and unlike the business firm, it is difficult if not impossible for government to declare a strategy a disaster and abort a national goal. How can the United Kingdom change its unbelievably expensive National Health Scheme or the United States abort its bankrupt Social Security plan?

The humanist can decry any attempt to apply the rules of private enterprise to the actions of government and rightfully relate quality of the environment to the incidence of crime, alienation, and apathy. Not every action of government can be related to some form of economic criterion. But three factors stand out starkly in the landscape of the welfare state: (a) is man better off by the diversion of resources by the state into various forms of welfare projects; (b) is the way in which the state allocates these resources appropriate —e.g., national health schemes versus private health schemes with compulsory and in some cases subsidized insurance premiums; and (c) what is the effect of the welfare state on motivation to work or to contribute?

Scandinavia, and in particular Sweden, provides an excellent case study of the establishment of welfare states. Scandinavia has a number of advantages over other industrialized nations: (a) homogeneous populations; (b) stable political systems; (c) high level of education and general standard of living; and (d) small populations. But serious problems plague these lands of milk and honey and the welfare state. The narrowing of net income after taxes paid to skilled and unskilled workers caused an unprecedented strike of college graduates in Sweden with the ludicrous effect of armed service officers being on strike. Unemployment in Sweden equals or exceeds that of the US in 1973, but is not complicated by the technological unemployment or the minority unemployment problem of the United States. Taxation has perhaps passed the point of dismotivation where workers will not work overtime because even with higher rates of pay, the net after taxes is lower than that paid for the normal working week. But even more serious is the potential loss of personal freedoms, '. . . just as the North pioneered social welfare with individual liberty, so it now finds itself called upon to define just where welfare must end in order that liberty may still be retained!' (*Scandinavian Times*, July 1971, p. 11)

All societies face the Swedish dilemma—how far should and can the government go in regulating the lives of its citizens? This is not in the sense of the police state of the totalitarian countries but rather as a regulated state where more and more constraints must be placed on organizational and individual freedoms to provide affluence to those unable to provide it for themselves. No country is immune. The United States has defined its poverty level at 3600 dollars per year for a family of four and yet that sum exceeds the per capita income of any other country in the world (however, this is a per capita figure comparison with family income).

Special programmes of rent subsidy, negative income tax, welfare payments, and food stamps have been initiated in the United States to raise the standard

16

of living of its poor. Welfare economists justify such payments not solely in the name of humanism but also as a transfer payment of funds from the hands of those who would save the money to those who would spend the money. This creates more demand and therefore new jobs. But other economists have established that saving creates the vehicle for investments which in turn also creates new jobs.

The welfare state exists and continues to grow in size and impact. What is its impact on nations, organizations, and individuals?

1. Total taxes and therefore government spending ranges have increased drastically in industrialized countries.

2. Motivational dysfunctions have been created with welfare recipients penalized in total income by working.

Exhibit 1.7
Welfare-state changes and impacts on motivation

Welfare-state changes	National impact	Organizational motivations	Individual motivations
Guaranteed economic security for all	Increased taxation and reduction of options on resource allocation	Require government guarantees of survival regardless of economic factors	Less desire to work and greater demands on organizations for psychological satisfaction
Levelling of all incomes through redistribution of income	Assumption of total leadership role by civil servants and politicians	Lack of creativity and innovation with high dependence on government policies	Tendency to reduce motivation for self-improvement through education and development

3. Populist governments are unable to reverse the trend toward more welfare and to eliminate existing benefits.

4. More and more resource allocation decisions are made on arbitrary philosophical or political criteria and fewer on economic criteria.

5. Worker motivation is affected directly by taxes, particularly on incremental income, and produces the Monday and Friday absentee problem.

6. Worker motivation is affected indirectly by the government-dependency syndrome and its attendant 'don't care' and 'don't worry' attitude.

Although there is little question that the average citizen supports the welfare-state concept, he seems to have little confidence in its economic outcome.

Whereas every third American feels better off than four years ago and anticipates being better off four years hence, only every fourth Briton, every fifth Frenchman, every sixth Dutchman, and every eighth German

17

feels similarly embedded in a continuum of progress. The feeling of cumulative progress proved to be positively related to discretionary purchases, consumption aspirations, and expressed willingness to put in more work. (Katona *et al.*, 1971, p. 171)

If individuals have no confidence in a welfare state and seemingly reject its humanistic ideals, they will tend to join a counterculture of apathy, hostility and alienation to society's organizations and institutions. The abandonment of the sensate values of the secular, utilitarian, and pragmatic aspects of Western society for what Sorokin (1937) terms the 'ideational culture of other-worldly ideals' may spell not only society's inability to maintain its present standard of living and quality of life but also to preserve any remnants of Western culture. Perhaps the greatest impact on organizations and individuals of the welfare state is that the standard motivational factors established by organizations will have to be changed to attract members to contribute. These impacts are summarized in Exhibit 1.7.

Structural changes in society

The welfare state and managed economies have drastically altered the role of government and its impact on society and its institutions. To support its involvement in the basic structure of society, government must necessarily

Exhibit 1.8

US personal income and government spending
($1000 million, current value)

Year	Personal income	Total govt. expenditure	Federal budget outlays	National defence*
1930	77·0	11·1	3·3	—
1940	78·3	18·4	9·6	2·2
1950	227·6	60·8	43·1	14·1
1960	401·0	136·1	92·2	44·9
1970	803·6	218·9	197·9†	79·2

* The apex of defence spending was $87·4 thousand million in 1944 out of total federal outlays of $94·0 thousand million.
† 1973 figures are $250 000 million for the federal budget and $74 400 for defence.
Source: *Economic Report of the President*, USGPO, Washington, DC, 1970, 1972.

increase its share of the gross national product. This shift is dramatically portrayed in Exhibit 1.8 with almost a 1000 per cent increase in personal income and over a 2000 per cent increase in tax revenues over 40 years.

Accompanying this massive change in the government's proportion of total income of a nation has been a plethora of government agencies. For example,

Denmark has one civil servant for every 2·6 private-sector employees. This has also resulted in a major shift in relative power between government and the private sector with major imperfections introduced into the equilibrium mechanisms of the free-market system.

Meanwhile, our actual economic machine is functioning in its own way, governed by its own imperatives and without much regard for the law of supply and demand. . . . It is an intricate, complex apparatus dominated by relatively few vast organizations that 'administer' prices not in response to consumer demand but in response partly to production costs and most to

Exhibit 1.9

Shifting percentage origin of gross domestic product
in three critical economic sectors*

	Agriculture (primary)		Manufacturing (secondary)		Public service† (tertiary)	
	1950	1969	1950	1969	1950	1969
United States	7	3	29	28	29	36
United Kingdom	6	3	37	29	28	32
Germany, F.R.	10	4	39	43	20	25
Sweden	12	4	33	28	22	28
Canada	13	5	28	22	24	32
France	15	6	38	35	21	28
Japan‡	23	9	24	33	20	22

* Sectors not included are construction, transportation, utilities, wholesale and retail trade.
† Public service includes: financing and banking, insurance, real estate, business services, community services, public administration, and defence.
‡ Figures are for 1952 and 1968.
Source: United Nations, *Yearbook of National Accounts Statistics*, vol. II, UN, New York, 1969, 1972.

the imperative that has even supplanted greed as the prime driving force— the imperative of growth. (Trippett, 1972, p. 25)

Japan's involvement of its government in business has led to the term Japan, Inc.

Where citizens habitually respect authority, a powerful elite bureaucracy and a ruling party which has virtually monopolized government for a quarter of a century can insulate themselves against change for a long time. The Japanese establishment is probably the most cohesive and exclusive leadership to be found in any democracy. (Pond, 1972, p. 22)

Although Japan has always been a monolithic state, its government–business complex far surpasses that of any other democratic society. Japan's model is unlike that of other nations since it allows private enterprise with the cooperation and collusion of government to share markets and promote efficiency through arbitrated company specialization. This has resulted in fantastic economic growth with the quadrupling of GNP in the last decade, and the reduction of the farm population to 18 per cent of the total working force.

The change in government expenditures has been accompanied by a major shift in the basic economic sectors of employment from primary to secondary to tertiary as depicted in Exhibit 1.9. Agriculture has shown perhaps the most dramatic shifts with the trend to scientific, mechanized, and large-scale farming to allow less than 5 per cent of the population to produce more than enough food for a country the size of the United States. The Green Revolution increasing the yields in rice and wheat has also allowed underdeveloped nations to feed ever-increasing populations.

Exhibit 1.10
Changing economic leadership of non-communist nations

	Total Real GNP* (US $1000 million equivalents)				Per Capita GNP* (US $ equivalents)	
	Rank	1950	Rank	1969	1950	1969
United States	1	434·7	1	890·0	2854	4380
Japan	5	33·1†	2	160·4	387†	1571
Germany, F.R.	4	44·1	3	143·2	822	2369
France	3	53·2	4	137·1	1275	2724
United Kingdom	2	63·4	5	105·0	1256	1892
Italy	6	27·9	6	78·9	598	1484
Canada	7	27·1	7	69·3	1974	3286
India	8	22·6	8	47·2	63	87
Brazil	12	10·2	9	31·9	197	354
Mexico	14	8·8	10	28·0	337	572

* Stated in constant 1968 prices.
† Earliest available year for Japan is 1952.
Source: Agency for International Development, 1970.

Another major change has been in the number of employees engaged in service industries. One estimate is that 60 per cent of the United States labour force is engaged in providing services (*The Wall Street Journal*, 2 October 1972, p. 1). Although this opens up new opportunities both for companies to supply services and for individuals to obtain employment, there is concern about the effect on overall productivity and real income increases. We do not share this pessimism but rather feel that the traditional manufacturing-oriented companies will restructure service industries. For example, television repairs in the future will be done by the owner with modular components for sale in supermarkets.

The increased affluence of the average citizen in the major developed nations has been spectacular. An intriguing part of such changed affluence has been the change in economic leadership as shown in Exhibit 1.10. The discrepancies in growth rates suggest a considerable mobility in positions of economic leadership. Exhibit 1.10 reflects the significant effect which differentials in growth rates can have upon positions of absolute and per capita economic activity. In two decades, Japan rose from number five in total GNP to number two, while Britain fell from second to fifth. In less dramatic change of positions, Germany moved ahead of France while two less-developed nations, Brazil and Mexico, acquired positions formerly occupied by European nations. The emergence of Brazil and Mexico into the top ten is not totally the result of business or economic superiority but is partially a consequence of additions to their population at rates five times faster than in Europe.

Exhibit 1.10 also shows that general standards of living as suggested by per capita GNP do not necessarily correlate with total GNP, except in the case of the United States. Although Japan was the number two economic power,

Exhibit 1.11
Twenty largest multinational firms*

	Base	Sales†		Base	Sales†
General Motors	US	28·3	ITT	US	7·3
Exxon	US	18·7	Gulf Oil	US	5·9
Ford Motor	US	16·4	British Petroleum	Britain	5·2
Royal Dutch Shell	Br./Neth	12·7	Philips	Neth.	5·2
General Electric	US	9·4	Volkswagen	Germany	5·0
IBM	US	8·3	Westinghouse	US	4·6
Mobil Oil	US	8·2	DuPont	US	3·8
Chrysler	US	8·0	Siemens	Germany	3·8
Texaco	US	7·5	Imperial Chemical	Britain	3·7
Unilever	Br./Neth.	7·5	RCA	US	3·7

* Multinational defined as sales over $100 million, operations in 6 countries, and over-seas subsidiaries accounting for at least 20 per cent of assets.
† World sales in 1971 US $1000 million equivalents.
Source: *Newsweek*, 20 November 1972, p. 96.

according to per capita measure she would rank far down on the list of developed nations. Nevertheless, Japan has had a growth rate in GNP more than twice that of the other nine nations.

Although the rate of growth of the United States has declined, its global economic impact must be recognized. It produces more than one-half of the total GNP of the developed non-communist nations, consumes 35 per cent of the world's energy and over 40 per cent of the world's resources with less than 6 per cent of the world's population. The United States owns 13 of the 20 largest multinational companies as noted in Exhibit 1.11.

In terms of comparison of the United States with other countries, the following facts emerge:

1. Only 14 non-communist nations had GNP's larger than the sales of General Motors (although sales and GNP are not the same, the relative significance cannot be overlooked).

21

2. Only 7 non-communist nations had GNP's larger than the combined sales of the five top US industrial corporations.

3. The original 6 EEC nations had a total GNP of approximately two-fifths that of the US.

4. The nineteen OECD European nations had a total GNP of less than three-quarters that of the US.

The conclusions are that the United States will continue to dominate world economic activity for perhaps another decade before the expanded EEC, Japan, and perhaps the Eastern Communist nations successfully challenge the US leadership.

Exhibit 1.12

Comparative university-level enrolment (1966)

	Enrolled students 1966	Enrolment as percentage of age group 20–24 years	Percentage increase in enrolment 1962–6
United States	5 526 000	43·0	72
Russia (est.)	4 000 000	24·0	67
Canada	205 000	20·5	77
France	500 000	16·0	100
Japan	1 370 000	13·2	80
Sweden	62 000	11·0	107
Belgium	54 000	10·0	80
Germany, F.R.	280 000	7·5	27
Italy	284 000	6·9	30
England	165 000	4·8	18
Switzerland	30 000	4·8	50
India	1 700 000	3·8	—

Source: Dimitris N. Chorafas, *The Knowledge Revolution: An Analysis of the International Brain Market,* McGraw-Hill, New York, 1970, p. 89.

A major structural change has been in university enrolments and in shifts to the physical and social sciences, particularly in the United States. Servan-Schreiber noted the effect of this change:

The growing 'technological gap' between America and Europe is due primarily to a paucity of higher education, and thus a relative weakness of science and research. But it is also due to an apparent inability—stemming from a refusal to make an investment, which is precisely the word, in man— to grasp and vigorously apply *modern methods of management.* (Servan-Schreiber, 1969, p. 75)

The United States and the Common Market have roughly equivalent population size, but the United States produces approximately four times the number of college graduates as shown in Exhibit 1.12. Perhaps even more critical is that the proportion of total graduates with science degrees in the United States is over three times greater than for the Common Market countries. In absolute terms, the US has some 14 times more scientific graduates available each year.

The complexity of modern society and its institutions has resulted in a major emphasis in the United States on university programmes in business administration or the management sciences with over 12 per cent of all college students enrolled in business administration. The United Kingdom has identified this need in the Robbins report and established two major graduate schools of business studies, one in London and the other in Manchester (Skertchly, 1968).

Other European nations are establishing university-related business administration programmes but not to the degree already accomplished in the United States and the United Kingdom. The management of technology has become a pressing problem for advanced industrialized nations and the university emphasis on business administration should permit the mating of science and management to provide the genesis of innovative technology.

Comparisons of the ranking of the economic impact of industries and companies show substantial shifts as mature industries become less important and totally new industries are created. Computer and data-processing companies provide the most spectacular changes, but equally companies in the leisure fields have expanded almost beyond the imagination of the business analysts of the late 'forties and early 'fifties. However, the displacement of the conventional forms of business enterprise and the rise of more aggressive and environment-responsive firms have been equally spectacular. Supermarkets in France displaced over 40 000 small retailers in 1971, and the rise of discount department stores in the United States changed the entire pattern of retailing.

Size rankings of large firms, as reported in *Fortune* over the years, show both the difficulty of maintaining growth and surviving in a changing world:

1. From 1956 to 1970, 15 out of the top 50 US firms were displaced, and 29 of the top 100 disappeared from the list of the largest 100 firms.

2. From 1956 to 1969, 29 out of the top 50 non-US-based firms were displaced, and 32 of the top 100 fell from the ranks of the top 100 firms.

Over a longer time period the changes are very great. For example, although US Steel was the first thousand million dollar corporation and controlled about two-thirds of the total US iron and steel market at the turn of the century, 70 years later it held only 20 per cent of the domestic market. The concentration of economic wealth and power is increasingly centred in fewer companies. Mergers totalled over 6000 in 1969 in the United States alone, and by 1969, some 115 firms with combined sales over 300 000 million dollars accounted for over 37 per cent of the total GNP generated by all private business. This concentration is even more pronounced in Japan. Interestingly, there have been great concentrations of power in the past:

C

Britain's East India Co., perhaps the archetype of the modern multinational, ruled a fifth of the world's population for nearly two and a half centuries. In the 1930's, United Fruit Company (now United Brands) commanded so enormous a presence in Latin America that it could topple governments, control 4 million acres of land from Cuba to Ecuador and earn the nickname 'el pulpo' (the octopus). In Africa, Liberia was once known simply as the Firestone Republic. (*Newsweek*, 20 November 1972, pp. 96–7)

Institutional rigidities

The structural and institutional forces opposing change outnumber those supporting and creating change. Institutional rigidities abound in all nations with either a strong tendency toward the status quo or toward their particular brand of change. Government agencies are often singled out for attack because their absurdities are more likely to be exposed and often seem totally illogical. Decision criteria are likely to be totally absent or completely political in nature. But business firms too are equally guilty of change resistance even in the face of overwhelming evidence of the magnitude and force of such change. Sometimes the commitment of resources is so immense that management does not feel it can suffer the short-term losses and trauma required to reorient the firm to the forecasted change.

Economic dislocation is the price paid for both the adjustment to change and the failure to adjust to change. In the former case it means potential hardship for some sectors of society if there is anticipation of change and restructuring. In the latter case, the economic dislocation occurs when the change occurs and no restructuring has taken place to soften the blow. There seems little doubt that the change-responsive model of adjustment to change by institutions, organizations, and individuals is far less costly to society than the crisis-change model.

Government creates institutional rigidities primarily because no mechanism exists to force an institution to justify its continued existence. The people have the right on a periodic basis in a democracy to end the tenure of any politician or political party. But no such mandate exists to terminate institutions. Politically it is difficult for an elected government to eliminate institutions because of the strong vested interests supporting their continuance. Even the phasing out of a naval shipyard brings great political pressure on the government to continue an uneconomic and unnecessary institution. However, it is quite possible politically to create new agencies and institutions, usually resulting in agency duplication and confusion. The United States government created a new Department of Transportation when it was found politically infeasible to consolidate or eliminate existing agencies responsible separately for air, maritime, and surface transportation. But the ensuing jurisdictional disputes have emasculated its effectiveness.

The cry is heard for governmental reform in every nation. The weaknesses of the United States' or United Kingdom's respective congress and parliament are well known. The former has elections every two years for the House of Representatives, and California and Nevada with 20 million and 100 thousand inhabitants respectively, each have two senators. The latter has over 600 members of parliament and poor utilization of its elected representatives. Such situations as overlapping jurisdictions, confusion of city and county governments, state and the Federal governments in the United States requiring residents to complete two different sets of tax forms and remit to two governments on the same income, obsolete subsidies, and ineffective government bodies plague all nations alike. These institutional rigidities cause tremendous waste of resources. But even more importantly, they create a crisis-change model rather than change responsiveness.

Business organizations likewise have institutional rigidities, more often than not created by organizational hierarchy and a tendency to manage by crisis. General Dynamics' loss of 425 million dollars in 1961 well illustrates this organizational rigidity when indicator after indicator pointed to the inability of the company to make a profit on its entry into the commercial jet aircraft field. At one point, an engineer calculated that the cost of the purchased parts exceeded the sales price of the plane when traditionally such parts constitute about 75 per cent of the total cost. Even this did not deter management from continuing its Monte Carlo strategy. Business journals in every issue report similar if not as great failures due to organizational rigidities.

Individuals are not immune to rigidity and an entire set of literature has emerged on individual resistance to change. Individual rigidity has perhaps its greatest effect in union jurisdictional disputes and the unwillingness of unions to permit innovative practices. Dock workers in the United Kingdom, and their counterparts in other countries, have resisted containerization to the point where container ships for the United Kingdom have been diverted to Holland. Estimates of inefficiency or higher cost due to restrictive practices by unions range to as high as 50 per cent and an average of at least 25 per cent, creating a rigidity of unbelievable magnitude in their effect on society and its institutions.

Creation of turbulent environments

Structural and institutional change with its concurrent technological and social–behavioural change will create increasingly turbulent environments in the last three decades of the twentieth century. Such change impact is further complicated by the following factors:

1. **Systems effect of change**—the concept of ecosystems can be expanded to think of the spaceship earth. The past approaches of thinking rather narrowly in closed systems must give way to open systems and, perhaps, even general systems thinking. This has been emphasized by the Club of Rome:

> It started with the premise that basic factors such as food production, population growth and environmental pollution all are interrelated. Each factor, it was decided, interacts constantly with the other factors—and with itself. For instance, a growing population increases the need for land to live on, thus diminishing the amount of land available for agriculture. At the same time, the demands for food from that diminishing farmland are growing. The study points out that growth and the drain on resources take place at an exponential rate rather than an arithmetic one. (*The Wall Street Journal*, 2 October 1972, p. 16)

Ecosystems studies provide excellent models for the systems effect of change. For example, the concept of a level, atomically blasted Panama Canal would permit the predator fish from one ocean into the other with perhaps the elimination of major fishing grounds, and there is the unpredictable effect of the eight foot difference in water levels between the two oceans. The systems effect of change is as yet unpredicted, primarily because the state of the art is quite primitive. One conclusion that can be drawn, however, is that it will impact to create ever more turbulent environments in the decades ahead.

2. **Multiplicity of variables**—the multiplicity of variables, like the systems effect of change, will create the need for the development of open-system, dynamic models to predict change and the effect of change. The polluting of the Mediterranean provides an example where the cause of the pollution may be identified but its quick solution is interdicted by a multiplicity of variables interacting with one another:

> Through the Straits of Gibraltar 31,600 cubic kilometers of surface water per year flow into the Mediterranean from the North Atlantic. The water is poor in nutrients but carries oxygen. . . . In this way, there is a complete turnover of Mediterranean water every 80 years. But even the life-giving, oxygen carrying Atlantic waters now are heavily polluted. . . . To supply oxygen to its deep waters, the Mediterranean has three 'lungs': the Provencal Basin, the upper Adriatic Sea and the Aegean Sea. The transfer of oxygen to the deep waters involves a mechanism by which the oxygenated surface waters, by cooling, become more dense and sink. This cooling takes place where continental air masses flow over the water. The chill winds spill down from the Alps into the Provencal Basin and, on the other side of Italy, onto the Northern Adriatic, and onto the Aegean from the mountains of Turkey. Because the Mediterranean is an enclosed sea, anything which affects the 'lungs' affects the whole system. (*Los Angeles Times*, 24 October 1971, p. 1)

3. **Acceleration effect of structural change**—this is due primarily to an accumulation of change needs caused by a reactive adaptation to change. The

failure to provide a change-responsive structure and climate in government, institutions, and organizations will result in an acceleration effect with cumulative impact on society. This, coupled with an accelerating rate of change, particularly in the technological and behavioural spheres, may cause a major overload on the economic and social system of countries. It can be likened to the effect of the National Health Scheme in the United Kingdom where years of neglect of health needs coupled with the accelerating effect of major medical improvements and changes resulted in massive health loads on the medical services of the country.

4. **Longer-term uncertainties**—technological forecasting and its companion, social systems change forecasting, are in their infancies, with the result that in longer terms there are very great uncertainties. Will the motor car be replaced by a personal-service public transportation system? Is welfare an unending sink hole which eventually will consume all the resources of a nation? Will education be automated? On one side we have the Club of Rome and other responsible agencies depicting the end of the world's resources within 100 years. On the other, we have forecasts of new energy sources:

> The machine is a sort of perpetual motion device that may be able to provide cheap electricity for centuries to come. . . . The fast breeder reactor is named for its ability to turn what are essentially useless rocks—uranium 238—into nuclear fuel. Because it creates, or breeds more atomic fuel than it consumes, it holds promise of opening up an entirely new and almost inexhaustible source of energy. (*The Wall Street Journal*, 20 November 1972, p. 1)

Institutional and structural change has multiple impacts ranging from the elimination of the livelihood of a worker to total reorientation of society. The companion change origins—technological and social–behavioural—intermesh and interrelate with institutional and structural change to mould an environment both benign and hostile to individuals and organizations. The dimensions of such change and their impacts are the subject of the next two chapters.

2

Dimensions of technological change

The origins of change can best be analysed in three primary categories as depicted in Exhibit 2.1. These three major sources of change feed upon and

Exhibit 2.1

Major origins of change

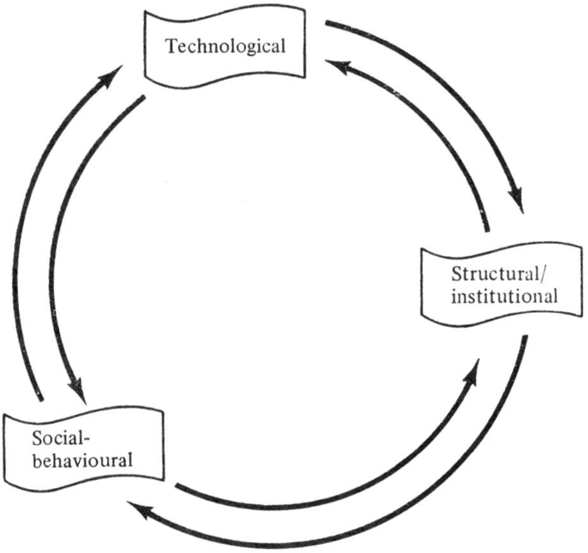

react with each other in an additive or multiplicative manner to create even greater change with an ever more pervasive effect on man, his life, his organizations, and his institutions. For example, the technological discovery and commercial intensification of television have had the following impacts.

Behaviour and social consequences

1. Rise in aspiration levels.

2. Revulsion against war.

3. Alienation and distrust of government actions and concentrated power.

4. Increased general anxiety and tension level as people feel burdened with the world's problems.

Institutional and structural consequences

1. Initial decline in cinema production and subsequent redirection.

2. Emergence of a new and powerful industry.

3. Change in advertising impact and buying habits.

4. Re-examination of freedom of the press.

It is not our purpose to speculate on the technological world of the year 2000 or beyond. We are firmly convinced that such speculations, although interesting and informative, do not provide individuals, business firms, or nations with adequate means for the analysis and management of change. Rather than catalogue and predict specific future technological changes, we prefer to categorize and examine the effects of technological innovations according to levels of impact upon society. The reader interested in comprehensive future projections can refer to Kahn and Wiener (1967) and Darling and Morris (1970).

Impact levels of technology

Technological innovations can be considered to have three levels of impact depending on their pervasiveness in the change and restructure of organizations, institutions, and society, as summarized in Exhibit 2.2. Column (1) of

Exhibit 2.2

Types of technological innovation

Col. (1)	*Col. (2)*	*Col. (3)*	*Col. (4)*	*Col. (5)*
		Potential		
Type of impact	*Identifying characteristics*	*Socio-economic consequences*	*Response implications*	*Time impact*
Primary (Type I)	Major invention and discovery	Restructures society and institutions	Pervasive opportunity	Long-term
Secondary (Type II)	Innovative breakthroughs	Enhances quality of life	Sub-system displacement	Mid-range
Tertiary (Type II)	Refinements and variation	Permits substitution and incremental choice	Localized competition	Short-run

Exhibit 2.2 classifies the types of impact. Although a particular technological change may seem at first glance to have a Type I (primary) impact, an in-depth analysis of change impact often relegates it to a Type III (tertiary) discovery. For example, a technological advance such as colour television seems

pervasive in the lives of those living in affluent societies. But when it is analysed, major technological advance that it may be from a scientific point of view, in the cold, dispassionate light of management of change it does not alter industries, institutions, or individuals in the way in which its predecessor black and white television did. Rather than having primary (Type I) impact, it has but tertiary (Type III) impact.

Few inventions have the potential to be a truly revolutionary primary Type I change. Only infrequently is a discovery, invention or innovation of such proportions that it will totally alter the character of society and modify the structure and behaviour of major institutions over the course of its development and public acceptance. To do so, the change must initiate a completely original and highly efficient method or system for performing an activity crucial to the society's functioning; and it usually takes years or decades for the full impact of a primary invention to become a reality.

Transportation technologies such as the locomotive, motor car, and aircraft or the communications development of the telegraph, telephone, radio, television, and computer are examples of primary inventions that eventually transformed or are in the process of reshaping vital processes, behaviour, and relationships within society. For example, commercial aviation has resulted in distance no longer being measured in miles or kilometres, but in units of time. Jet transportation also has altered the conduct of business, government, education, and personal pleasure, and the computer permits mathematical calculations in minutes which two decades ago would require months or years. Communication satellites, hooked to radio, telephone, and television make two-way communication only seconds away. Video records of events anywhere on earth or even between here and other celestial bodies are transmitted for instant impact on the world. A critical and almost frightening fact is that the majority of these technological advances have happened not only in the lifetime of the reader of this book but in less than half a lifetime! This is overwhelming evidence of the accelerating rate of technological change.

Characteristics and consequences

Column (2) of Exhibit 2.2 defines change characteristics resulting from different types of technology impact:

Type I (Primary)—Major invention or discovery
Type II (Secondary)—Innovative breakthrough
Type III (Tertiary)—Refinement and variation.

Prior to the Second World War, *Type I inventions* with potential primary social significance did not necessarily create threats for established business, organizations, and individuals as great as those of the post-war period. A time dimension seemed to exist which permitted organizations, individuals, and even societal change to evolve more gradually and to permit adaptation to change. It is true, however, that this time lag did not permit the growth or even survival of those organizations or societies which failed to identify primary technological change.

A number of Type I technological changes have already been discussed. A further analysis of one of them, the motor car, will help in understanding the dramatic effect of a Type I technological change. For example, the original development of the motor car only gradually replaced the horse and buggy and to a lesser extent railway and tram travel. The motor car stimulated growth of established but relatively infant industries such as rubber, petroleum, and steel. It created the motel, automotive accessories, and highway construction industries. The principle of a self-propelled vehicle even altered the conduct of war as supply logistics became more flexible and tactical vehicles such as tanks and motorized assault weapons became employed on a large scale.

Coinciding with a substantial increase in personal income, in many countries the motor car is now more of a convenience or necessity than a luxury. This widespread ownership of motor cars has stimulated a revolution in urban planning and retailing that was in full force in the United States during the 'fifties and recently has begun to alter and transform other nations. Urban extension into suburban areas has not only changed residential demands but has also precipitated development of suburban shopping centres with department stores, supermarkets, and specialist shops bounded by spacious parking lots.

Switzerland, Germany, France, Japan and Sweden began in the late 'sixties the inevitable experiment with this car-based retailing concept. Many of these regional centres, such as the Parley II, 15 miles west of Paris, have subsidiaries or affiliates of established central shops. Perhaps the slowest rate of change is in Japan, which despite its industrial efficiency, maintains the costliest and perhaps most archaic distribution system of the developed nations. In a country built on layer upon layer of wholesale distribution to service the 1·5 million small neighbourhood shops, the recent birth of 9000 supermarkets with more direct distribution methods suggests gradual reform. Europe and Japan, cultural traditions notwithstanding, will probably see food retailing, as but one example, shift from a small-scale neighbourhood base to large-scale, free-standing, and shopping-centre supermarkets within the next decade.

Type II technological changes are secondary innovative breakthroughs which add new dimensions to established technologies, often giving a boost to a primary type of invention to extend the scope of its influence or to broaden it into new directions. The development of the jet engine certainly improved the capacity of military and subsequently commercial aircraft, but it was primarily a sequential development of the Type I invention of aircraft. As commercial jetliners became operationalized in the late 'fifties and early 'sixties, the airline industry experienced a growth surge. Air travel and air cargo became more convenient and less costly because added capacity combined with faster speed and less maintenance requirements reduced direct operating costs and fares per seat- or ton-mile. Jet transportation also accelerated growth of satellite industries such as car rentals, air freight forwarding and an expanded range of airport services.

At the same time, however, displacements occurred within the aviation industry. High and risky development costs involved in converting from a piston to jet technology resulted in some shakeout of the number of firms which could successfully compete in this new secondary technology. The Convair Division of General Dynamics lost 425 million dollars in its poorly developed and loosely controlled strategy to produce its 880 series of commercial jetliner (Smith, 1963). Other firms in Europe and the United States underestimated the operational cost advantages of jet power for commercial aircraft and pursued what at the time appeared to be a safer strategy of using an intermediate technology, that of propeller turbine engines.

But because the turbo-props were introduced only two to three years before jets, the selling period was brief and sales were low. The Britannia 320 sold only 60; the Viscount 800, a much smaller aircraft, sold 145; and the Lockheed Electra managed to sell 172 before closing production (Stratford, 1967). In Europe, manufacturers began to work in concert with and fully supported by governments through the entire process of development, manufacture, and sale of aircraft. In the United States commercial development and production remained largely private and narrowed to two firms until Lockheed's attempted re-entry into the commercial market encountered financial difficulties and brought the government back into the business of administering some form of subsidies.

Similarly, the development of the transistor by Bell Laboratories of American Telephone and Telegraph in 1948 represented a secondary Type II technology affecting the communication industry. In the pioneering days of computers when vacuum tubes were still used for switches and relays, many computer experts forecast a potential computer market of possibly 100 large government agencies, firms, or research universities. But the transistor helped shatter that conservative forecast. Faster computing speeds and greater reliability were possible with transistors which made the computer more economical for a wider range of users.

Subsequent development, first of the integrated circuit by Texas Instruments in 1959 and more recently of LSI, or large-scale integration of hundreds of integrated circuits into a single tiny silicon chip, contributed to further advances in computer capacity and speed, coupled with lower output cost (Diebold, 1969; Brand, 1970). By 1970 computers were a 7300 million dollar industry with over 50 000 installations in the US and nearly 20 000 in Western Europe. But it was still the computer which was the Type I invention and the transistor the Type II, since solid state was an add-on technology to permit even greater impact and subsequent institutional dysfunctions by the computer.

Satellite industries mushroomed to service and support computer applications, and new firms emerged to develop software programming, time sharing, data transmission, and peripheral equipment to capture the potentials of the second-, third- and fourth-generation computers. American Telephone and Telegraph predicts only a doubling of telephone traffic during the 'seventies compared to an expected nine-fold data-transmission increase.

Critical scientific discoveries such as plastics, nuclear reactors and fission for energy generation, electromagnetic force fields applications, air-cushion track vehicles for an improved form of rail transportation, short-range take-off and landing aircraft, hovercraft, and computerized guidance systems for personal vehicles are of secondary or Type II impact even though they represent new technological advances. This is because they do not restructure society and its institutions. Yet their impact on business firms may make entire industries obsolete, and drastically change the cost and profit structures of individual business firms.

Type III technology, or tertiary level innovation, is the most prolific form of technological change. Yet the consequences of this type are minimal in major impact on society. From a tactical or even strategic point of view for the business firm, Type III technology permits the firm to develop new products and services for its competitive advantage. This competition through product research and development ranges from the introduction of new food and household products in an attempt to gain additional shelf space in food and convenience markets, to style and size variety in cars for the purpose of offering a complete and differentiated line, to the construction of special purpose ships such as container vessels or very large crude carriers, to improved drugs, chemicals, and products of all types.

Society can benefit by allowing the consumer greater choice and substitution between competitive products or services. But society as a whole may pay a higher cost with endless proliferation without sufficient economic justification. Private enterprise rationalizes such proliferation as satisfying psychological needs for diversity, individuality, and personal choice.

But not all Type III technology is frivolous and oriented to minor product style change. For example, IBM's 1000 million dollar plus investment in the engineering design of the System/370 can best be classified as Type III technology. IBM's fourth-generation computer, the System/370, delivers about twice as much computing for each dollar of machine cost as its seven-year-old cousin, the System/360. Such a scientific breakthrough, despite its tremendous development cost and user advantages, is really Type III technology because its addition to the aggregative impact of computers will not change society and its institutions, except in an incremental fashion.

Of course, the diffusion of computer technology has not come solely from designing larger and greater capacity machines, but also by branching the principles of computers into hundreds of specialized small-scale computing and memory devices. The next few decades will probably bring the application of electronics and computing technology into thousands of uses not even imagined today, extending even further the impact of computer technology. But even with major scientific breakthroughs such as voice-command self-programming, and unprecedented memory capacities, the impact of change is one of incremental extension.

Type III technology is not, however, risk-free and may involve sizeable research and development investments, as in the case of IBM's System/370. Another example is DuPont's Corfam, its intended substitute for the forecasted shortage of shoe leather. After an investment of 300 million dollars the company abandoned the project in 1971 because of quality and cost problems. Even a research-oriented firm like DuPont, which was responsible for adding totally new dimensions to the textile industry with its introductions of synthetic fibres beginning in 1939, was unable to manage technology without great risk and some subsequent failures.

Similarly, while the various new varieties of jet aircraft provided little additional convenience or speed for the passenger, they potentially increased the profitability of airlines by offering savings through variation in stage length or flight distance, operating performance, and payload capacity. These Type III innovations did not change society or even the airline industry. However, they resulted in an increase in risk for airlines as new aircraft were purchased at the very time when airline travel was declining due to recession in the United States, which caused temporary overcapacity.

The response implications, Column 4 of Exhibit 2.2, vary according to the stage of economic development of a country. For example, the development of a new strain of seed for agricultural purposes would be imperceptible in a developed economy except to those directly involved in that specialized area of agriculture. But such an innovation could be revolutionary to under-developed economies. Recent introductions of high-yielding rice hybrids with improved plant quality coupled with new methods of cultivation are shifting economic patterns within and among Asian nations.

Rice-poor countries such as the Philippines, India, and Ceylon, long dependent on rice imports to sustain domestic food supplies, have moved more toward self-sufficiency. The Philippines began exporting rice surpluses in 1968 for the first time in recordable history. If reform of feudal land ownership and tradition-bound cultivation practices were to accelerate, far-reaching consequences could result. With a possible glutting of the rice market and disruption of major sources of foreign exchange for the established rice-exporting nations, first-order consequences would be a realignment of economic and political relationships among the Asian nations. Secondly, peasants, no longer needed in agriculture, would be shifted into a domestic labour pool, potentially to be used as resources for industry and other institutions, making possible further productivity increases and economic growth.

34

The technological growth process

Few nations or firms have discovered the key to sustained technological development as a means for producing a greater abundance and variety of products and services. Why is there such a discrepancy, especially between countries, in levels of growth and development? What determines whether one nation will lead in technological innovation while another will lag far behind? The answer to these questions requires examination of the interrelationship between key socio-economic contributors and the national growth process. Although highly simplified, Exhibit 2.3, the wheel of progress,

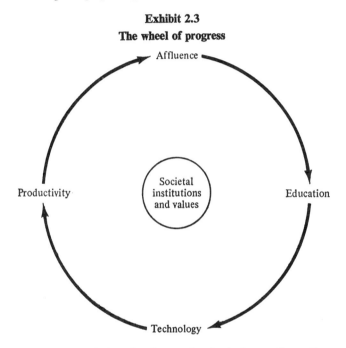

Exhibit 2.3
The wheel of progress

describes the essence of the circular, technological transformation process. By breaking into the cycle at any point, the course of events which lead to a potential for growth can be traced and analysed.

To develop technological capabilities, a society must make major investments in all levels of education. But higher levels of educational investment are dependent on growing affluence and availability of discretionary income. In turn, rising levels of real per capita income occur only as a result of increases in the productivity of human and physical resources. Finally, the expansion of productive output requires a growing base of technology as an input factor of production, and so the cycle repeats itself. But the activation of this process is dependent on a society's values, aspirations, and institutional framework. The central ideological framework of a country can (a) encourage expansion of this process, as in many of the North American and European countries, or (b) stimulate growth in selective sectors, as in the more prosperous communist nations, or (c) retard and be a detriment to technological expansion and its concomitant transformation of a socio-economic system, as is the case in most undeveloped countries.

This conceptual model can help explain the realities of the growth process. Education in the more developed Western nations has generally originated as the result of a personal-value system that views education as a route to personal and societal advancement and well-being. Barring prejudicial deterrents, the individual has been free to choose whatever route and means of education he desires within his range of cognitive, motivational, and financial capabilities. The result has been a system of primarily governmentally

Exhibit 2.4

Expenditures on education and research as a percentage of general government expenditures*

	1958	*1967*
Finland	21·9	22·4
United States	15·1	18·4
Denmark	13·7	17·4
Australia	13·4	16·4
United Kingdom	12·7	15·8
China (Taiwan)	12·6	14·7
Italy	10·9	14·2
Bolivia	8·0	11·6
Germany, F.R.	7·8	8·3

* Few countries separate educational expenditures as a separate national account item, thus the countries which do report are biased in favour of larger proportional educational expenditures.
Source: United Nations, *Yearbook of National Accounts Statistics,* Vol. 1, New York, 1969.

funded and controlled basic education coupled with mixed private and government systems at higher levels. Expenditures on education in selected nations are shown in Exhibit 2.4.

Within communist countries, particularly Russia, the decision to pursue educational investment has been largely the product of governmental policies to develop selected skills. The outcome in either case has contributed not only to populations with basic skills which enable potentially greater productive efficiency, but has more precisely led to an expanding knowledge base in highly specialized technological areas. It is through the efforts of these educated and skilled specialists that basic and applied research, which leads to still further advances in man's frontiers of knowledge, is possible.

In North America, Japan, and several of the more productive European nations, education or knowledge is not necessarily pursued as an end in itself, but rather as a means to the end of useful and practical application in developing and producing the products and processes which affect work, society, and life itself. As technological advances for new methods and equipment are utilized in factories, offices, hospitals, governments, and homes, the human resource is able to extend his effective output and become more productive. The farmer who utilizes the technology of more efficient equipment and improved seed and methods expands his capacity to produce and frees or displaces other farmers to pursue different types of jobs. Similarly, the factory worker equipped with automated machinery can produce more per hour than with labour-intensive equipment, requiring less manpower to produce the same level of output. A business-accounting department using a computer can provide more detailed control records faster than a department using non-automated methods.

The end result of the utilization of new technology is higher productivity, lower costs, or higher quality. As the use of technology diffuses throughout society, the collective productivity, as measured in GNP per capita, rises, and with it levels of income, which facilitates further expansionary investment in education and a consequent greater range of technology. This process is not, however, a simple closed-link system which evolves as a matter of routine. Quite the contrary, the process is highly turbulent and volatile and is accompanied by tremendous dislocations.

Assimilating technology to generate higher productivity may result in the displacement of large numbers of individual workers, firms and even industries. Displacement of skills, products, and organizations in turn results in major shifts of populations with the decline of some towns and cities, and the growth of others. The ramifications of technological change can stretch across continents as educated and skilled but under-utilized human resources migrate to countries where organizations will use and reward their skills. In his study of the international brain market, Chorafas pointedly recognized this fact:

> The men leaving England and the rest of Europe today are no longer mainly peasants and factory workers. They are scientists, technologists, doctors, planners, and professional men who are still proudly British, French, German, or Italian, but who have abandoned hope of proper recognition and progress in their country of origin. This is the essence of the brain drain. Migration is the reaction of disappointed men. (Chorafas, 1970, p. 14)

Technological ramifications and change

Technological research objectives include improved quality, lower costs, extended capacity, or user convenience, all of which are intended to benefit mankind. Quality, a multi-dimensional characteristic ranging from extended serviceability, reliability, precision, aesthetics, health and sanitation, to comfort and convenience, is difficult to measure. For business, technological breakthrough does not necessarily lengthen the product life cycle, since other inventions may make a product obsolete overnight. Technology cannot receive all credit or blame, because many new products are almost frivolous with package or formula changes; products have shorter lives in the 'sixties and 'seventies than in prior decades.

New technology can make existing products obsolete, producing truly lower costs, even though the initial capital outlay for new-generation hardware may be several times greater than earlier versions. The product innovation may so greatly increase speed, range, rate of output, or may so reduce variable costs such as labour and materials, that savings per unit output repay research and development cost in two or three years or less. These types of technological cost savings in computers, xerography, communications electronics, aircraft, ships, lasers, and large durable goods such as refrigerators and televisions have resulted in both a lower cost and greatly enhanced standard of living for the individuals, organizations, or nations which have a high utilization of these products.

Even if unit costs increase, the additional satisfaction or convenience may greatly outweigh the increased costs. Rental cars, disposable baby diapers, non-returnable bottles and cans of beer and soft drinks, air mail, and many similar everyday products and services may all require a higher per unit cost or charge than alternative means, but convenience and satisfaction outweigh increased costs. Technological advances, even in an industry not noted for them, have resulted in the construction contractor finding it cheaper and better to raze and destroy an old building and construct a completely new one than to remodel a technically or aesthetically obsolete structure.

Technology's main thrust is to obtain quality, cost, capacity, and convenience advantages, but its consequences for society as a whole go far beyond these relatively simple objectives. The attainment of these objectives may, and often does, impact on individual life style and economic well-being, on the birth and demise of organizations, on the standard of living of a nation, and even on world geopolitical strategies. Cars and buses have changed life styles in all the nations of the world and the very structure of cities and towns. The jet aircraft has altered even the economic income of Masai tribes in the central highlands of Kenya and Tanzania. The invention of synthetic rubber changed the economic structure of South-East Asia, and that of atomic weapons the balance of world power.

The prediction of both technological advances and the specific impact of such advances is not possible in the 'seventies with current techniques and methods. At most we might be able to do a vector analysis which will determine the direction and rate of technological change. It is for this reason that change responsiveness must be built into individual, organizational, and national strategies.

Technology has both first-order and second-order or by-product consequences. The first-order consequences are those usually programmed as the target of research and development activities. They are expected to have a direct positive bearing for the innovating organization and its immediate customers. The initial or first-order consequences diagnosed and predicted for a technological advance include (a) the expanded availability of a range of products and services, (b) substitution of capital for labour leading to higher productivity and lower costs, and (c) increases in sales or power for the innovating organization relative to competition.

By contrast, second-order consequences are usually poorly diagnosed and predicted as to the effect on (a) organizational methods, processes, or structure; (b) the initiation of changes in behaviour among customers, suppliers, employees, or society; (c) side effects on the quality of the physical environment; and (d) the stimulation of general or specific regulatory constraints enacted by governments in response to social and legal pressures. Currently many managers, scientists, economists, and politicians are prone to look only at the first-order consequences of technological innovation, with resulting dire potential dangers.

But in some instances, especially where governmental funding is involved, a systems-oriented analysis including the multiple interrelationships between first- and second-order consequences has been made. The atomic blasting of a new sea-level Panama Canal is recognized as having not only the potential hazards of atomic pollution but a major change in the ecosystems of the Atlantic and Pacific Oceans. Similarly, a major reason for termination of further development and production on the United States supersonic transport was the systems prediction of the potential effect on the upper atmosphere of exhaust pollutants, which was linked with economic infeasibility. A few commentaries on the supersonic transport by United States' Senators captures part of the flavour of both the logic and emotion behind the debate:

Senator Percy. I simply ask now, if the airlines and the manufacturers and the banks will not finance it, why then stick the customer—the taxpayer—with these enormous costs in order that a businessman might save a couple of hours, two or three times a year, when he flies to London, especially when that same businessman often cannot in less than 3 hours commuting time get from his home to work and back every single working day of the week? . . .

Senator Goldwater. The only industry in which this country leads the world is the aircraft industry. . . . Either we are going to have this airplane or someone else is going to have it. I imagine the same arguments were made when Henry Ford started to make automobiles. . . . The world someday will have SST. Not today, not tomorrow, but it is coming, just as sure as we stand here arguing about it. . . .

D

Senator Percy. Testimony by the Council on Environmental Quality raised the possibility of climatic change as a result of high-altitude exhaust emissions by a fleet of SST's. This possibility was later substantiated by a MIT study of critical environmental problems. . . .—that stratospheric smog, consisting of both gases and particles, would be created that would raise the stratosphere's temperature by 6 to 7 degrees. . . . I think we should know the effects on the atmosphere before we commit ourselves further. (*Congressional Record,* 1970)

The second-order consequences from any significant discovery can be extensive and could include (a) obsolescence of individual skills with the elimination of products or services with further dislocations of unemployment, need for retraining, and even the death of a city or region; (b) bankruptcy or restructuring of an organization; (c) the stagnation or demise of entire industries; and (d) economic or social shifts within and between nations. Organizations which have not predicted second-order consequences are unable to adapt to the new competition or changed methods because they have been change resistant rather than change responsive. The list of failures or setbacks includes many extractive industries throughout the world; the traditional segment of the office equipment industry when computers and xerography were introduced; and several shipbuilders in the UK, US, and Europe which relied on proven methods while Japanese firms experimented and captured most of the world's shipbuilding market.

Governments and institutions fail to recognize shifts in relative power and importance as different resources become necessary to provide the material wants of a nation and as desires and needs shift to a different plane, perhaps with more intangible satisfaction through services, knowledge, and diverse experiences. The undesirable and frequently unpredicted by-products of technology—pollution, congestion, discrimination, urban decay—become of greater concern to an increasing segment of society aware that life has qualitative as well as quantitative dimensions. International imbalances in technological capabilities become apparent through trade deficits, brain drains, and shifts in centres of world economic power. Stop-gap first aid is applied on an international scale through the exercise of protective tariffs, subsidies, import quotas, and occasional abrupt changes in relative currency values. Politicians and managers alike tend to treat major technologically induced changes through symptomatic relief of pain rather than major corrective surgery.

The failures to diagnose and predict second-order consequences are far easier to identify than are the systems and means to avoid such failures in the future. As subsequent events develop, the management of technology may require major shifts not only in strategies but in the very structure of society.

Challenge of technology

Two widely read books have emphasized the impact of technology on society. Servan-Schreiber in *The American Challenge* (1969), dramatized the schism between American–European technological and managerial capabilities now and in the future. It is generally recognized by astute scholars today, however, that the gap between the US and Europe is converging, not widening (Brooks, 1972). Peter Drucker (1969a) assumed a more global perspective in *The Age of Discontinuity* with an analysis of the technological/aspiration gulf between developed and undeveloped nations. Despite some overstatements in the Servan-Schreiber thesis, the important point is that both suggest that technological disparities have and may further precipitate imbalances of crisis proportions both among the developed countries and between the haves and the have-nots as nations vie for positions of world economic leadership. Solving or improving technological problems associated with resource allocation, assimilation, confusion of means with ends, and dislocation side effects will be major strategy challenges in the years ahead.

Development of major technological innovations is restricted to the minority of the world's population in the developed nations. The power centres of North America, Western Europe, Japan, and the USSR enjoy superior economic and skill resources unavailable to less developed nations with low per capita incomes. Since it annually produces and consumes nearly half of the non-communist world's GNP and more than half the PhD's and other graduate students, the United States has the lion's share of technological resources, although its relative position is declining. A combination of government and private investment has enabled almost 28 000 million dollars per year to be devoted to basic and applied research and development projects within the United States. Utilization of industrial laboratories, universities, and not-for-profit think tanks or research laboratories has permitted a simultaneous exploration of most major technologies, even though resources may have been concentrated in a few primary areas.

The US has achieved significant unification of cooperative efforts in major large-scale programmes, most notably in aerospace and in particular with NASA's successful milestones in extending the frontiers of space and telecommunications technology. However, few technological projects have had such clear-cut goals as did NASA's public mission of transporting men safely to and from the moon. Undoubtedly this tangible and easily measured goal, spurred by the 1957 success of Russia's Sputnik I, helped sustain financial support of space exploration.

During the first ten years of its existence, NASA accounted for somewhat less than 3 per cent of total federal government expenditures, or about one-half of 1 per cent of GNP. With this budget, NASA organized thousands of subcontractors into a planned, integrated network of total space technology, void of either excessive duplication or omissions in critical subsystems. But the true success of NASA is not so much its space missions *per se*, but the knowledge and skills that were developed and acquired by these far-flung independent contractors in diversified technological areas such as chemicals, ceramics, adhesives, electronics, guidance systems, ultrasonic machining, powder metallurgy, plasma-gun welding, laser metal-forming techniques, and similar capabilities found only among participants in complex projects requiring new materials and techniques. Furthermore, a major lesson learned by involvement in such endeavours consisted of new insights into the managerial and organizational processes and requirements for success in large-scale projects (Sayles and Chandler, 1971).

Despite the relative abundance of resources in the US and the effectiveness of NASA and similar system-oriented projects, US approaches to technology have not been without accompanying social and economic wastes. The above-mentioned fall-out from space and defence technology occurred primarily in basic research and not the more heavily funded design and development of specific-end items. In many industries there is a tendency toward fragmented and duplicated effort as competing organizations push their research and development subgroups to come up with new, better, and more profitable products. Likewise, many governmental agencies at all levels still expend massive resources for programmes and projects ranging from social welfare and poverty to sophisticated forms of transportation without clearly defined goals, systems-management approaches, fiscal accountability, or measurement of performance against goals. In social welfare alone in the US in 1966 there were 170 different programmes of federal aid, financed by over 400 separate appropriations, administered by 21 federal departments or agencies further aided by 150 Washington D.C. bureaus and over 400 regional offices (*New York Times*, 23 November 1966).

For a nation to afford competition in any line of technological development, major organizations must have a large critical mass of skills and financial resources to carry projects through to successful completion. This has caused problems in European technology as national ties and identity tend to fragment and duplicate major technological efforts, forestalling the amassing of sufficient integrated resources to develop and advance superior technology. One study showed that of 50 major industrial innovations in the pre-Sputnik twentieth century, 32 were initiated wholly or in part in the United States and 38 were brought to commercial application in that country (Ben-David, 1968).

But with all of the highly publicized accomplishments of US leads in space, managers, politicians, and scientists frequently assume that the US dominates technological invention. While it is true that the US enjoys greater absolute research and development resources than any other nation, for the past decade the expenditure of US resources has been heavily skewed to space and defence missions. In citing data from the OECD, Brooks (1972, pp. 114–15) shows that on a relative basis, US government support of science and technology, which amounts to about 60 per cent of total research and develop-

42

ment expenditures, has virtually ignored areas with a direct economic pay-off. Exhibit 2.5 shows the comparative shares of 1968–9 public research and development expenditures in support of economic objectives in manufacturing, services, and agriculture among seven nations. Brooks (1972) concludes that the major developed nations of the world are reaching a common level with superiority less distinguishable and more internationally diffused.

Europe has shown a tendency to seek greater cooperative efforts in science-intensive projects, such as the Concorde and the seven-member European Launcher Development Organization (ELDO). But to date the fate of both projects is questionable; the Concorde because of possible lack of a market, and ELDO because of an under-capitalized and less than fully integrated approach to design, produce, and launch rockets capable of orbiting communications satellites. Both ventures reflect status-need overtones, coupled with lack of total system planning.

Exhibit 2.5
Public research and development expenditures (1968–9) in support of manufacturing, services and agriculture

	Per cent of Total
United States	6·0
Canada	48·8
United Kingdom	22·1
France	16·5
Japan	25·0
Sweden	13·1
Netherlands	18·0

Source: Brooks (1972, pp. 114–15).

The Japanese have been more selective and organized in their research. Most of their efforts have been directed toward perfecting and improving established technologies rather than producing major breakthroughs in new fields. With close planning among government, business, labour, and universities, Japan has achieved rapid economic growth by developing competitive expertise in basic industries such as chemicals, optics, steel, plastics, textiles, and shipbuilding.

In textiles, for example, Japan is committing large funds to research into new synthetic fibres. Japanese inventions in textile machinery such as water-jet looms coupled with a government edict which scrapped 790 000 obsolete looms in five years, plus consolidation of mills to improve economies of scale, have boosted Japan to a position of world leadership in textiles. Although textile manufacturers, particularly in the US, argue that lower labour costs are the reason for Japanese success, labour-cost differentials of five times more expensive labour in the US provide only a partial explanation. Japan's total textile industry is more automated, less fragmented among small inefficient firms, and more productive than the US industry (Mecklin, 1970).

How do less developed countries fit into the technological picture? Clearly, the developing and undeveloped nations will be consigned to positions of technological followership, at least throughout the rest of this century. Lacking both financial resources and scientific–managerial knowhow, it is doubtful that any major technological achievement will come from a non-communist nation other than those in Europe, Japan, the United States, or Canada. For the undeveloped countries of Asia and Africa, the phenomenon of having to run faster just to keep pace with the present is an unfortunate reality.

This is not, however, an indictment that less developed countries have no future in the use of technology. Quite the contrary, it is highly probable that firms in the developing areas of Latin America and the Middle East will gradually become major centres for the mass production of established labour-intensive technology, similar to the strategy which transformed post-war Japan. Their critical key to success is to develop and utilize managerial and organizational skills together with sufficient engineering capabilities and production skills to imitate and manufacture established products.

Because these nations generally are late entrants into technology-based industries, they do not have to overcome the obsolescence problem of earlier entrants. In effect, they can leapfrog to purchase new, more economic equipment. Provided policy makers select industries for which there is a mass outside market and which will not overly tax their thin resource base, these newly emerging firms can start fresh, using highly productive equipment to complement their relatively low-cost human resources. The gravest threat to their future success lies in political attempts to acquire instant status by blundering into capital-intensive industries such as steel and auto manufacture where they will continue to be at a technological and managerial disadvantage.

The underdeveloped countries of Asia, Africa, and Latin America are prime markets for used equipment which is no longer competitively productive in the major markets. Firms in Europe and North America trade up in technology and export low-technology machines to the capital-impoverished countries. But this transfer is far from perfect. Firms in the maturing industries of Europe and North America are not always receptive to investing in improved equipment and an up-graded product line. The laggards in these industries within Europe and North America find themselves increasingly at a competitive disadvantage with the largely standardized products which flow out of low-cost firms in the underdeveloped areas, produced on machines scrapped by firms more responsive to technological improvement.

As long as the underdeveloped nations have limited financial and human resources to operate and maintain their factories, they become potentially superior competitors to less productive and declining segments of once prosperous industries in Europe and the US. With the combined pressures from highly productive, imitated technologies in developing countries and low-cost manufacture from low-technology transplants to the underdeveloped areas, firms within the major economic powers will have to continue to extend technology or lose market share because of astigmatic perception failures to utilize new technologies.

Prediction astigmatism

Accelerating technological change has impacted to render obsolete organizational, national, and even international strategies. It has invalidated past premises and assumptions normally relied upon for the formulation of future strategies.

Technology is now transitory and system wide in its impact—it is not subject to conditions of static equilibrium or of a continually steady state. Yet the strategies of the past which enabled large-scale organizational growth assumed static conditions—change was abnormal, a variation from the norm, and something to be quietened down to bring the organization back to its normal functioning. A highly structured and routinized managerial hierarchy with specialized staffs and elaborate control procedures traditionally has been thought of as the organizational form to foster orderly and rational incremental growth. But such an organizational form has great rigidity and little ability to adapt to change.

General Motors has achieved annual sales in excess of 30 000 million dollars by functioning within a relatively stable product environment void of major technological change other than automation and newer manufacturing methods. In basic engineering design the motor car today remains essentially unchanged from models of 50 years ago. Annual style changes as practised in the US are rarely technologically based but are more a strategy designed to achieve competitive advantage because General Motors' economies of scale enable it to utilize dies and tooling more efficiently than smaller firms.

But further strategies face the uncertainty of even higher standards for pollution emission, the possible action of government to rescue cities and even countries from over-crowding and strangulation by cars, and even a technological breakthrough on personal transportation, perhaps funded by governments in a similar fashion to NASA.

The strategies of General Motors and thousands of similar large firms, not necessarily in sales, but in product, production, and organizational strategies, have been appropriate for successful growth in past decades. But there is considerable doubt that the past strategies of differentiated basic product lines with manufacturing and distribution economies of scale may any longer be the key requirement for future success. All too often past successes lead individuals, firms and even nations to tangible and psychological commitments which increase vulnerability to future change. Mature, bureaucratic organizations often generate managerial inbreeding to a high degree by selecting and promoting their like kind—managers who have spent entire careers learning about that firm, organization or industry. This can produce a form of perceptual biasing reminiscent of astigmatism, or that perceptual affliction characterized by distorted images of reality. By concentrating so long on internal or routine, industry problems, the rest of the world appears as an out-of-focus blur, irrelevant for strategy decisions.

The tendency to see only one's own actions in clear focus is potentially dangerous if external changes are occurring which may disrupt strategy effectiveness. One handicap of this astigmatism is the failure to anticipate or predict encroachments upon established markets, both from new technology and from innovative marketing and organizational practices. Firms are likely to monitor competitors' changes in products, processes, or marketing techniques. But rarely do they scan the larger frame of the general environment for technology transfers or innovations. Few major technological innovations have originated from companies within an industry. Schon (1967, p. 169) notes that the main sources of major technology advancement emerge from firms traditionally outside of an industry. In his observation: 'major technological change has tended to come from outside established firms in the industry, from independent inventors, new small firms, foreign countries, and invading industries'.

New vectors of technological innovation by invasion from unprecedented points of origin may completely change and revitalize an industry. When General Motors and the automotive industry invaded the locomotive industry with a new power plant called the diesel engine, steam engine manufacturers such as the Baldwin Locomotive Works, at that time the world's largest producer of locomotives, were displaced and many were bankrupted. On the other hand, DuPont's introduction of synthetic fibres revitalized the overly mature textile industry within the US.

Countless service industries based on human skills have evaporated or been reshaped by automation and more productive uses of technology. Even the construction industry, traditionally a customized on-site business, is being altered by off-site technology ranging from precast concrete apartment walls and rooms to modular factory homes, to preassembled plumbing fixtures, to completely manufactured mobile homes. Technological invasion is not achieved without resistance, however. In some instances an industry's growth becomes crystallized or hardened in one direction and competitive advances are impeded or blocked. Such was the difficulty Westinghouse had in replacing the established Edison direct-current system of power transmission with their more effective alternating-current system (Olken, 1969).

For any organization or nation to cling to the past for sake of past glories is a tenuous posture. In an age of shifting technology the past is irrelevant except as it prepares a firm for current and future actions. Many firms and organizations attempt to extrapolate their past into the future simply because

46

they have become so entrenched in committed courses of action that they have little flexibility for future options.

Future growth industries within Europe, North America, and Japan will differ from traditional growth industries of the past by being less capital intensive. Large-scale manufacturing firms typically have huge investments in assets and equipment designed to produce volumes of mass-produced or processed output such as steel, cars, food, petroleum, or chemicals. Future technologies will emphasize investment not so much in productive equipment as in developmental research, employee skills, and flexible organizational processes. Except for development costs, much of the cost element will be variable in materials and labour. The production of computers, for example, requires considerably less fixed productive capacity than the more basic, mature industries.

A major reason for the shift to lower investments in large, fixed-asset, long pay-off projects will be the increasing cost of technology with higher risks. Not only will technology be increasingly costly to obtain major discoveries but the probability of obsolescence of discoveries will be higher. The exception will be the natural monopolies, particularly public utilities which have shown a faster rate of economic output than any other basic industry in the past four decades with over a sixteen-fold increase in the US. Much of this is attributable to expanded investments in technological equipment to upgrade quality and capacity of service. In many cases such as telephone services, current levels of demand could not be met without extensive investments in facilities. Likewise, other public services such as hospitals will have large investments in elaborate labs and diagnostic equipment plus expensive life-support monitoring and extending equipment in individual rooms to treat illnesses more effectively.

Technologically induced shifts from origins outside the traditional fields or industries will force obsolescence and even bankruptcy on unwary and unresponsive organizations. Entire industries may be eliminated because of an unwillingness or inability to shift direction. This predicament is especially real for firms in mature industries which face loss of market share on one hand from a wider range of more suitable product substitutes generated by advanced technology, and on the other by lower cost and more productive foreign producers who erode the market for standardized products.

Although the reasons for lack of responsiveness to technological change varies with the individual organization or industry, some of the more common inhibitors include:

1. Psychological and social commitments to existing products, processes, and organization,
2. Sizeable capital investments in long-life single-use facilities,
3. Low profits and reduced rate of growth,
4. Small size or fragmented activities,

5. Complacent top management,

6. Industry norms and associations or cartels which perpetuate industry-bound thinking,

7. Lack of successful entrepreneurial models to emulate, and

8. Powerful labour resistance to methods changes.

With slight modification these danger signs might equally apply to some countries which fail to identify a changing role in an increasingly technologically based world. Countries limited to natural resource exports, whether by choice or imposed by colonialism, certainly face this possibility. Even the world's richest country, Kuwait, may soon be strangled by its own wealth. With its oil-rich income, the government has given its people many benefits, including university education for the more educable. But the government has failed to consider how these people are to be effectively utilized. Not everyone prefers leisure to work. Nation-wide dismotivation, apathy, unrest, and alienation will accelerate and restrict social and economic development of this small nation if it continues to ignore its social and technological responsibilities.

Management of technology

Technology is a high-risk, costly, and uncertain activity. The world has entered an age in which many of the easy inventions and discoveries have already been produced. To achieve breakthroughs which have social significance and profit potentials for the originator, increasingly larger investments in research must be made. Quantum leaps forward in technological benefits require greater managerial and financial commitments. But while costs of discovery are increasing at an accelerating rate, the incremental pay-off results seem to be growing at a decreasing rate over the short-run.

Seldom is an organization able to successfully carry through an innovative project within management's original cost estimates (Waters, 1970). Yet conservatism of expected developmental costs is probably a necessary requisite for innovation, as many projects would not be undertaken if management really knew in advance how much would be required. One of the greatest challenges of technological innovation facing management is knowing when to abandon a research project. Often there is a feeling that 'success is almost within reach, all we need is a little more time and money'. But that little extra can at times be likened to pouring water into a bottomless pit—the resources continue to vanish without so much as a ripple. Financial failure before a venture is able to generate a positive cash flow has been the fate of many firms large and small.

To obtain cost–discovery effectiveness and justify research and development expenditures, firms require potentially high pay-offs. Pharmaceutical drug

48

companies have been criticized for prices excessively higher than the cost of production and materials. But the uninformed public fails to consider the high research investment that preceded production of an effective and successful drug and all the dead ends and unsuccessful formulations that must be recovered from the successful ones.

There is also the added risk that a new product will quickly be duplicated or closely imitated, thereby reducing the market and profit potential for the original innovator (Baldwin and Childs, 1969). As the technology of any industry becomes easier to duplicate, the motivation for further innovation declines. Undifferentiated competitive advantage, whether in drugs, petrochemicals, electronics, or building materials, ultimately leads to a slowdown in the rate of product improvements generated within the industry. In seeking more profitable potentials for future growth, management turns more to manufacturing or distribution process improvements.

One sign of a maturing industry is a shake-out in the number of participants with increasing concentration among a few key oligopolistic suppliers. In technology-intensive ventures, where the potential magnitude of loss is great, the shake-out is usually accelerated.

In some cases failure may be accentuated because the aspiring firm was too widely diversified in several major technology projects. Before selling most of its computer business to Honeywell, General Electric drained some estimated 500 million dollars from profits between 1965 and 1970, because of simultaneous resource-consuming ventures into computers, nuclear power, and commercial jet engines (Demaree, 1970). And in 1971 the colour TV pioneer, RCA, also announced the termination of its computer operations with a similar massive loss. By contrast, IBM has concentrated research efforts along a fairly homogeneous base of data-related technology and has successfully captured the major share of the world's computer market. The only contender who enjoys a larger market share than IBM in any major market is the British firm International Computers Ltd., but it is finding technological advances more difficult and costly because of its smaller, more limited resource base.

Recently, managers of technology have had to consider a new form of cost—social costs. Water, air, and noise pollution are slowly becoming cost items which no longer can be produced free of charge to the polluter. In addition to its contributory role in funding and directing many high-priority technology efforts, governments are beginning to act as monitors of disturbing technological side effects. The legal and police powers of the state are being used through economic sanctions to force various industrial groups to begin curbing their effluents—effluents which are the product of management looking only at first-order consequences. Although such controls will be threats for many firms, with resulting higher costs, they also create new technological opportunities. Firms responding to the issues of physical ecosystem protection are finding new growth opportunities in a market that a decade ago was practically non-existent because of lack of concern: crime prevention, solid waste disposal, environmental landscaping, noise and smoke abatement, water purification, forestry, and others.

Awareness over technology's social costs also waves a danger flag warning that the pursuit of technology should not become an end in itself. The US decision to abort the development of the supersonic transport was primarily a move to manage technology and avoid its detrimental by-products. Large-scale, multi-channel, three-dimensional, audio-visual space communication between continents could theoretically be a reality in the 'eighties at a user cost comparable to today's long-distance telephone rates. Such an eventuality might reduce the need for business-oriented air travel with all its associated disadvantages and costs. Certainly the technological benefits would be many times greater than those to be gained from adding to supersonic-transport capacity. The challenge is one of establishing economic and socially accepted priorities to serve as policy guides in the management of technology.

This chapter has outlined some of the major consequences, impacts, and challenges associated with managing technology. While the emphasis has dramatized the need for adaptiveness on the part of institutions, organizations, and individuals who come into contact with technological change, a word of caution must also be given against a run-away infatuation with change. Although the rate of technological innovation has greatly accelerated, not all products, industries, or societies are changing simultaneously. Low-technology industries with few research and development needs may go for years or decades without significant change. The most predictable thing about invention is its unpredictability. Even a tertiary-level innovation can be highly disruptive in a tradition-bound industry.

The management of technological change is not easy. Few organizations have found the desired balance between doing too little and pursuing too many rainbows. Technological management begins with understanding the origins and nature of change within the science-based environment of mankind. It is possible to alter managerial and organizational practices to become more change responsive and adaptable to technology innovation, whether initiating change or using it as an input to improvement in internal processes and in new ways of relating to the external environment.

3

Social and behavioural change

Technological change has freed man from devoting all of his time and energy to physical survival. It has created great surpluses of material goods, permitting man to allocate time and resources to educational and cultural goals, and to enhance the physical well-being of man in industrial societies. Man's new freedom from the problems of survival and his development as an educated being, with all the knowledge or past experience of the world at his fingertips, has resulted in massive social and behavioural changes in the nineteenth and twentieth centuries. But social and behavioural change has always been the mark of civilized man.

> The early Romans had been instilled with the simple virtues of self-reliance, personal integrity, family cohesion, and discipline. The Greek influence softened the ways of the Romans, making them less harsh and insensitive, but it also inculcated habits of sophistication which were often corrupting and even decadent. Furthermore, the Roman conquest of the Hellenistic world paved the way for the spread to the West of various oriental cults, often based on superstition, divination, and other-worldly antidotes. (Wallbank and Taylor, 1954, p. 177)

The old Latin phrase, *Tempora mutantur, nos et mutamur in illis* (the times are changed, and we are changed within them), is just as applicable to the twentieth-century man as to his counterpart in the Roman Empire during the first two centuries AD. Rapid technological change of the twentieth century has spawned social and behavioural change, creating great social turbulence. Such change both affects and is affected by institutional or governmental change and by business adjustments to change. What are the principal social and behavioural changes taking place in the 'seventies and 'eighties? What are the origins of such changes, and more importantly, their consequences?

Man does not adapt easily to behavioural and social change. His cultural heritage, his education, his family upbringing have all provided him with a set of norms and role expectations (Thompson and Van Houten, 1970, pp.

21–36). A father should behave one way, a child another. Some behaviours from unions or business are acceptable, others are not. Schools and governments are expected to perform some functions and services, but not others. Adjustment problems occur when the behaviour we see fails to fit our preconceptions of normalcy. Our traditions and conceptual framework may be challenged, producing symptoms of anxiety. Alternatively, we may adhere to our expectations, considering that no real behavioural or social change has taken place and that dysfunctional behaviours are solely random events.

Attempts to ignore or minimize the magnitude of behavioural and social changes lead to inadequate or improper assessments of reality. Individuals and organizations cannot escape the consequences of social–behavioural change. Within organizations, motivational patterns, skills, aspirations, and job roles at all levels are undergoing seemingly subtle yet profound shifts which challenge traditional organizational and management practices. At the interface level of organizations with their environment, changing social–behaviour patterns require strategy modification and revitalization if the organization is to remain responsive to its external environment.

> Powerful environmental influences from human demands are evident. The major demands involve *human* rights as defined differently by different individuals; an *identity* that conforms to one's desired self concept; and *freedom from authoritarian and regimental social* situations. Corporate presidents and key executives are now challenged by the choice of leadership obsolescence or leadership appreciation. (Mee, 1969, p. 39)

A general systems perspective

The tendency to evaluate or moralize the behaviour of individuals or factions of society from a personal frame of reference is not unnatural. Such an assessment is based on personal values, of ideas of right and wrong and what is important and not important, which thrust perception and assessment into a judgemental frame of reference. Such personal perspectives view the actions of others as desirable or undesirable.

While such a personal normative frame of reference simplifies views of reality, its major shortcoming is that it blocks understanding of behaviours which lie outside expected limits. In a situation of 'I am right and you (they) are wrong', there is little hope of recognizing and comprehending reasons for the actions of others and of recognizing major changes in behavioural and social patterns. This results in a polarization of perceptions, as in Northern Ireland between Protestant and Catholic, in Belgium between Flemish and Walloons, or in the United States over the question of the Vietnamese war.

An alternative conceptual scheme which specifically focuses on behavioural purposes, interrelationships, and changes in behaviour that modify the impact of value judgements is the *general systems model*. Long used in the biological and physical sciences, the systems model is an inter-disciplinary tool of description, analysis, and prediction useful for studying many types of interlinking phenomena (Miller, 1955; Boulding, 1956). This is a particularly useful conceptual model for the manager, minimizing the biases of personal frames of reference and even cultures. It is not subject to the biased distortions which arise when judging actions in terms of one's own beliefs and expectations, a frame of reference which may be totally inappropriate for the situation under observation.

Several common characteristics are present whether a system be biological, physical, mechanical, or social. All systems consist of a hierarchical arrangement of specialized subparts, each purposively linked into structural and behavioural relationships with the others. This structural linkage between the subparts or subsystems serves to maintain and develop the total system by the process of exchanging and transforming materials, energy, and information between the system and its external environment. There is thus an interdependency, not only within the system but between the system and other separate yet interrelated systems, which comprise its environment (Duncan, 1964; Katz and Kahn, 1966).

All of these properties and processes are found in the social systems we identify as organizations, institutions, and societies, as well as in man himself. As the most basic form of social system, the formal organization, whether it is a firm, hospital, union, government, or university, provides a simple illustration of the systems model application. Any formal organization:

1. is created and continues to exist to achieve a common purpose that is greater than could be achieved by individual action alone,
2. develops a division of labour or specialized subsystems to subdivide goals and to increase productive efficiency,
3. uses patterns of authority and communication relationships to link and integrate specialized subsystem activities, and
4. depends upon transactions with external clientele and suppliers to provide inputs or absorb outputs necessary to maintain and develop the system (Schein, 1965, pp. 7–9; Hage and Aiken, 1970, pp. 6–13).

Our primary concern in this chapter is not with behaviour in organizations *per se*, but with identifying individual and collective behaviour within a society in order to understand and predict behaviour. Society typically is thought of as a stable but evolutionary outgrowth of cultural customs and heritage, infused with distinctive values and mores. Certainly historical antecedents play a major role in shaping the contemporary character of a society just as an adult's childhood and past experiences shape his predispositions to behave in patterned ways. However, for the purpose of managerial diagnosis of the causes and consequences of social–behavioural change, it is necessary to view society as a system or constellation of interacting individuals, organizations, and institutions.

This network of loosely coupled subsystems is not static but rather in a state of dynamic equilibrium which is always shifting and moving toward a new, yet temporary, position or equilibrium. A state of transitory or fluid balance exists because of the fundamental principle of interdependence. At the same time some relationships are being broken up and dissolved, others are being created and expanded. As one institution or sector of society seeks to improve its relative advantage, its changes in output or interrelationships induce changes in other parts of society.

For example, as unions press for higher wages, employing organizations seek either accommodating cost economies, pass along higher operating costs through price increases in their products or services, or absorb higher costs through reduced profits. One nation which attempts to strengthen its position by waging political or economic war on another changes the structure and behaviour of both nations and probably others as well. A firm which develops a new technological process or product will disrupt former transactional patterns and threaten other firms with loss of customers. A group of people who oppose the actions or products of another group or organization may exert political, legal, social, or market power to bring about change in the other's actions. Such interdependencies of behaviour and action are the contributory forces that transform society, and for most societies the transformation process is accelerating.

Some individuals, among them the eminent psychologist B. F. Skinner (1971), relegate the changes within society to a non-emotional, almost machine-like rationality. But changes within a society or organization are seldom of the simple cause–effect or stimulus–response variety. Neither are they always the result of purely cognitive actions; feelings and affective-generated behaviour may in some cases supersede thought-out rationality. Wars and revolutions are often more the result of differences in religion, values, or culture than they are of economic or power motivation. But since any change with significant impact on society is a product of many interacting forces, little useful purpose would be served in isolating precise origins of change within a complex social system.

Because of the interweaving nature of society, organizations, and widely differing value systems of individuals, any major change inevitably has several contributory causal factors. Thus, while we have taken the conceptual licence to distinguish major change origins as being primarily structural–institutional, technological, or social–behavioural, there is actually a circular or reciprocal interaction among change origins (Buckley, 1967). Recall that the model of socio-economic growth in the preceding chapter (Exhibit 2.1) had circular inputs among affluence, education, technology, and productivity.

54

Many of the misunderstandings or clashes between sectors of society are due to over-simplification of change origins. For example, it is naïve to claim that pollution is caused by technology alone, or that welfare aid goes to recipients who have social values that prefer non-work to work, or that Japan has become a power in world trade simply because of wage rate advantages. Such perceptions of cause–effect are so over-simplified that they distort reality and an accurate understanding of the situations.

Herein lies one of the major dilemmas in the management of change. On the one hand there is a practical need to simplify one's conceptual image of the background and causal factors of a particular change. In effect, the manager or strategist has to ignore much of the irrelevant noise associated with any critical change in order to understand:

1. Why is it occurring (problem identification)?
2. In which direction is it headed (vector analysis)?
3. What is its rate of change (time-horizon determination)?
4. What are its consequences on individuals, organizations, and society itself (magnitude and consequences projections)?

But at the time there is always the other danger of over-simplification, of eliminating so much of the informational detail that is presumed to be irrelevant that the strategist creates an inaccurate map of the environment and of change dimensions.

Admittedly, the current state of the art in social–behavioural analysis is limited and conceptual simplifications have to be made. While economic and technological forecasting have undergone years of refinement, concern with social forecasting and interpretation is more recent and less developed (Darling and Morris, 1970). More precise analytical approaches will surely be forthcoming within the next decade, but recent computerized attempts at macro social forecasting as recently developed by Forrester (1971) remain questionable. Even quantitatively oriented scientists usually agree that for highly complex phenomena such as social–behavioural change it is more appropriate to develop a reasonable qualitative explanation and analysis than to jump prematurely to quantified prediction that is tenuous at best (Miller and Starr, 1969).

A major objective of effective change management is to develop conceptual–analytical tools which enable the manager to make decisions that have a higher probability of being successful than if he relied on experiential-based hunches, intuition, or judgement alone. The remainder of this chapter presents an approach within the systems perspective for analysing several of the underlying reasons for social–behavioural change. Emphasis is upon understanding and uncovering patterns of change as well as explanation for change divergence and vectoring.

E   **55**

Social structure and behavioural ethics

Despite instant communication through television and telephone and a commercial ability to travel at 600 miles/h and soon at almost twice the speed of sound, contemporary societies are more heterogeneous than any in past history. The person of average means living in any of the more affluent societies enjoys a way of life that physically is more comfortable than realized by even the wealthy of a few generations ago. At the same time much of the world's population find conditions and life little changed from what their ancestors experienced as much as 2000 years ago. But the differences between societies are not simply those of material standards of living or of haves versus the have nots. Disparities are found not just in degree of economic or

Exhibit 3.1

Societical stage and behavioural ethic indicator scale

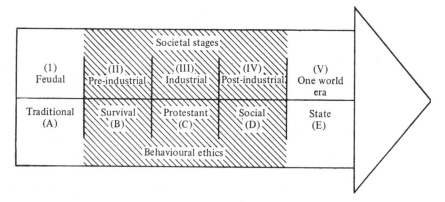

structural development, but even more fundamentally in the ethics or value structures that guide human behaviour within society.

Historians and anthropologists often attempt to capture the Zeitgeist or prevailing spirit of an era in a single descriptive word such as primitive or Renaissance. But analysis of the ongoing changes within and between societies, especially as they impact on organizations and managers, has greater meaning if the twin dimensions of structure and behaviour are separated. The model in Exhibit 3.1 is a continuum of these two basic dimensions, differentiated and labelled as *societal stages* and *behavioural ethics*. Although for historical and futuristic diagnosis each continuum contains five levels of eras, contemporary managers of change are most concerned with transitions occurring within the pre-industrial to post-industrial stages and the survival to social ethics (the shaded zone in Exhibit 3.1).

Societal stages I–V reflect major differences in degree of structural growth as characterized by: (a) level of economic development per capita, (b) complexity and diversity of institutions, (c) involvement in science and tech-

56

nology, and (d) occupational diversity of the population. With an emphasis on the more tangible and measurable components, these societal stages are similar in concept to Rostow's (1959) stages of growth: traditional society, preconditions for take-off, take-off, drive to maturity, and age of mass consumption; or to Farmer's (1969) country types: developing, take-off, industrial and post-industrial.

By contrast, the behavioural ethics represent the less tangible aspects of society with differences between A to E a function of (a) the methods and sources of pre-adult socialization; (b) the content of professed values, beliefs, and mores, and (c) the scope of personal orientations and aspirations. Each ethic personifies substantial differences in the patterning of learned behaviour as individuals become socialized or indoctrinated in what Riesman (1950) calls the prevailing social character or mode of conformity.

A time dimension does not appear directly on the social–behavioural indicator scale as the possible stages and ethics are not bound to any common time frame. The concept of time relevant for social change is the time required to bring about a shift from one societal stage or behavioural ethic to another. Under ideal conditions there is a tendency for stage and ethic to parallel one another as suggested by the balance within the model in Exhibit 3.1. But as a society moves toward the right of the scale, there is a profound time compression as changes between stages and ethics move at accelerated rates. Society experiences a growing cleavage between individuals and groups who are in various stages of adjustment to the new ethic.

History books are replete with examples of feudal stages and traditional ethics among former European, Hindu, Japanese, Chinese, and Arab societies, so there is little need to dwell on dated history. And since the possible evolution of a one-world era of supranational sovereignty probably lies beyond the lifetimes of today's youngest managers, there would be limited value in speculating about the long-term future. Currently the societies of the world function somewhere along a pre-industrial to post-industrial continuum and within corresponding survival to social ethics. Exhibit 3.2 suggests several of the changes which occur as societies move between these levels. However, since most of the world's economic activity occurs within advanced industrial or youthful post-industrial societies, the most meaningful analysis of social–behavioural change is found in the transition between protestant and social ethics.

Weber (1930) (originally published in 1904) and Sombart (1913) stimulated an outpouring of theories which link the early emergence of European industrialism with basic values closely interwoven with Judaism and Protestantism. The widespread acceptance of values which stress individualism and independence, thrift, hard work, and the accumulation of property are all ingredients of the type C (or protestant) ethic necessary to advance industrialism within a free society (McGuire, 1963, pp. 18–26). Although we have followed accepted Western convention in identifying this as the protestant ethic, the label is symbolic of a set of closely held values and attitudes, regardless of any established religion. An influential sector of Japanese society, for example, subscribe to values characteristic of this ethic, even though the principal religion of Japan is Shinto.

Exhibit 3.2

Characteristic shifts between stages and ethics

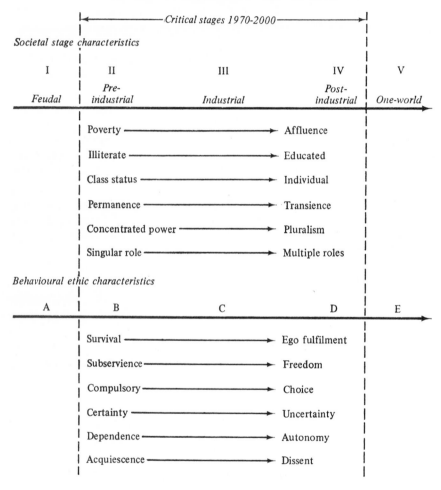

For several generations the protestant ethic has prevailed among a majority of society in highly developed nations—a group commonly called the middle class. But the long-standing protestant ethic now exists in an uneasy coexistence with an evolving social ethic in the United States, throughout much of Western Europe, and inevitably in Japan as well. It is not uncommon for an executive, politician, or professor to adhere to a protestant ethic while

58

some of his colleagues and many of his subordinates, constituency, or students aspire to a social ethic.

The success of the protestant ethic and the stage of industrialism to which it is linked actually sows the seeds for its own transformation. With its emphasis on security, achievement, personal enrichment, and general external conformity to commonly accepted norms of morality and social appearance, the protestant ethic stimulates economic growth. Economic growth in turn facilitates a structural shift into post-industrialism, as evidenced by several signs: (a) the population becomes highly urbanized with metropolitan hubs the centres of progress; (b) government becomes monolithic and a dominant force in interlinking all institutions; (c) power becomes concentrated in the hands of large bureaucratic organizations among several institutions; (d) technological efficiencies require a minority of the population to produce society's physical goods; and (e) revolutions in information processing, communication, transportation, and cybernetic controls diminish time and space obstacles.

As any society moves from feudalism or pre-industrialism toward a post-industrial stage and beyond, the correlating ethic fosters a wider range of behaviour—conformity is less uniform. Despite some common values and aspirational objectives, each successive ethic becomes internally less homogeneous. Ideational or other worldly spiritual values yield to the sensate with their secular, pragmatic, humanistic, and contractual character (Sorokin, 1937). The protestant ethic with its support of individualism certainly allowed for less conformity to societal expectations than did either the traditional or survival ethics. And now with the emergence of a social ethic there is even greater diversity of values and beliefs among its numerous clusterings of social groups.

Under the social ethic, the standards and guidelines which one adopts for shaping and limiting his behaviour are taken not so much from family or vague notions of societal expectations but from peers and one's contemporaries. Individuals seek belongingness and peer approval, not for external appearances or for what one has in a material sense, but for what one is as a person. Belongingness, in the protestant-ethic context, meant attachment and identity with one's community, home, and job. In the social ethic the ties to place and organization are more transitory and belongingness or sense of individual identity is found in deep, but often short, experiential relationships with friends and colleagues (Packard, 1972).

For some the superordinate goals of involvement in an activity or cause for the good of society provides a sense of moral commitment and means for self-fulfilment. Such a sense of higher than personal mission may be found either as a member of a conventional institution or by identity with an association or movement that is new or perhaps extremist in its attitude towards conventional standards of wisdom. For others, expression may be found in dropping out of the mainstream of society to cultivate personal talents or interests or

59

perhaps to cross over into a totally new institution to broaden self-perspective. Dropping out in the social ethic does not necessarily mean the traditional connotation of an escape from or denial of inability to cope with realities—a pathological symptom that applies to the executive who doesn't want to be bothered with new problems just as much as to the long-haired lad fed-up with school.

Above all, the social ethic does not accept things as they are just because they happen to be that way. Apathetic complacency is overpowered by intent to bring about meaningful change in oneself, in organizations, in institutions, in society—if change is viewed as necessary. The individual seeks to be responsive to his environment, but believes that the environment should provide meaningful experiences and opportunities for as much self-fulfilment as he is prepared to pursue.

The transition to the social ethic is perhaps the behavioural–social change with the greatest impact on society in the second half of the twentieth century. Not only are there major adjustment requirements for society to seek out a new ethic, but also the potential economic consequences are as yet unknown. Will the search for a new involvement and the rejection of the protestant ethic lower the standard of living? Would a hippy generation willingly give up the trappings of the industrial state produced by a protestant ethic—the conveniences of the motor car, television, and frozen foods? Perhaps the social ethic will necessarily have to encompass many of the motivational virtues of the protestant ethic in order to produce the economic surpluses required to implement the social ethic and attain the affluence of the industrial and post-industrial societal stages.

Management theory and man

Stripped to their most basic common denominator, management and organizational theories are essentially approaches to *behaviour modification*. Underlying practically all theories of management developed during the twentieth century is a central theme: how can the organization modify and adapt the behaviour of its managers and non-managers so that individual behaviour will support the task requirements and objectives of the organization? This does not imply that behaviour modification is necessarily either good or bad from an external viewpoint, but simply the reality that the individual's efforts are channelled to further the goals of the organization.

Fundamental to any theory of behaviour modification are implicit assumptions about the nature of man. These assumptions about his motivational characteristics, capabilities, dignity, beliefs, and feelings underlie the final product of any practical theory—the prescribed relationship between the organization and its individual members. Such tacit notions of man reflect the temporal nature of management and organizations theory. The theory emerges

60

to meet critical needs of the times, and as basic organizational needs shift with the development of society, the theory reflects a mirror image of prevailing thoughts about man and the conditions which affect his behaviour.

Scientific management, the earliest well-developed theoretical approach to management, was fathered by Frederick W. Taylor shortly after the turn of the century and was closely followed by the bureaucratic theory of Max Weber. In some respects these two approaches were as different as they were similar. Scientific management was really a supervisory and engineering theory of management since Taylor and his followers were concerned with improving the productive efficiency of the factory worker. Their answer to the efficiency issue was measurement of workers' activities and motions to achieve the highest possible degree of specialization coupled with a differential piece-work economic incentive. By contrast, the total organization was Weber's domain, where depersonalized roles within a hierarchical structure of status and authority relationships became the mechanism which enabled collective task coordination.

Scientific management was the mechanical or industrial engineer's explanation; bureaucracy, the sociologist's—yet both subscribed to a comparable view of man. The human individual was viewed as a passive, security seeking, economically motivated, largely dependent resource or instrument to be utilized by the organization. In return for economic remuneration and sometimes position advancement, the managed and the manager were expected to perform given tasks defined and designed by management as the thinkers and planners. Such mechanistic views of individual behaviour seemed consistent with the youthful growth of industrialization, when employee skills and productive processes had to be developed where none had existed before, and when production—not marketing or systems management—was the primary concern of management.

Are these theories, developed over fifty years ago when economic, political, and social conditions were vastly different, still in vogue today? There is little question that these pioneering theories continue to have a deep influence on the practice of management. It may not be an overstatement to say that these mechanistic, efficiency-oriented theories still serve as important management guidelines in the 'seventies, although naturally with some evolutionary changes. They have been expanded and modified to include behavioural inputs, particularly the contributions of the human relations movement of the 'forties and early 'fifties, and the more recent quantification inputs of operations research.

The philosophy and methods of scientific management and bureaucracy continue to influence managers with (a) the central emphasis on efficiency, (b) the concepts of task specialization and task interrelationships, (c) the motivational devices of extrinsic rewards such as income and status, and (d) the structured and systematic form of rationality for the organization and control of large organizations. But are these theories appropriate to manage the change from the protestant to the social ethic, and the industrial to post-industrial societal stage?

An examination of the impact of the motor car as one of the early Type I technologies which has widely altered society indicates a failure of traditional management theories. Except for those concerned in the manufacture of some luxury cars, the factory worker in any of the world's automotive parts or assembly plants is essentially skilled or semiskilled, and his job narrowly specialized and machine paced. The worker is an extension of the machine, tolerated either because he is less costly than investment in more fully automated machines, or because the individual is more flexible to adapt to production change than machines. This mechanistic approach to the factory worker is encouraged by the higher productivity of automated plants as shown in Exhibit 3.3. Although the car production worker is highly paid with

Exhibit 3.3

Assets and sales per employee for the ten largest motor manufacturers

	1971 Sales US $ millions	Assets per employee	Sales per employee
General Motors	28 264	23 600	36 564
Ford	16 433	24 273	37 951
Chrysler	7 999	22 026	35 238
Volkswagenwerk	4 967	15 381	24 589
Daimler-Benz	3 460	9 843	23 537
Toyota Motor	3 308	45 729	61 622
Nissan Motor	3 129	49 424	39 342
Fiat	2 943	13 457	16 076
British Leyland Motor	2 836	10 029	14 643
Renault	2 747	10 426	17 720

Source: *Fortune*, **85**, 5, May 1972; and **86**, 2, August 1972.

wage rates often 25–50 per cent higher than those in other industries (one-third more in the US in 1971), highly motivated employees are not attracted to the industry.

Despite his good pay the car worker in many plants is unwilling to work a five-day week. Absenteeism runs high. Contract negotiation strikes are often long and bitter, interspersed with walkouts and wildcat strikes. Alcohol, and even drugs, are used on the job as means of psychological escape. These symptoms of tension, boredom, and dissatisfaction are especially pronounced at General Motors' most modern plant at Lordstown, Ohio:

What workers object to finally is the thing that *is* the automobile industry: the assembly line with all its regimentation and monotony. . . . What a man does on the line, he does at the line's pace. Nothing of any complexity is required of anyone, because the cars roll past each man too rapidly—one every 36 seconds. The jobs may not be especially strenuous, but the pace is gruelling; the repetition maddening. (Norman, 1972, p. 98.)

In addition to various psychological escapes, work-group performance norms may emerge that often run counter to management's expectations, even including sabotage, but which allow workers to occupy their thoughts and feelings with divergent monotony-breaking activities (Jasinski, 1956; Wyatt and Marriott, 1956). Such actions suggest that, under highly routine work conditions, it is difficult for individuals to find meaning even in a protestant ethic, much less a social one. Unless the individual uses his income and discretionary time to find satisfaction away from the job, his self-concept, attitudes, and behaviour on and off the job become even more negative and self-defeating.

General Motors, the world's largest corporation, and many thousands of firms requiring similar job roles, are faced both with a hostile external environment and a hostile internal environment. Worldwide competition, aggressive labour unions, governmental controls, and a society that questions the car's social desirability, even while buying more cars, are external forces impacting on management's strategic actions. At the same time the behaviour of employees at lower status levels thwart management's attempts at higher productivity. Lower levels of managers also fail to find personal challenge and fulfilment, falling into a similar pattern of routine conformity, boredom, and largely cognitive–emotional disengagement. Even the unions are faced with similar hostile environments as leaders cling to traditional strategies but fail to control the demands and actions of their membership in any real sense.

The difficulties for mass-production firms such as General Motors in a post-industrial era are bound to increase. The motor industry has been a pioneer in efficiency and task specialization through scientific management and bureaucracy, and implicitly has accepted the philosophy that views man as a passive instrument of the organization. Economically, this has been highly successful in the first half of the twentieth century. But will it work in the 'seventies and 'eighties?

Any attempted overlay of social consciousness on a scientific management base may generate even greater internal as well as external turbulence in the years ahead. As more of society moves toward a social ethic and if society moves in the direction of preparing each individual to reach his fullest potential, the ideals of structural rigidity in organizations will become more dysfunctional and will further aggravate the problems of complex organizations.

Does this mean that such management concepts as task specialization, standardized procedures, and hierarchical authority are completely out of date? Some management theoreticians, most notably Chris Argyris (1957, 1964), feel that the requirements of formal organizations are basically incompatible with the self-actualizing needs of the mature personality. Our position is that the conflict between the economic and the social missions of the firm cannot be resolved simply by denying either mission. The diversity and individuality of human behaviour will not permit one mould, be it self-fulfilment or a mechanistic use of man's labour.

Not all workers react unfavourably against repetitive work that is void of intrinsic satisfaction. The notion that happiness and personal satisfaction on the job are positively correlated with productive output simply does not hold true in all cases. Not all individuals are challenged by the pursuit of complete self-fulfilment. As Seeman (1967) concluded from his study of Swedish factory workers, it is probable that people in low-skilled jobs in which the work itself is unrewarding come to accept the terms of their employment for what it is—a condition necessary to earn income with momentary sources of satisfaction sought whenever and wherever they might be found.

However, localized examples of complacency and apathy should not cloud the fact that many societies are in a transitory state of ethics. If we look at prevailing central tendencies it becomes obvious that the general environment of society has substantially changed over the last 20 years and will continue to change at an even faster pace. Behavioural changes in aspirations and ethics are being accentuated by changes in the structure of societies—through higher levels of affluence and education, through growth in the bigness of organizations, through greater central government involvement in subsidizing individual needs, and through a communication–transportation revolution that permits instant awareness of conditions and behaviour throughout the world.

In the post-industrial societal stage, the number of minimally educated and low-skilled individuals who will tolerate organizations that demand extreme conformity to tasks devoid of personal and social meaning is expected to shrink. Similarly the assumption that technical and managerial personnel can be motivated, governed, and organized using the assumptions of a protestant ethic will become more tenuous as this broad base of organizational members become more attuned to a social ethic. Unfortunately there has been a tendency to treat the symptoms of social–behavioural change with partial solutions rather than recognize the basic social–behavioural changes.

In the search for solutions to human behaviour problems, many firms have attempted to merge individual aspirations and needs with organizational requirements through job enlargement or enrichment, limited participation in the decision process, and supervisory leadership-training, utilizing techniques ranging from simple role playing to non-structured T-groups, laboratory or sensitivity training. The current level of dissatisfaction by employees and outsiders with business organizations suggests that management has not yet developed means to satisfy changing social and behavioural patterns (Fitzgerald, 1971).

Modifications of the scientific management–bureaucracy model to attempt the integration of the economic and social missions of business firms are not adequate for the turbulent environments ahead. The managing of human resources in the future must bridge the gap between managerial attitudes, philosophies, and practices and the realities of changing human behaviour and the underlying work ethics. Aspirations and expectations about the nature of work and leisure are different. But management has no reference points or experience, and management theorists have not provided concepts to permit management to achieve both economic and social missions. The protestant ethic is rapidly becoming obsolete as an explanation for the behaviour of post-industrial man, but no prescriptions exist on how to deal with the new social ethic. And while an influential managerial elite holds firm to one ethical frame of reference as society moves on to a far different one, the consequences can only accentuate alienation and social turbulence.

Aspiration–alienation hierarchy

Against this background of imperfections among theory, practice, and reality, we can probe more deeply into the causes of upheaval in social ethics. History reveals that there is social turbulence in shifts between structural stages of development and behavioural ethics. Once a sizeable segment of society realizes that they could be better off, their rising aspirations make present realities seem more insufferable. DeToqueville noted this phenomenon in eighteenth- and nineteenth-century France:

> The evil which was suffered patiently as inevitable, seems unendurable as soon as the idea of escaping from it crosses men's minds. All the abuses then removed call attention to those that remain, and they now appear more galling. The evil, it is true, has become less, but sensibility to it has become acute. (Quoted in Jacoby, 1972, p. 71)

However, most past transitions in stable societies have stretched over a century or more, allowing a series of less drastic adjustments, whereas the current shift from a protestant to social ethic is more abrupt and uncertain. There is no cohesive goal to unite the populace, such as might have been served by religion or the desire to overthrow poverty-maintaining oppression during earlier transitional states. Society has become fractionated with each faction pushing its own cause in the name of improving society or restoring human dignity. Such a period challenges the responsiveness of institutions, organizations, and leaders to manage the change process if cleavages are not to become so deep and hostile that society borders on anarchy and teeters on the brink of self-destruction.

Paradoxically, the renewal of society is advanced by the self-destructive tendencies of behavioural ethics. Any ethic embodies the aspirations, ideals, and values of a prevalent majority of society. But as these aspirations and ideals become realities, the unity of the ethic diminishes as a source of inspira-

65

tion and guidance for the average citizen. The success of any ethic is reflected in the extent to which the structure of society becomes more complex and in the degree to which a greater number of people are made better off in terms valued by the ethic.

In evolving this transition within and between ethics, a few basic factors signal and contribute to social change. Exhibit 3.4 presents a hierarchy of six phenomena which lead to growing dissatisfaction with and the eventual demise of one ethic while giving birth to another. As one factor becomes developed, it stimulates the emergence of another, which feeds into yet another level within the hierarchy. And out of the ultimate social turbulence a renewed society and ethic takes form.

Exhibit 3.4
Hierarchical social change factors

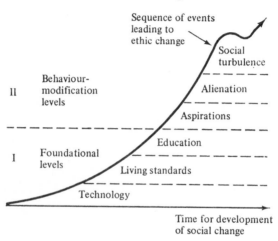

Technology is essentially a base condition which places limits on the form of social behaviour. Used in the anthropologist's meaning of the word, technology is any tool or means by which a society extends the range of human capabilities. The degree of technological elaboration thus determines how extensively humans will be used as sources of physical versus mental energy. Any minimal technology society such as a feudal or pre-industrial stage, will only allow subsistence living standards for most of the population with education and the dissemination of knowledge and beliefs passed largely by word of mouth from generation to generation. In such early stages of development the behaviour modifying upper-level factors may appear almost non-existent, since the transition is normally gradual.

Once society is well into the industrial stage–protestant ethic, it becomes possible for the individual to see that greater change is possible within his own lifetime. Spurred by widespread growing affluence in which average real

66

personal incomes might double within 20 years or less, higher levels of education throughout the entire population become possible. Education becomes a major vehicle for attaining influence, prestige, and wealth. With better-developed skills and understanding of the world about him, aspirations elevate to higher levels beyond purely creature comforts of life. Concern with one's self-identity, purpose in life and role in a larger society rise to a conscious level of awareness for a larger number of people (Reich, 1970). The individual modifies or channels his behaviour toward realization of higher aspirations, whether they be a more affluent and leisurely life style, intellectual or artistic development, self-expression in one's work, or the more ideal pursuit of making some contribution to humanity and society.

Aspirations are many sided. Sometimes they are tangible, such as wanting a job promotion or a new home or apartment. At other times they are illusive and exist as vaguely defined ideals or even wild pipe dreams, such as desire to help build a stronger Europe or a more peace-loving world. Seldom however is the realization of individual aspiration totally within one's self-control. Although strong motivation, commitment, and personal capabilities may draw an individual along a path toward an aspired objective, his course must frequently be indirect as he manoeuvres to overcome obstacles, follows dead-ends and occasionally crashes headlong into failure.

Man's pursuit of aspirations is not played alone on a field with competition removed. Throughout life, contenders vie for positions in school athletic teams, for scholastic honours, for positions of responsibility and leadership, and for the expression and acceptance of ideals and philosophies. There is a constant jousting for positions to win the mantle of success for personal efforts. It is not that society is what the mathematicians would call a zero-sum game—one person's gain not necessarily being another's loss. But neither are the benefits of society gained simply by following the economist's theory of exchange—that two or more parties will engage in exchange only so long as everyone comes out ahead in his own mind. The oft-used example of trading five apples for four oranges because oranges are preferred more than apples by one trader and the second trader is indifferent in his preference is applicable only for limited types of market interactions. Furthermore, behavioural ethic shifts could change individual aspirations to abhor any exchange or the rewards from material and individual success.

In social interactions—whether they be within a family, an organization, between racial or income groups, or between institutions and nations—adding up the score of wins and losses is no simple matter. As millions of individuals and thousands of larger groups and organizations pursue widely differing objectives, interactions inevitably cause the actions of some to thwart the progress of others, while for others they are mutually advantageous. At any point in time society's resources are relatively finite. Not all goals can be realized, whether personal or societal, but it would seem that the social ethic has failed to recognize the problem of conflicting goals.

An excellent example is the acceptance of the goals of full employment and price stability by the majority of the Western industrialized nations as well as by the Eastern European Communist Bloc countries. The prestigious OECD (1970, pp. 23–9) has categorically stated that these goals are incompatible, utilizing existing fiscal and monetary tools. Poland has had riots in a police state over rapidly rising prices, and inflation is one of the most critical issues in all industrial nations with obvious failure by any country to contain it.

The economist may belabour this dichotomy of goals as over-simplified because desire for economic growth, budget deficits, and the like are perhaps even more important contributors to inflation. But this example well illustrates the emergence of the social ethic in national goals. In 1972, the Netherlands instituted a government policy to forbid layoffs, because unemployment doubled from 1971 to 1972, reaching a high of 129 800 in a total population of 13·3 million. The obvious result will be higher costs and therefore higher prices in Holland. The social ethic dictates one course of action but the societal stage interdicts its successful implementation. The hard facts of economic reality may not be acceptable in the social ethic, but economic failure will only further accelerate societal turbulence.

Achieving a victory requires hard work and effort but there are rewards of self respect and a sense of accomplishment. But what about those who never taste victory—those who constantly taste the bitterness of failure and defeat? As education makes individuals more skilful and knowledgeable, so also does it elevate expectations and aspirations. However, repeated failure to attain just and accepted aspirations leads to alienation. Individuals or groups with common aspirations who find their efforts to bring about change or advancement consistently blocked will become alienated from society, or from certain classes or groups within society or, most tragically, even alienated from themselves if their sense of self worth is reduced (Schacht, 1970).

The teenager bored by educational experiences which are not meaningful for him may become alienated from an educational institution. If his efforts to find employment are similarly blocked because of restrictions and barriers to entry, he may become alienated from all of institutional adult society. He physically and mentally rejects the norms of acceptable society; or he may sublimate and seek personal meaning through daydreaming or other activities.

The minority member of society who because of race or religion finds countless doors slammed in his or her face rightly recognizes that the prejudiced majority employ discrimination for their personal gain (Basil, 1972). His alienation turns to hostility and hatred and finds expression through collective demonstrations, violence, or revolution.

Even the average citizen—the epitome of the ideals of the protestant ethic —becomes resentful of having to contribute his taxes for the support of programmes he rejects or for a direct subsidy to individuals he feels are less worthy than himself. His alienation is a sense of frustration and resentment toward the system over which he has no control or power. He complains about the wastes of government, high taxes, and social misfits when among friends, but seldom takes action to change the situation because of the futile feeling he is just one among millions. The entrepreneurial businessman typically feels powerless and resentful about government policies which erode his managerial freedoms. This is aptly illustrated in the experience of French businessmen as they are confronted by national economic planning;

> Obviously, the plan's emphasis on efficiency, economies of scale, and industrial expansion is in direct conflict with the traditional conservative behavior of a majority of small family-owned firms. Since the governmental authorities provide inducements for compliance with the plan's objectives in the form of subsidies, the firm that doesn't let itself be 'induced' may soon find itself at an impossible competitive disadvantage. (Schollhammer, 1969, p. 83)

The two extreme symptoms of alienation are futility and revolution. Both extremes as well as gradations in between will be found in any modern society in the throes of social transition. Those whose behaviour reflects complacency and futility are usually the stalwarts of the past—they abhor change and become more entrenched in accustomed ways of doing things. In organizations they are equivalent to dry rot—they attempt to protect personal vested interests and resist change, further contributing to overall alienation. Because such people are more prone to inaction than action, they are often overlooked, and yet from a management-of-change perspective, they represent one of the greatest obstacles. The behavioural disease is apathy. Management and society have few effective cures for those already affected.

By contrast, the activist or revolutionary backs up his visionary idealism with a sense of zealous mission. He champions the clash with convention and established authority for the publicity it brings to his cause. Television follows his actions, whether leading an anti-war protest demonstration, rioting because of racial or religious inequality, revolting against foreign-government domination, or speaking out publicly against institutional practices that undermine health, safety or justice. The newsworthiness of the activist further infuriates the anti-change member of the old ethic, causing increased anxiety, resentment, and unwillingness to yield or negotiate.

Somewhere in between these extremes of do nothing/do anything are found most members of society. They feed on and react to the behaviour of the extremist as well as promote their own aspirations. Social turbulence is both caused by and creates other reactions. In an open societal system, widely differing actions and reactions interact. With disparities in ethics and desired objectives, society simmers in constant turmoil and at times boils over into direct confrontation or violence. The attainment of both personal and national goals are thwarted, leading to further alienation.

69

This state of social turbulence is not abnormal or atypical. Nor is it necessarily a sign of the break-up of society. *Social turbulence is the natural condition of a transitional shift in behavioural ethics.* It can be expected to erupt whenever a society functions on two ethics simultaneously. Turbulence is further augmented by institutions and organizations that are committed to the past and are reluctant to effect major reorientation except in time of crisis.

Social turbulence is not the limited domain of North America and Western Europe. Japan is quickly developing as a mature industrial nation and will soon join in the prosperity and problems of other more affluent nations. Some authors predict that by the 'eighties Japan will become the most prosperous post-industrial society (Hedberg, 1969). But such prosperity will not insulate Japan from increased social turbulence in the next few decades. Signs of behavioural change have already appeared in several large firms, such as the Matsushita Electric Industrial Co. (Panasonic and National products) whose work force at average age 25 gradually grow sceptical about paternalistic and ritualistic practices:

> There are also early, surface signs of a deeper generation gap; Japanese who have grown up since World War II generally do not revere work as life's primary activity. 'These young people are different. They're always asking why,' observed Executive Vice-President Takahashi. (Kraar, 1972, p. 98)

Japan, through its cultural heritage and its close coordination of the efforts of government, labour, and business, has fostered a protestant ethic or hard work, thrift, savings and economic security. Although the protestant ethic is reinforced by Japan's cultural heritage, economic prosperity and the contamination of the Japanese culture by foreign influences are creating a new social ethic, particularly among youth who are impatient and unwilling to undergo personal sacrifice for the sake of national economic growth. Japan is experiencing the same phenomena as the traditional Western nations, and even Russia and its Eastern European satellites.

No central authority can develop and control behavioural ethics. Although the state can influence underlying ethics and behaviour, society as a whole determines the norms for its members regardless of superimposed political or religious influences.

Turbulence from changes in ethics can revitalize society to produce institutions and organizations more responsive to the changing needs of society. But unmanaged turbulence and change results in a high price by society for change. The question is not whether society will undergo massive change in the next few decades, but rather can managers in private and public life manage the change to minimize disruptive turbulence. The effective management of change to minimize turbulence is a major challenge for managers, government leaders, and all men of wisdom to work toward change responsiveness in all parts of society.

Complexities of modern life

Turbulence from societal and behavioural ethic changes results in a corresponding turbulence in the individual's personal environment. The turmoil inherent in society's transformation increases complexity and causes uncertainties for the individual. In an era of environmental turbulence, new situations, often far removed in impact and nature from those experienced by the individual, occur at faster rates, and force choices between a greatly increased number of options. The final result is an increase in the general level of anxiety and inability by the individual to deal effectively with the ever-increasing complexity of modern life.

Contemporary industrial society has created material wealth and cultural advantages far beyond that experienced by kings like Louis XIV and Henry VIII. And society in the last hundred years has continually reduced the hours of work, and will undoubtedly further reduce them in the 'seventies and 'eighties. But society has simultaneously created new demands on man's discretionary time. The complexities of modern life result in the individual devoting more and more hours outside of work to what might be termed life maintenance. This includes additional time to commute to work as urban sprawl separates the worker spatially from his work, shop for daily necessities, repair and service possessions, pay bills, and fill out tax returns and other government forms.

Man also is challenged by loss of identity and feelings of impotence in impersonal dealings with large institutions and organizations. The punched-card syndrome in which identity is reduced to a series of numbers on credit cards, insurance policies, and memberships can be potentially demoralizing to those who see themselves as nameless cogs in the system. Except in the small town or self-contained neighbourhood, there is little or no individuality in the numerous interactions which are required for carrying on life's maintenance activities. To the shop assistant, Richard Jones is just another faceless customer, to the telephone or electric utility he is just another account, and to the government taxing authorities he is just another number to identify taxable income. Even the private car designed for mobility and travel flexibility fails to allow individuality because the infrastructure provides insufficient highways or roads to allow true mobility.

It is increasingly difficult to circumvent this loss of identity. And man, as his values shift from the protestant to the social ethic, is ambivalent. On the one hand, the standardized, routinized, impersonal methods of handling masses of people and their transactions becomes his servant. They free him from needless explanation and involvement in carrying on the tasks that simply have to be done, but from which he expects to derive little or no personal satisfaction.

On the other hand, the punched-card syndrome is symptomatic of the ills of society with its no-one-cares attitude and the feeling of conformity and

F

control. Not only does it foster impersonal transactions but it also contributes to a loss of privacy. The same computer which handles an individual's numbered account at a department store is capable of tapping a central credit file which can retrieve a record of his financial past and present. Man's entire public life is on file with commercial credit agencies, government tax and licensing departments, police departments with dossiers on non-criminals as well as criminals, unions, association rosters, employment records, educational transcripts, and other sources of recorded information.

Unfortunately, the advantages of modern technology with its computer-technological capabilities require that individuals lose some privacy in exchange for financial credit, employment, safety and other benefits. But much remains to be done to prevent abuses and further loss of privacy, identity, and individual freedom. The widespread alienation of the man in the street from society in general and governments in particular testifies that the loss of identity is indeed a product of the 'seventies.

Television plays a special role in influencing behaviour in the latter half of the twentieth century as both an educational stimulant and a placebo. It has not attained the horrors predicted by George Orwell in his book *1984* as a brainwashing and behavioural device. But television is an unbelievably powerful instrument of influence. It can placate the populace by providing a means whereby man can escape from the complexities of life. But equally it contributes to man's anxiety by its ability to bombard him with information.

Television is symptomatic of the information overload to which every member of advanced societies is subjected, even though television presents a simplified view of selected subjects. This information overload is not only generated by television, but also by radio, newspapers, books, magazines, signs, correspondence, and interpersonal communication in all forms. But even with the availability of these massive information sources, man knows relatively less and less because total knowledge is growing exponentially. Furthermore, man's mind only processes the smallest fraction of informational input to store it in his memory as raw data. And even most of this data bank remains as unrelated facts and opinions with little of it restructured and integrated in a way which is useful for understanding and making decisions.

In a turbulent environment in which the individual is confronted by more experiences and information occurring at faster rates, perceptual inputs of information may overload his capacity to think and to make decisions. He becomes bewildered and confused and finds great discomfort and difficulty in making even simple programmed decisions. Yet the life of post-industrial urban man in its complexity provides an ever-increasing number of options. The individual is faced with both information overload and option overload or what Toffler (1971) calls overchoice.

Individuals in a post-industrial society seldom have answers to pressing personal questions, often are uncertain of the alternatives, and may not even know the real question or decision facing them. Major uncertainties have been created by the complexities of technology, institutions, organizations, knowledge, and human behaviour. Since man is untrained in how to cope with either complexity or uncertainty, and rarely has a well-defined value system, he has few adequate criteria to serve as a frame of reference for decision making.

Institutions have failed to innovate or create means to aid the individual coping with uncertainty and option overloads. In fact, in many instances they have increased rather than decreased both complexity and general turbulence and uncertainty. These failures have further alienated the individual from society and hastened the substitution of the social for the protestant ethic. The failure of the protestant ethic to create the conditions to permit individuals to nurture their capabilities, accept responsibility, and make decisions has resulted in man becoming a dependent rather than an independent human being (Argyris, 1957, 1964).

Change responsiveness with its concomitant ability to accept ambiguity and uncertainty must be developed in a society which wishes to have independent, self-sustaining members. The potentially most powerful institution for developing this adaptive capability is education. But most societies have a long way to go before they attain what Glasser (1969) calls *Schools Without Failure*.

Education and human potential

Education, one of the major means for developing a change-responsive society, is itself in crisis. Failures in primary schools, secondary schools and the universities plague every nation and have exposed the dangers and short-comings of educational systems that attempt to perpetuate stability and uniformity. A recent outpouring of books characterizes the flaws in long-practised curricula and pedagogical approaches to education. Authors such as Holt (1970a, 1970b), Dennison (1970), or Weinstein and Fantini (1970) are representative of many who charge that the basic uniformity and tradition of educational systems has failed both the student and society. Formal education has not prepared citizens for living, experiencing, and learning in, or coping with the dynamics and turbulence of contemporary societies.

An integral part of the crisis is financial and revolves around the ineffective expenditure of funds for which questionable value is received. This is the resource-allocation problem which has dimensions both of (a) an investment for the future, and (b) the short-term limitation of the conflict in resource allocation among the many demands of society from police protection to road building. How much of a society's current wealth should be channelled into developing human resources and individuals for future generations? Unfortunately, increasing social turbulence often results in the withholding of resources for education even though such an allocation might result in solutions in the next decade.

In addition to the resource-allocation crisis, there is a major unresolved issue of content and methodology—what should be taught and how should students learn? Most of the nations of the world have a time lag in education with methods and content lagging behind current needs and conditions, and almost total failure to educate for the future. The structure of modern education is largely a product of a past period in which values were different, skill needs were basic and constant, and the multi-dimensional roles of man's life were of less concern.

Mass education—the ideal that every child, regardless of family income, class, religion, or sex, should receive some basic state-supported educational indoctrination—was originally a proactive strategy for nations entering early industrialism (Gardner, 1969). Factory output and economic wealth could be increased (a protestant ethic value) by increasing the ability of youth to think, read, analyse, and understand as he entered the world of industrialization. The structure of the system that evolved parallelled that of the occupational system into which youth would probably go—courses were highly structured, clear hierarchical authority was established between student and teacher, and everything revolved around prescribed time periods. As Toffler (1970) suggests, such a process of education provided an indoctrination model for youth that would mirror that which he would find in the world of work.

For a period in which stability was the norm and conformity was a contributory asset, such an educational process played a functional part in helping people adjust to the work-oriented dimension of their lives. Since the earliest beginnings of education, a primary aim of the process has been to inculcate future generations in the tradition and heritage of the past. Education insures that ancestors and culture, both myth and fact, will be remembered and preserved. The impact of this phenomenon of education has been passed along by every generation of teachers, even in the 'seventies. Does this history-bound system today prepare the individual for a future-oriented world of change, both in work and in the more personal realm?

Unquestionably there is value to be found in a liberal or classical approach to education. But how far should this be extended? Should every child from primary to secondary schools receive the same enlightenment? How extensively should a society's higher systems of education promote the humanities rather than the more pragmatic or career-oriented disciplines? Few individuals in today's world can afford the luxury of an education in which knowledge is sought after for its own sake. To be viable, knowledge, or better still, education, must be useful as a tool for improving the satisfaction of work and play, and contribute to the overall ability of society to survive and serve its members.

There is little doubt that today's standardized education, which is highly structured even at the university level, contains much wasted time and effort in attempting to provide each student with an equal dose of the medicine of knowledge. Students may ply through the pages of texts on academic subjects and perform adequately on tests of their memory ability. But are they really learning to conceptualize and integrate what is going on about them or are they merely playing the expected student role because it is the only option available to them? Are they able to learn at the understanding and reflective levels of reasoning? The reader can easily make his evaluation of his own education by reflecting on how well it prepared him to understand society and its complexities, and to make a personal contribution.

The educational expert will reject the validity of this text on either of two scores: (a) education must be broad based; or (b) the need for educational by-products, e.g., for mathematics to teach logic, is a justification for all students to study algebra and geometry. These are powerful arguments except for one fact—what students have learned and have been able to utilize in managing the complexities of life is far removed from the claims made by education. Modern education by most tests is just neither very efficient nor very effective!

France's violent May 1968 student revolt in Paris dramatizes the need for reforms in higher education. It led Georges Pompidou to react: 'The university is dead and must be rebuilt'. But subsequent changes initiated by the Fauré law to streamline administration and allow greater student participation have not resolved the problem that the universities still need skilled engineers, scientists, mathematicians, and administrators. This relative neglect of the pragmatic side of education is underscored in a statement by Servan-Schreiber in his controversial *The American Challenge*:

> The growing 'technological gap' between America and Europe is due primarily to a paucity of higher education, and thus a relative weakness of science and research. But it is also due to an apparent inability—stemming from a refusal to make an investment, which is precisely the word, in man—to grasp and vigorously apply modern *methods of management*. (Servan-Schreiber, 1969, p. 75)

The United Kingdom has grappled, perhaps more effectively, with a similar problem. Until the 1963 *Report on Higher Education* prepared under the chairmanship of Lord Robbins, England had virtually neglected graduate studies in business and management which were pragmatically oriented. Although several advanced management curricula have been initiated, subsequent experience has shown that for business education to become viable and relevant for the student and business community, there must be a re-orientation or replacement of traditionally economics-minded faculty and greater interchange between the university and the business community (Skertchly, 1968; Central Training Council, 1969).

Recent United States experience shows the dangers of imbalances within the professional disciplines. The crisis in the aerospace industry in 1971 dramatized that universities can over-specialize within a profession, as evidenced by an over-supply of highly educated aeronautical engineers. Again the past, even if only immediate, obscures the future, and universities continue to educate for a profession long after the absorption capacity of society becomes saturated. Although this example signifies a structural rigidity within the overall system, it is possible that the US, with its high percentage of young people with postgraduate degrees, faces a serious question of utilizing graduates for relevant and meaningful work. While some nations may produce too many graduates to employ them effectively, others are not producing enough to keep up with the demands of professions and more complex occupational roles. In 1966, only 4·8 per cent of England's population age 20–24 years were enrolled in higher education compared to 7·5 per cent in Germany, 13·2 per cent in Japan, 16 per cent in France, 24 per cent in Russia and 43 per cent in the United States (Chorafas, 1970, p. 89).

Education can be the fundamental change agent of society. But to achieve this potential, education must promote the fullest possible development of individual growth. The idea of individual development makes built-in flexibility mandatory within the process of education. This parallels the expectation that education in turn will help the individual to become more flexible in his own life as he faces an uncertain future. Structural flexibility requires more than the elitist–commoner separation of students as prevalent throughout Europe, or racially separated systems as still found in the United States. Class or racial barriers notwithstanding, the entire institution of education needs to reassess both its objectives and its means.

Fortunately, experimentation, albeit on a piece-meal basis, is widespread to develop greater responsiveness and flexibility within educational systems. As teaching becomes more soundly based on a foundation of psychological learning theory, coupled with an integration within the classroom of encounters with present-day realities and anticipations of the future, education will become more responsive to the needs of societies in transition. Greater opportunity for student exploration within the class to seek out the events which have meaning for enriching his life and furthering understanding of the environment about him is being tested in some schools. The element of some student choice in deciding what he will learn is compatible with preparing him for an active role in making responsible decisions in his post-student life. Still further, the concept of career or lifelong education will undoubtedly expand as a significant element of college and university education.

Education is not an end in itself but a means to furthering society's ends. However, in the midst of transitional stages and ethics, society has difficulty determining what those ends should be. In such a condition of uncertainty, the greatest resilience comes from the diversity promoted by decentralized education systems. Diversity also prevents resources from being allocated to what may be an inappropriate strategy for education and society.

In many respects the changes and reluctance to change within education are symbolic of the dynamic era within which all modern societies must function. Education illustrates the complexities of the general systems model as it is an institution truly affected by entry into the post-industrial structural stage and the conflicting coexistence of protestant and social ethics. Effective management of change, whether involving a redirection of educational strategies and resources or strategies and organization for a marketing-oriented firm, begins with the identification and analysis of change origins that affect future performance.

The past three chapters through theory and example have sketched out a basic conceptual framework for understanding change origins and their interrelationships. All of the changes analysed thus far provide foliage for the three main branches of our origins of change model: structural–institutional, technological, and social–behavioural. These multiple change origins impact on society's organizations, individuals, and institutions.

Now we are entering the second phase where these three zones of impact are analysed and assessed to diagnose how they have functioned in their attempts to cope with change. Before individuals, organizations, or institutions can move toward more change-responsive philosophies and strategies, current orientations to change and limitations to more effective change responsiveness must be diagnosed. As the reader will soon learn, many of the obstacles to a clearer identification of change and willingness to innovate and manage change result from clinging to behavioural ethics, structures, and ideologies which are inappropriate to the realities of the present and expected future.

Part 2

Transitional response to change

Man is an adaptive creature. He can live in the tropics of the Amazon jungle or on the ice-covered mountains of Greenland. He adapts his institutions and his society to change. What have these adaptations been, and how effective are they in light of the massive changes described in Part 1?

The motivations of man, his skill requirements, and his adaptibility provide the setting for any transitional response to change. How has the transition from the protestant to the social ethic affected man's basic motivational pattern? What contributions has behavioural science made to an understanding of man as the twentieth century comes to a close?

Organizations have to cope with the change in man's motivational patterns. The traditional concepts of control and conformity are under attack in organizations, but organizational development and its allied solutions have fallen short in substituting more effective concepts. Organizational climate is perhaps one of the most important components of a change responsiveness, but organizations have not yet created the mechanisms and means to use it well.

Strategic gaps are all too common in industry and government. Organizational inflexibility, ignorance of complexity and open systems effects, and organizational scanning failures have contributed to strategic gaps from the EEC farm policies to RCA's loss of almost 500 million dollars in the manufacture of computers. Such strategic gaps result in immense misallocation and waste of resources. Transitional responses in strategy formulation leave much to be desired.

4

Organizations
in transition

A major managerial challenge in the 'seventies and 'eighties is to prepare for future change through an orderly and planned transition without excessive turbulence and uncertainty. The tendency in man to polarize positions creates internal turmoil when man and society are in transition from the old to the new. The cleavage between apparent stability and the need for flexibility is more than a simple conflict between opposing managerial attitudes and philosophies. Under conditions of turbulent change, the outcome may mean the death or survival of the organization.

Darwin's survival model applies just as much to man's creations of firms, institutions, and even governments as it does to the survival of finches in the Galapagos Islands. Formal organizations, such as the business enterprise, belong to that special class of systems known as *ecosystems*, in which individual parts and organisms can be replaced to prolong effective functioning of the overall system. Malfunction of the brain, heart, or other vital organs speeds the single biological organism towards death, and even the marvel of medical transplants cannot prevent the eventuality of death brought on by old age and a worn-out system. By contrast, in a forest or other biological community, the death of singular animal and plant life is compensated for by the reproduction of the species, to keep the entire interacting ecosystem alive and resilient even to major disasters. Theoretically an organization is more like the forest than like the individual organism. It is capable of adding to and nurturing healthy and adaptive subsystems, while killing off or allowing to die those aged or outdated parts which consume more energy than they contribute.

Such are the possibilities of organizations. But more frequently than not, the gulf between the real and the possible is wide, deep, and inherently unstable, like the geological fault which produces an earthquake as the earth moves in opposite directions. Few organizations are subject to predetermined laws that limit the life span of the organization, except in rare instances of special charter. Yet, in activating the capacity for renewal, most organizations appear to be more analogous to separate biological systems than to perpetuating ecosystems. Few organizations survive the hostility of their environments during the first two or three years of existence. Fewer still develop beyond adolescence, stave off the blindness of past achievements, and function in sustained harmony with their environments.

Organizational models of change

How have organizations sought to cope with changes evolving around and within them? Why do they differ so widely in ability to achieve adaptiveness? What features of organization affect the degree to which an organization either lags behind, keeps abreast of, or initiates changes in its transacting

Exhibit 4.1

Progressive stages of organizational characteristics

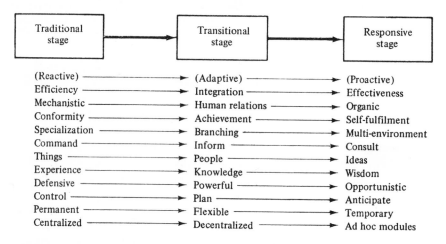

environment? As suggested by Exhibit 4.1, organizations can be described as containing a mix of characteristics which are either traditional, transitional or change responsive. Many, if not most, organizations still display those time-tested characteristics which deserve the ignoble title of traditional. But increasingly we find business firms, professional groups, universities, and even governmental agencies which are more transitional in their orientation; organizations that can adapt to new pressures and opportunities although not without difficulty. But the final change-responsive organizational form still remains elusive and uncertain.

The philosophies, strategies, and organization for developing change-responsive organizations are the prescriptive domain of the third part of this book. The task here is to examine the contemporary response of individuals, organizations, and institutions towards improved change responsiveness to cope with technological, social–behavioural and institutional–structural change.

The traditional management model, widely practised although deeply questioned by management theorists, defines organization as a structure of authority and task relationships. These interrelationships are considered in a mechanistic way to design an organization to standardize and coordinate economic output. In the behavioural model, organization is defined as the embodiment of collective purposes, processes, values, norms, beliefs, and relationship—a complex network of thoughts, feelings, and actions that is more accurately understood as a social rather than economic phenomenon. The decision-centred model accepts many of the tenets of the two preceding models but considers that the principal function of a manager is decision

Exhibit 4.2

Comparison of strategies and management-of-change models

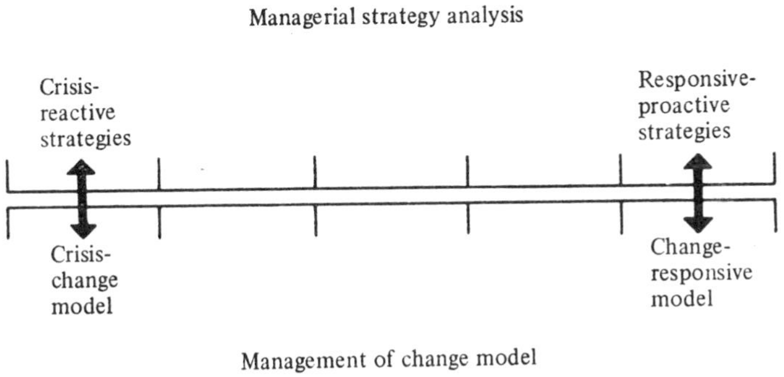

Managerial strategy analysis

Crisis-
reactive
strategies

Responsive-
proactive
strategies

Crisis-
change
model

Change-
responsive
model

Management of change model

making and all organizational design should be structured around decision making and decision makers.

Current managerial models are more preoccupied with differentiating between traditional, behavioural, and decision-centred attributes than with crisis-change and change-responsive models. Consideration of environmental impact is severely limited in contemporary management theories. Environmental impact is best approached by an analysis of the strategies used by firms with the primary differentials identified on the upper continuum in Exhibit 4.2. The appropriate management-of-change model corresponding to the strategies is found on the lower continuum. But it must be recognized that the utilization of occasional responsive–proactive strategies does not mean that the firm has developed and implemented a change-responsive model of management. In the 'seventies, responsive–proactive strategies have been more the result of the recognition of the potential impact of a hostile environment than of purposely developing change-responsive organizations and philosophies.

Crisis-change model in action

Few organizations have begun to approach the responsive–proactive ideal. They are engulfed in a system that perpetuates conformity, precedent, and procedure and allows past commitments to bear heavily on current decisions. Reaction to crisis continues to be the primary model of adjusting to change. Building on past successes and rejection of uncertainty is to be expected of man and his institutions. It is only as change accelerates and companies enter turbulent environments that the impetus to develop change-responsive organizations will occur.

The chemical and plastics industry provides an interesting example of crisis–reactive strategies with traditional and transitional organizational forms. It utilizes relatively sophisticated technology and has undergone structural competitive changes as it matured. A trio of interrelated events—relative ease of product duplication or technological imitation, expanded international competition, and undifferentiated commodity characteristics of most non-consumer products—led to a 1971 worldwide condition of manufacturing over-capacity. In a period in which prices typically are rising, the capacity glut in the chemical and plastics industry has forced prices downwards to some 65 per cent of the level 15 years ago, and reduced return on investment.

Union Carbide receives a substantial part of its 3000 million dollars annual sales from this industry and has witnessed a drop in its return on equity from 15 per cent to less than 9 per cent between 1961 and 1971. Faced with these technological and market-structure changes Union Carbide pursued a strategy intended to preserve its traditional organizational processes and orientation. Rather than diversify out of commodity chemicals which manufacturers in any country can produce, Union Carbide opted to invest nearly 2000 million dollars over five years into protecting its share of market in basic chemicals and plastics, products which accounted for 40 per cent of 1971 sales but only 22 per cent of pre-tax net profits. It committed 250 million dollars, for example, into one of the world's technically most sophisticated chemical complexes. But while computerized controls and modernized equipment reduced unit cost on the annual output of 3500 million pounds, it also added to world capacity at a time when firms in other countries, many of them under-developed, were doing likewise.

Chairman of the Board, F. Perry Wilson, realized Union Carbide must make a transition away from dependence on commodity products, as noted in his remark, 'Some day I'd like to see us with 50% of our sales in consumer products but . . . We won't reach that figure in my lifetime' (*Forbes*, 1 July 1972, p. 42). Transitional organizational change is occurring, for example, in reshaping research and development, but the process is slow. A new management system using a modified management by objectives is being introduced to focus attention on critical objectives and to incorporate a shorter time horizon into long-range planning. But as the chairman realized, turn around for Union Carbide will be slow and expensive.

The world's largest chemical company, Imperial Chemical Industries, is a firm largely characterized as transitional, but wishing to employ traditional tactics on occasion. Shortly after its founding in 1926, ICI worked out patent-sharing agreements with DuPont and I. G. Farben in exchange for a geographical division of markets—DuPont and Farben would stay out of Britain and ICI would stay out of the US and Germany. The dissolution of this restraint of trade agreement by the US Federal Trade Commission in 1952 opened up the possibilities of a new competitive restructuring of the world chemical markets. Not until the early 'sixties, however, did ICI begin to show signs of transitional adaptation by branching into international marketing and production outside of Great Britain. Unlike Union Carbide, ICI invested capital in shifting out of dependence on commodity chemicals into higher-margin pharmaceuticals, fine chemicals, and agriculture products. Such a major shift in product-market strategy required a transitional shift in perspective away from economies of scale to reliance on cost controls as a measure of effectiveness.

But at the same time that ICI was expanding into foreign markets, largely via acquisition, at least some of its top executive management group were pushing for a return to the days of a chemical cartel where market conditions were more certain. During a September 1971 meeting in Düsseldorf of chemical and plastic executives from several companies, the chairman of ICI's plastics division, Edmond Williams, argued for 'some legally recognized procedure for better international and intercompany consultation'. But this desire to turn back the clock came at the same time that the EEC Commission was emphasizing greater competition among European firms to protect the economic health of firms which in the long run could not ignore Japanese, US, and other world competitors. For ICI, transitional approaches appear to have a strong chance of winning out over tradition, since a negotiated control of competition seems unlikely in today's environment.

The motor industry, and in particular General Motors, provides another example of crisis–reactive strategies and the need for change responsiveness. Despite the success that had made it the world's largest firm with a financial budget larger than any enterprise or government other than the US and USSR, General Motors is having trouble adjusting to a transitional organizational mode. Its difficulties stem from the combined impact of technological, social–behavioural, and institutional–structural changes. United States car manufacturers, and General Motors in particular, long have doubted the market impact of small cars. But under market pressure initiated by the popular success of the Volkswagen Beetle, and more pervasively the stream of Japanese imports, by 1972 subcompacts and compacts represented 39 per cent of the US market. This dramatic shift in buying behaviour toward a view of the car as simply a necessary mode of transportation caused General

Motors' standard-sized car, long its mainstay, to slip from 45 per cent of the US market to 33 per cent within five years.

Market pressures and government concern about car imports on the balance of trade eventually led General Motors to react to the small-car pressure by introducing the Vega subcompact. Seeking to turn a delayed reaction into an innovative production strategy, the firm built a 250 million dollar showcase example of the most automated assembly factory in the entire motor industry. To escape traditional union pressures of the Detroit labour force, the new Vega plant was located in rural Lordstown, Ohio. The company expected to find hard-working young men eager to get off the farm. But reality has turned a dream into a nightmare.

The Lordstown plant has one of the youngest work forces in the country with an average age of 25 and a 29-year-old union president. There is no protestant work ethic at Lordstown—shoulder-length hair, mod clothes, peace symbols, drug addiction, and imported cars—these are some of the outward manifestations of the Vega production workers. While management carefully researched and planned its computer-directed 100 car per hour assembly line, it apparently failed to use the same thoroughness in selecting, training, motivating, and generally understanding its workers. Ranging from indifference and absenteeism to outright sabotage, worker attitudes and behaviour led to an enormous pile-up of cars waiting for repair and completion after having passed through this supposedly infallible automated line. Productivity is far below standard and disciplinary action is high, as evidenced by this bulletin board notice in one of the plant buildings:

> Management has experienced serious losses of production due to poor-quality workmanship, deliberate restriction of output, failure or refusal to perform job assignments and sabotage.
>
> Efforts to discourage such actions through the normal application of corrective discipline have not been successful. Accordingly, any further misconduct of this type will be considered cause for severe disciplinary measures, including dismissal. (Smith, 1972, p. 47)

These words signify that General Motors' management has taken a highly traditional organizational posture; one that will probably intensify employee hostilities before it improves productivity.

Such examples suggest that in business as in the theatrical arts, there are relatively few star performers who continually dominate the centre stage spotlight. Firms such as General Motors, Imperial Chemical Industries, Union Carbide—or Unilever, British Petroleum, Ford Motor Co, or Nippon Steel—are commonly familiar to more than one generation, but their positions of prominence are often due to sheer power of size and forward momentum than to excellence as a transitional or change-responsive organization. Market and economic power can long suppress the disturbances of change and mask the internal inefficiencies that sap both the will and capacity to improve or renew the organization. But few even large organizations can escape yielding to crisis when hostilities become so intense that power can no longer hold every antagonist in its proper place, as Lordstown and General Motors so readily illustrate. And as the traditional firm struggles to regain its footing, others rush in to steal the centre stage and prove to the business community and society that they have a more sensible, appropriate way—whether the ideas be an innovative method of transportation, energy production, washing clothes, population control, data processing, medicine, or entertainment.

The difficulties of sustained adaptation and success have been crisply captured in the words of a noted British historian:

> The go-ahead company of one generation—like Distillers' or Dunlops'—can often become the laggard of the next: and to a remarkable extent corporations behave like individuals, becoming middle-aged, corpulent, and sometimes just dying from old age. (Sampson, 1968, pp. 513–14)

In a more pragmatic vein, one corporation recently emphasized in an advertisement how lack of adaptiveness in crisis management can spell disaster:

> When we started out in 1920 there were a lot of companies around that are only memories now. And some that were around then still are today, but they're far down the list of leading U.S. companies.

The firm was ITT, which then boasted sales of 7600 million dollars, making it the ninth ranked industrial firm in the non-communist world.

Even the innovative and change-responsive firm all too often fails to recognize that it was not some specific market or product it developed but its change responsiveness which created its success. In a totally new market a well-managed firm will have a rate of growth that cannot be maintained simply because eventually there will be a maturing of the market. United States Steel was the first 1000 million dollar corporation, but during the twentieth century its market share has contracted three-fold and it has fallen out of the top ten US industrial rankings. Had US Steel maintained a compound growth rate equivalent to the economy as a whole during that period, in 1969 it would have assets of over 80 000 million dollars instead of less than 7000 million dollars (Vance, 1969). A change-responsive firm would have predicted such market maturity, and diversified unless prohibited by law.

Most organizations initiate change only in crisis, and often then only when it is a case of survival. Managers have become acclimatized by experience and education to *solutions*, not to *predictions*, of problems. Where this latter quality does exist it is often more a function of individual willingness to take risks—to put one's job on the line—than a product of intentional organizational development. As Greiner's (1970) studies of patterns in organization change indicate, managements and especially top managements have adopted a

G   87 passive role in managing change. Successful change, Greiner states, does not begin until strong environmental and internal pressures 'shake the power structure at its very foundation. Until the ground under the top managers begins to shift, it seems unlikely that they will be sufficiently aroused to see the need for change, both in themselves and in the rest of the organization' (1970, p. 221).

In the absence of more responsive and flexible change models, a crisis-reactive approach will prevail. This crisis-reactive tendency is the result of underlying uncertainties, misunderstandings, and rigidities in most organizations. One such critical area of uncertainty and misunderstanding is the effect of complexity on the organization and the management process.

Complexity in organizations

Business firms vie with one another to manage technology, gain market power, manipulate financial resources, and further domestic and international growth. Central governments, the largest single organization in any country (a) alter monetary, fiscal, and incomes policies to manipulate conflicting socio-economic goals; (b) compete with business and universities in introducing new and improved social and economic services; (c) adopt conflicting and discriminatory policies to protect special interest groups; and (d) act to promote national sovereignty while proclaiming the need for an expanded international posture. Labour unions demand more of everything except reform of their own organizations and promote the status quo through restrictive labour practices. Individuals aspire to a higher standard of living and quality of life, are more highly educated and knowledgeable, tend to become more sophisticated and cosmopolitan in outlook, and offer organizations a resource that has more potential than is currently fully utilized.

These events and ideas, although profoundly interconnected, do not present an integrated pattern. Organizational environments have become complex, difficult to predict, and almost impossible to manage. Environmental ambiguities are now of a magnitude unknown even during the Second World War, when uncertainty and complexity seemed the rule of the day.

Traditionally, complexity in organizations has been most associated with the phenomenon of size, of managing the activities and tasks of tens of thousands of employees. The benefits of economies of scale—allocating costs over a larger output–revenue base, sustaining longer production runs, or moving a larger volume of output per resource unit—have been expected to more than offset the complications of managing large organizations. But economies of scale can be an illusion in an era where changes in markets, technology, laws, and even human behaviour occur very quickly. The tax laws of several countries favour firms selling out part of their holdings and periodically consolidating activities to reap the advantages of capital gains. Multi-industry or conglomerate organizations view the purchase of heterogeneous companies whose price–earnings ratios are lower than their own as the strategy to multiply financial worth rather than traditional economies of scale.

Large-scale organizations produce managerial–behavioural discontinuities because of feelings of impotence and failure to associate individual productivity with organizational success. Size is thus but one symptom of complexity, but often it is the focal symptom because so many other aspects of complexity feed into it. The true level of complexity of an organization is a product not simply of the number of job titles and people in the table of organization but of the depth of specialization, segmentation, and professionalism that enables the organization to acquire knowledge from current operations, the latest developments in the research disciplines, and from the environment generally (Hage and Aiken, 1970). It is thus possible that a research-intensive organization of only 1000 people might be organizationally more complex than a mining, manufacturing, or transportation firm employing 100 000.

The complexities of formal organizations are most readily apparent in the conflicts that erupt within the organization and between it and transacting external constituencies. Over the years a number of tools or processes have been devised and implemented by organizations as a means towards coping with complexity and the recurring conflict so closely linked with it. Some of the processes for coping with complexity and uncertainty adopted by organizations in recent years include:

1. Cooptation or absorption of environmental elements
2. Decentralization
3. Management by objectives (MBO)
4. Long-range planning
5. Environmental forecasting (economic and socio-political)
6. Management information systems (MIS)
7. Operations research (OR)
8. Task forces or team management
9. Programme or project management
10. Product management
11. Organization development (OD)
12. Subcontracting
13. Use of outside scientists and consultants
14. Coordinating decision-making committees.

These strategies, techniques, and structures provide some means for keeping complexity under control and using it as a tool for organization development rather than as an uncontrollable enemy. Many of these coping mechanisms have been theoretically subsumed into the twin concepts of differentiation and integration. Organizations become more complex as they take on the characteristics of greater differentiation, which is the segmentation of the organization into functions or units to deal with specialized external environmental sectors. Each of these functions or units becomes more distinguishable from other parts of the organization through orientation toward specialized goals, differences in time perspectives, uniqueness in interpersonal orientations with colleagues, and variations in formality of structure (Lawrence and Lorsch, 1969).

The production department of a consumer-products firm, for example, might be differentiated from the research department in the same organization by focusing on control of unit costs rather than innovation and creativity (goals), by thinking about daily rather than annual tasks (time), in a concern for getting the job done efficiently more than with concern for peers (interpersonal), and function more within a structured command hierarchy than one built on consultation and collaboration (structure).

As subgroups become more differentiated, their linkages with other organizational units with whom they must interact become more strained. Conflict rather than cooperation consequently becomes the behaviour of individuals who identify themselves with groups that have little basis of similarity and accord, other than involvement with the same product. When marketing is clamouring for more product–package variations to satisfy customer idiosyncrasies, when production is trying to stabilize or reduce line change-over times or to become more automated to reduce costs, and when finance is pushing to reduce inventories and investment in fixed assets to speed up cash flow, the chances for subjugating self-interest for unselfish collaboration seem remote. Yet traditional thinking assumes that structure alone will suffice in bringing about necessary cooperation between the parts—what differentiation has split apart, chain of command can join together. Seldom is this the case except in small entrepreneurial firms under one-man control.

Complex integration and the tolerant confrontation of conflict are difficult to achieve for an organization steeped in a traditional ideology. Even organizations in a transitional state of adaptation and using combinations of MBO, task forces, and project management or other adaptive mechanisms typically encounter major problems in change responsiveness. Problems often begin to grow with a past success, such as in the building of a bureaucratic organization that is highly efficient in stabilizing the administration of specific tasks. But the needs of routine management are opposed to those of change, and institutionalized policies and procedures lead to organizational sclerosis.

A form of hardening of the arteries develops where new ideas and sources of information become choked in procedure and edited as they pass through level upon level of informational filter, each narrowing the passage in the corporate pipeline. Accurate monitoring of the environment becomes nearly impossible as critical clues fail to reach the appropriate decision maker. Internal entrenchment in established ways and lack of sensitivity to the external environment blocks or dilutes attempts by managers who do try to modify structure, objectives, or actions. Frequently, even top managers simply go through the minimal motions of reforms to satisfy the activists who press for change, but when the changes fail to produce positive results, they use the failure as a mandate for a return to old ways.

Complexity in large organizations, however, can be very forgiving of weaknesses in strategy or structure. Often the forward momentum of an organization is enough to sustain it during troubled times. The slack built into complex organizations allows a certain amount of coasting and resting on one's laurels. Ironically it is the existence of organizational slack, or under-utilized resources, that provides the resilience for innovation to occur; yet, during periods of stress and reduction of profits, the first line of defence is usually to cut or reduce resources (pare costs is the usual policy statement) rather than attempt to utilize them more fully (Guetzkow, 1965).

Although complexity is not well understood, it allows organizational slack and has great resilience, which permits some degree of change responsiveness. Less complex organizations, such as a small manufacturing firm with one or two industrial products, or a retailer in a single neighbourhood, are more certain and easily understood by the management, but they have far less power over their environment and are more vulnerable to sudden shifts in customer expectations, competition, or supplier practices. As an organization develops in complexity, its abilities become more diffuse and its transacting environment more heterogeneous. As this occurs, dependence on any single sector of the environment decreases and the organization increases its ability to adapt to environmental change by shifting priorities.

Yet as the environment and the internal organization become more complicated, many organizations experience difficulties and uncertainties in shifting organizational forms to cope with change. This inability to deal effectively with change often results in a pendulum swing from centralization to decentralization.

Centralization–decentralization syndrome

One of the most common methods for managing the twin problems of direction and control in complex organizations has been the concept of decentralization. The word concept rather than structure is used judiciously, since in the true meaning of the word, decentralization involves more than simply structure alone. Carried to its fullest fruition, decentralization embodies a philosophy that individuals are capable of thinking for themselves and should be allowed to do so in the economic interests of the organization. Rice and Bishoprick (1971, p. 101) highlight the essence of this ideal: 'It holds that any individual in the organization needs only to be given some broad policy guidelines, which, in addition to the value structure which he holds, will allow him to make his own decisions for the benefit of the organization'.

Such an egalitarian brand of decentralization is seldom, if ever, found in complex firms and governments. Instead, decentralization becomes a compromise by top management with limited delegation of authority but total delegation of responsibility. Deciding the balance between functions which are centralized and those that are delegated remains a highly pragmatic matter in the eyes of top management (Holden *et al.*, 1968). Chandler's (1962) widely quoted thesis that 'structure follows strategy' is in reality much like the proverbial chicken and egg question of which comes first, but the implication remains valid that organization structure should be compatible with and facilitate the achievement of organizational goals and strategies.

Centralization–decentralization is not a simple either–or issue. Nevertheless, a great amount of managerial thinking is focused on the question of centrality as if it were the main substance of organization. Failure to accept the fact that organizations are not simply one or the other has caused confusion among managers at all levels.

Such confusion was exemplified in a medium-sized bank where the president felt that his regional branches constituted a decentralized operation. However, interviews with regional managers found that open conflict and apathy existed. There were ambiguities in operational responsibilities; communication between headquarters and the branches was grossly inadequate in both directions; all personnel decisions were centralized; loan jurisdiction varied according to branch size and the personal history of the manager; hours of public operation were set by top management. Was this decentralization? The difference between what the president expected and what actually occurred was not highly correlated. Ambiguity was a more appropriate description, with confusion accentuated because the president did not understand the concept of delegation.

A former chief executive of General Electric (US) clearly stated what is necessary for effective delegation. He indicated that clearly thought out, simple, and understandable systems of objectives, policies, assignments, schedules, and methods of evaluation; and completely trained and developed people who know what is expected of them, are critical for successful decentralization (Cordiner, 1956). Like many large firms, General Electric found that explosive post-Second World War growth made obsolete its traditional method of highly centralized decision making. Decentralization, started in the early 'fifties, became almost a fetish in dividing the organization into manageable units. As a result there was an extreme division of market sectors into product groups with a resulting loss of strategy formulation for markets as a whole.

Decentralization at General Electric was not linked with a philosophy and strategy of change responsiveness. Organizational difficulties climaxed in the inability to manage effectively three risky ventures—computers, nuclear power, and commercial jet engines—resulting in an estimated 500 million dollar reduction in after-tax profits from 1965 to 1970 (Demaree, 1970). Despite successive management changes and the acquisition of the French computer manufacturer, Machines Bull, and Italian Olivetti's data-processing division, the chairman of the board at General Electric, Fred Borch, found himself in command of an organization unable to orient itself to the computer market.

Borch had several opportunities in the late Sixties to make a run for a larger market share by investing more money and effort, buying other foreign manufacturers, or introducing an advanced product line. He chose instead to delay an aggressive strategy and cut G.E.'s losses. Borch now admits a fundamental reason for what seemed, at the time, a dithering approach to the business. 'We didn't have the competence to pursue it,' he says. 'It would have been foolhardy.' (Demaree, 1970, p. 156)

Although many large firms make organizational changes periodically, few of these are as far-reaching as the effort involved to re-orient an organization from a more traditional philosophy of centralization to one embodying a substantial degree of decentralization. There have been many outstanding successes with transitional decentralization, but the record is marred by equally impressive failures. The centralization–decentralization syndrome has been one of vacillation between opposing sets of seemingly valid and logical arguments.

The *arguments for decentralization* include the following points:

1. An increase in scale of operations (geographically, product line, projects, or diversity of functions) creates so much complexity that tasks must be divided into manageable units.

2. Profit centres are created to delegate revenue and cost performance to a single responsible position.

3. The granting of autonomy to one manager in charge of plant A, territory B, division C, or product line D, permits decentralized decision making and coordination without the necessity of channelling information for decision making to one central authority.

4. The creation of autonomous units permits top management to concentrate on critical policies and strategies affecting the entire corporation.

5. Top management provides overall guidelines to integrate the operating divisions and professional services from the headquarters staff to assist in planning, monitoring, and problem solving (Basil, 1970, p. 90).

6. The behavioural advantages of decentralized decision making are the utilization of man's unique thinking and creative resources; feelings of involvement and coordination of managers' personal goals with organizational goals; and the introduction of a humanistic philosophy of management with the development of effective and responsible human beings.

The *arguments for centralization* which seem equally powerful include these points:

1. It is a fallacy that lower-level decisions are better simply because the decision maker is directly responsible for the consequences of his decisions.

2. Decisions are qualitatively limited both by the analytical capability and knowledge of the individual decision maker and by the adequacy and organization of data; and lower-level decision makers are less qualified and lack much of the critical information available to the headquarters staff (Simon, 1957).

3. Computers permit higher levels of management to make fuller utilization of management science models which an operations-research staff has programmed to test alternatives or schedule and allocate resources more quickly and accurately than can be done by human judgement alone. Not only does a centralized computer give top management greater control access to current operations, but also industry simulation models permit the projection of future environments by varying sets of assumptions.

4. Centralization of expensive capital items such as computers as well as supportive services such as research, personnel, public relations and finance reduces waste and duplication of services.

5. Centralization of decision making prevents managerial crisis by a more objective point of view by the decision maker.

6. Speed of decision making is greater with quicker implementation through centralized decision making.

The arguments and rebuttals are more involved than the summary positions presented here. But it is obvious that current management theory and practice does not provide one organizational form as a panacea for this problem. Current centralization and decentralization models do not solve the problems of increasing organizational complexity.

The failure to develop change-responsive modes of organization structure leads to a management-by-crisis approach. This lack of change-responsive organization has created major problems of organizational change for United Air Lines, the largest airline outside the Soviet Union. Organizationally, the firm remained highly centralized throughout the 'sixties during a time of substantial growth and introduction of new technology. The chief executive officer was relatively isolated in his Chicago headquarters and practised a style of deferring decisions which was emulated throughout the organization. The economic recession of 1969–70 caused a general slump in the airlines industry for which no effective strategies were developed, due to the sluggishness of the decision system. A former customer-service manager of United Air Lines notes: 'The company was very centralized. . . . It took so long to justify things that by the time you could get it justified you didn't need it anymore' (Loving, 1972, p. 73).

The failure of the organizational form to respond to the new environment resulted in the board of directors appointing a new chief executive officer who could build a system which would respond to environmental change. The new executive, although inexperienced in airlines management, recognized

94

the failure of the existing response mechanisms and established regional divisions to initiate a thrust toward decentralization. He created a new managerial philosophy of commitment to problem solving and individual responsibility for decision deadlines. The result was widespread acceptance of the concept of accepting responsibility for service and profits with elimination of redundant services, especially in the central headquarters.

A change-responsive organizational form would have permitted the early recognition of the obsolescence of the centralized organizational structure and the development of appropriate proactive strategies. Unfortunately, the crisis-change model, with its dependence on the values and judgement of a key or a few key managers, usually requires major replacement of top management to change an outmoded organization with its dependence on the rigidities of a self-perpetuating hierarchy (Chandler, 1962).

Hierarchy and flexibility

Questions of centrality of power and the breadth of delegation practices naturally confront the issues of integration and flexibility. But even more fundamental to adaptability is the formalization or degree to which organizational procedures, positions, status symbols, and communication become institutionalized. Only during the past two decades have an increasing number of organizations begun to express concern about the emerging need for flexibility in structural design. Most, however, are still geared more to a system based on stability and predictability than one of capacity for innovation and change responsiveness.

Organizations have had few guidelines from management theorists directed to the problem of opening up structures, to make them less conforming and more responsive to environmental possibilities. Katz and Kahn (1966) observe that:

> The typical models in organizational theorizing concentrate upon principles of internal functioning as if these problems were independent of changes in the environment and as if they did not affect the maintenance inputs of motivation and morale. Moves toward tighter integration and coordination are made to insure stability, when flexibility may be the more important requirement. (p. 26)

Management theory has tended to do little more than reflect the state of the art in organizational practices (Kroos and Drucker, 1969). Organizational practices largely reflect a mode of behaviour that was placed in motion and given definition by the industrial giants that launched society into an industrial era. Both theory and practice in management thus bear the burden of decades of acquired tradition, learned during a time in which organizations identified closely with a narrow line of endeavour, when corporate missions were more definable and operational, and when the environment was fairly certain and controllable. Given this combination of circumstances, it is understandable why the central force in organizations today is one akin to classical patterns of bureaucracy.

Most interpretations of bureaucracy spring from the original work of Max Weber (1904) who considered this to be an ideal organizational form to maximize rational decision making, provide for administrative efficiency, achieve stability and perpetuate continuity. Essentially bureaucracy in contemporary organizations is characterized by:

1. A well-defined chain of command—a hierarchy of explicit authority-status relationships.

2. Highly specific division of labour through task specialization.

3. An impersonal codified system of rules and procedures for handling all routine activities and expected contingencies.

4. The acceptance of tenure, seniority, and technical competency as the basis for promotions and remuneration increases.

5. The separation of administration from ownership.

6. The assumption that given such a structuring, and impartial treatment, members will work in an organizationally rational manner.

Such a set of concepts has largely served as the model of industrial and governmental organizations during the past 50 years. Taken in perspective, this system is an improvement over the personal whims and idiosyncrasies which prevailed when businesses were owned and managed by captains of industry for whom management was an extension of personality. But with the institutional–structural, technological, and especially social–behavioural changes in the post-industrial era, the assumptions and functioning of traditional bureaucracy are suspect as a cause of much maladaptive performance. Bureaucratic structures are intended to provide for routine, stability, and continuity—the tenets of the industrial rather than the post-industrial societal stage.

Recent research by behavioural scientists provides more insight into why highly structured systems are negatively correlated with adaptive flexibility. The pioneering study of major significance was an investigation of Scottish electronics firms by Burns and Stalker (1961). This team was responsible for popularizing the terms *mechanistic* and *organic* as indicators of extreme types of organizations. The mechanistic form epitomizes the bureaucratic tradition, with its precise definition of organizational form and technical requirements for each function. It emphasizes structure and hierarchy for control, authority, and communication to achieve goals and accomplish tasks. By contrast, the organic form relies more upon individuals with specialized knowledge and recognizes unique individual capabilities. The organic system allows for a continual readjustment of individual tasks through an integrated network of communication, authority and control. Central to the distinction between the two is how integration within the system is achieved—whether by rules and norms to perpetuate stable behaviour, or by functional interdependence as generated by system-goal requirements.

Subsequent research has confirmed and extended Burns and Stalker's findings (Pugh *et al.*, 1969; Lawrence and Lorsch, 1969; Hage and Aiken, 1970; and Child, 1973), isolating the following *characteristics causing decreased adaptiveness*.

1. An increase in the number of levels of supervision coupled with a narrow span of control—a tall rather than a flat organization.

2. Control by detailed inspection of work methods and procedures rather than by evaluation of results—emphasis on conformity and uniformity rather than outcome.

3. Standardization of communication channels closely linked with the authority of hierarchy, and communication content consisting more of instructions and decisions to be implemented rather than exchange of advice, consultation, or information.

4. Decisions reached by use of power and bargaining with suppression of conflict rather than reliance on knowledge and open analysis of reasons underlying conflict—confrontation of a win–lose nature rather than collaboration.

5. Low task complexity based more on physical than on mental skills and a low ratio of managerial and professional staff people to those employees directly engaged in tasks of producing, handling, and selling the organization's output.

6. An insular attitude of top management more inward looking than outward, with a sense of commitment to and vested interest in past decisions.

7. Self-selection of managerial incumbents with managerial in-breeding through a highly restrictive internal promotion system.

Obviously these characteristics are relative rather than absolute and the way in which they, and other factors, are combined will affect overall levels of adaptiveness or responsiveness. It is paradoxical that organizations cannot rid themselves of all the undesirable features of hierarchy to achieve greater adaptiveness. Stability, and thus some form of hierarchical structure, remains necessary for the conduct of current, more routine operations, particularly in business and government. Furthermore, the concept of fixing responsibility to specific positions is a highly ingrained and necessary part of the twentieth-century organizational system. What is necessary, however, is flexibility in the structuring of subsystems so that components and positions are not necessarily subject to the same degree of standardization in procedure, control, and planning.

A modified bureaucratic organization is the form usually designed to provide transitional adaptiveness. The completely free-form, temporary, democratic organization, such as advocated by Bennis (1966, 1969) and other behavioural scientists who suggest the removal of structure, remains an ideal and possibly unrealistic dream. Bennis (1969, p. 34) visualizes organizations of the future as: 'Adaptive, problem-solving, temporary systems of diverse specialists, linked together by coordinating and task evaluating executive specialists in an organic flux—this is the organizational form that will gradually replace bureaucracy as we know it'.

Experience has yet to produce any major successes with such an idealized system among large mission-oriented organizations. Organizations, other than a few professional types such as small research institutes, colleges, or hospitals, have not been able to decentralize decision-making completely to participating or democratic groups (McGregor, 1967). In the first place an attempt to do so on a large-scale basis fails to consider the organizational need for orderliness and coordinated activities towards mission goals with continuity for some subparts. And secondly, it clearly ignores the differences in needs among individuals.

Past conditioning makes twentieth-century man demand a fairly predictable, quasi-dependent atmosphere. Only a few feel at ease with the high uncertainty of transitory structures. In a state of constant reassignments people tend to become emotionally distraught over the feeling of homelessness. This has been particularly noticed in large organizations when high-ranking individuals, familiar with line positions, have been temporarily reassigned to special task forces for several months. The conflict between the need for flexible structures and resistance to them together with guidelines for coping with this dilemma is a major focus of Part 3.

Numerous attempts to achieve greater organizational adaptability and at the same time increase member satisfaction have used group processes aimed at developing more democratic–participative processes. Most such efforts in industrial organizations have produced at best mediocre results, but even transitional improvement is better than rigid insensitivity to change needs. One pioneering effort deserves special attention as it shows some of the limitations in expecting too much from democracy in industry.

A British engineering and metals concern, Glacier Company, was one of the first post-Second World War companies to experiment in using group therapy combined with democratic processes to change an industrial organization (Jacques, 1951; Brown, 1960). Tavistock Institute was the source of therapists who acted as change agents at several levels, primarily by listening and providing feedback about group processes. The overall effort was a quasi-democratic attempt to improve member understanding of organizational interrelationships and to achieve a restructuring of the organization by members themselves rather than as a result of directives from management. But as the group-diagnostic process progressed over time, no restructuring occurred. If anything, the system moved toward a more authoritarian hierarchical structure as role relationships became more clearly defined.

The originally intended shared-decision mechanism of a union–management works council became more limited in scope. Restriction of participation in management decisions by non-managers involved a compromise necessary for survival of a marginal performer in a competitive industry. Katz and Kahn (1969) summarized the major results of this change-inducement effort:

> The group therapy process at Glacier thus helped management clarify its policies and procedures with respect to management responsibility, making unambiguous the character of the executive structure as an order-giving system, and stipulate the part to be played by the representative system and by the union. In the past management had suffered from confusions about the use of consultative democratic procedures, the pretense of democratic participation, and the abdication of management from some of its responsibilities. (pp. 413–14)

In retrospect, the limited scope of success about participative practices at Glacier may have been as much one of timing as in method of implementation. Glacier may simply have been ahead of its time, and given the subsequent social–behavioural changes, the experiment might have been more successful. Additionally, the experimenter–innovator venturing into uncharted territory does not have the benefit of the lessons of forerunners, greatly lessening the chance of success.

Hierarchy and some degree of leader-centred decisions remain unavoidable in organizations during the transition period between the protestant and social ethic. But firms are beginning to decrease the overbearing degree of management-imposed structure that stifles innovative ideas and ignores the realities of environmental change. When firms adopt responsive–proactive orientations, organizations will reflect more the hierarchy of goals and programmes and less the pyramiding of authority bounded by role specialization.

Institutional–personal goal conflicts

Organizations represent groupings of human and physical resources to achieve collectively those purposes which could not be attained practically or economically by individuals alone. This principle is so basic that managers seldom question its significance or ponder its implications. Yet intertwined with this concept are all the underlying feelings and behaviours associated with organizational membership. The leaders of any organization where membership is voluntary (as opposed to involuntary penal incarceration or military conscription) are either foolish or ignorant if they cannot reliably answer these questions: (a) what is it about our organization that attracts people who seek to belong to it; (b) what conditions or factors motivate individuals to continue their association with us; (c) what causes individuals to lose interest in us and go elsewhere; (d) do dissatisfied members continue to retain membership with our organization, and if so, why; and (e) what impact do answers to the above four questions have on the attainment of our organizational purpose?

We purposely used the term members rather than employees so that we might illustrate how institutions differ in the reasons why individuals are attracted to them. For churches, fraternities, social and service organizations, and possibly political parties, membership is largely because individuals accept the norms or ideals represented by the organization. Normative organizations thus have a high degree of congruence between the goals or ideologies of the individual and those represented by the organization (Etzioni, 1968). Apart from any personal material benefit, there is intrinsic satisfaction gained solely from the association which links individual with organization so long as neither changes ideologies.

Once the focus shifts to organizations entered for employment, the subject of individual goals vis-à-vis the organization becomes more unclear. There are some professional types of institutions where organization membership becomes a way to further one's personal aspirations, as in academia, medicine, entertainment, or law. Such organizations permit the individual to practise his profession and to pursue achievement of self-fulfilment objectives rather directly. But for most of mankind, the job is a means to a more diffuse end. The traditional management assumption is that employment is simply a means of producing income which can then be spent to satisfy personal objectives, and the substance of the work is irrelevant. While this remains true for some, for others the job not only provides income but also serves to absorb time and prevent boredom, provides a sense of doing something useful, offers an outlet for social interaction, conveys status, or permits attainment of power, success, and scores of less tangible objectives. Outwardly, the job may appear to satisfy one or two personal needs, but subconsciously the individual may evaluate his employment and shape his behaviour in the organization on the basis of a dozen or more criteria.

With all the exhortations by theorists such as Maslow (1954), McGregor (1960), and Herzberg (1966) about the complexities of man's needs, goals and motives, it is ironical that organizations still ignore personal goals. Batten (1966, p. 48) states two straightforward reasons for this failure: '. . . first, sheer laziness and lethargy, second, the fundamental fallacy that the average employee's personal goals are somehow not in tune with those of the company or, at best, are irrelevant'.

This suggests that somehow, through ignorance or intent, managers have not come to grips with answering the four questions which introduced this subject. If this is so, then it can be fairly certain that managers have also failed to evaluate thoroughly the fifth question—the impact of possible individual–organization goal incongruence on performance in the organization. What happens if the individual finds that the organization frustrates his personal goals?

Some researchers and activists proclaim almost with evangelical zeal that

100

individual–organizational goal conflict is dysfunctional for both parties. Much of the problem about goal conflict links back with the previously discussed issue of what management conceives the organization to be. One principal critic of traditional organization, Chris Argyris, concludes that most conventional organizational practices deny the individual an opportunity to pursue personal goals within the organization and that this condition causes negative consequences for both. Argyris (1957) frames his argument by evaluating traditional assumptions:

> Thus the planner makes the assumption that administrative and organizational efficiency is increased by arranging the parts in a determinate hierarchy of authority in which the part on top can direct and control the part on the bottom. . . . The leader, therefore, is assigned formal power to hire, discharge, reward, and penalize the individuals in order to mold their behavior in the pattern of the organization's objectives. . . . The impact of such a state of affairs is to make the individuals dependent upon, passive, and subordinate to the leader. As a result, the individuals have little control over their working environment. At the same time their time perspective is shortened because they do not control the information necessary to predict their futures. (p. 10)

Essentially the same conclusions come from André Gorz (1968) who proposes radical strategies for labour unions in France and elsewhere. Suggestive of his condemnation of the failure of business to recognize the personal goals of a more trained, affluent work force is his synopsis of the plight of the semi-skilled worker:

> . . . the dominant contradiction is between the active, potentially creative essence of all work, and the passive condition to which they are doomed by the repetitive and pre-set tasks dictated by assembly line methods, tasks which transform them into worn-out accessories to the machine, deprived of all initiative. (Gorz, 1968, p. 36)

Where individuals feel frustrated and thwarted by the structural and impersonal requirements of organization, any of a number of defensive adaptive behaviours may be evidenced. Some simply reject the organization and leave. Others attempt to join or beat the system by climbing the organizational ladder. Defensive reactions may trigger aggression, ambivalence, regression, and daydreaming with the individual becoming apathetic and disinterested in his job and the organization. Dissidents may seek strength in numbers and create informal groups to sanction defence reactions by cheating, restricting output, making errors or mistakes, and generally shirking; and given time and success these behaviours will become entrenched in emergent work norms.

Additionally, individuals may outwardly orient themselves less towards the human factors of the job and seek increased material satisfaction through union pressures and even stealing. Argyris (1964) contends that the development of the above behaviours negatively affects organizational goals and causes management to counter by (a) increasing the degree of pressure-oriented directive leadership, (b) increasing the use of management controls, or (c) increasing the number of attempted participation and communication programmes. Management at the General Motors Vega plant clearly used tactics one and two while the Glacier Company attempted tactic three. Such managerial behaviour usually intensifies the clash between organization and individuals.

However, the reader should be cautioned against accepting these findings as conclusive. Because humans are extremely divergent in their individual patterns of behaviour, uniformity in the values and goals of employees cannot be assumed. Some individuals will tolerate a high degree of job dissatisfaction if the remuneration, including leisure time, enables satisfaction to be found in non-work activities. A study of Swedish workers found that work which is intrinsically dissatisfying may be accepted rather easily and counterbalanced by substitute satisfactions. Seeman's (1967) research offered an explanation:

> One such alternative would suggest that workers simply come to terms, more easily than our theories imply, with the only work life they know and can reasonably expect for themselves. . . . And the big task for the worker is not to convert it into a major source of intrinsic satisfaction, but to manage it so that it can be an acceptable life of the moment by creating occasions, however small, for humour, sociality, decision-making, competition, argument, etc., that are at once trivial and remarkable. (pp. 283–4)

However, the toleration of an organizational life that leaves little room for individual accomplishments other than financial income does not mean that it is the most effective or efficient system. Creating those 'trivial occasions for competition and argument' often erupt today as work stoppages and wildcat strikes, sometimes closing down entire industries in the UK, France, Italy, or the US to protest alleged mistreatment of a few or to voice general dissatisfaction. The traditional assumptions that money motivates and that direction, coercion, and control can bring about desired employee behaviour still retains a certain amount of validity depending on the situation and the individual. But such managerial considerations are subject to increasing doubt as they frequently result in erroneous judgements about individual expectations and willingness to produce.

This is particularly true in the case of younger workers who have developed in an environment so radically different from that of the current world leaders—a world with no major economic depressions or war between developed nations, with commonplace but major technological achievements like jet aircraft and television, many of which are questioned and even rejected by youth, and where personal leisure and gratifications are taken for granted by many. Such a changing reality is underscored by an industrial-relations manager for Ford Motor Co in a memo to his superiors. His message applies with equal validity to practically any routine job, be it factory, sales, clerical, technical or service:

> For many, the traditional motivations of job security, money rewards, and opportunity for personal advancement are proving insufficient. Large numbers of those we hire find factory life so distasteful they quit after only brief exposure to it. The general increase in real wage levels in our economy has afforded more alternatives for satisfying economic needs. Because they are unfamiliar with the harsh economic facts of earlier years, new workers have little regard for the consequences if they take a day or two off . . . the traditional work ethic—the concept that hard work is a virtue and a duty—will undergo additional erosion. (Smith, 1972, p. 46)

Conflict between protestant and social ethics and discrepancies between organizational and personal goals are not limited to non-supervisory employees. In the long run a more serious detriment to organizational viability is the goal conflict experienced by managers and professionals who feel confined in their ability to effect changes in the organization. Such frustrations are connected with the previously discussed highly centralized and restricted delegation hierarchy, where higher levels of management have opportunity for challenge and achievement but those in lower echelons experience confinement and limitation.

From a cross-section sample of 1072 American managers, England (1967) located several areas of major agreement and disagreement between personal and corporate values and goals. Those values and goals which were held to be important for the individual he termed *intended* and those which were judged important to organizational success he labelled *adopted*. The thesis of the study is that intended values affect managerial perception of problems and information, but that adopted values—those which are rewarded by the organization—are more instrumental in directly channelling managerial behaviour. Because of the demands and expectations exerted by the job, managers tend to suppress personal intended values, unless the conflict between inner ideals and job demand are so sharp that the individual stands up for his personal convictions at the possible cost of his job.

In examining the personal goals of individuals, England found that there was a high intended–adopted congruence on the values of achievement, success, and creativity. Some values judged low as intended goals were deemed to be important for organizational success as noted in Exhibit 4.3. England's research found high congruence on the business goals of organizational efficiency, high productivity, profit maximization, organizational growth, industrial leadership, and organizational stability; but the goals of employee welfare and social welfare were much more important to the individual than to the organization.

Reluctant compromises between individually and organizationally sanctioned values and conflicts in the priorities of goals generate pathological behaviour ranging from boredom and alienation to strikes and sabotage. Perhaps the most universal symptom is boredom arising from lack of challenge and opportunity in work itself. Organizations have long been accustomed to using human resources for tasks which would better be handled by machine, but human labour costs less as well as being a variable rather than a fixed cost.

This failure to recognize the need for challenge and opportunity applies equally to managerial positions and clerical and factory jobs. The manager is expected to be more tolerant because the carrot of future promotions is held before him. The stick must be used to prod clerical and factory workers whose future holds no promise of job liberation. Job enrichment or enlargement may provide temporary relief by restructuring jobs into more complete whole tasks,

Exhibit 4.3
Ranking of selective personal goals of managers

	Intended or personally induced (*per cent*)	Adopted or organizationally induced (*per cent*)
Achievement	83	69
Success	70	64
Creativity	70	63
Job satisfaction	88	41
Individuality	53	29
Money	28	46
Influence	18	47
Prestige	21	35
Power	10	52

Source: Adapted from England (1967).

but without further occasional change, routine and boredom again set in. Once a task is mastered, the challenge of further improvement fades. And simply because a person carries the title of vice-president does not mean that his job is interesting or that he is realizing a high achievement of personal goal realization on the job.

Social and behavioural adaptation

Business firms are only a mirror reflection of society. Although managers sometimes become enamoured with their progressiveness as leaders of industry, all industry lags behind the changes in society. True, firms contribute to change through the abundance and diversity of their product output, but the intent of business is not really to change values and behaviour except as a possible by-product of selling products or services. Firms are thus in a position of having to adapt and respond to societal changes—they are not the pace-setters which modify values and the contemporary societal ethic.

Collectively, firms—as do most other forms of organizations—still function almost exclusively according to a protestant-ethic constellation of values. Achievement, self-control, joy in work, independence, rationality, endurance of stress, cognition above feelings—these remain the foundation of the business ideology. While firms usually keep pace with the advancing stream of technological change, seldom do they display an equal regard for keeping abreast of shifting values and the ethic reconfiguration. Just as a firm cannot long ignore competitive technological advances, neither can it long remain in conflict with the values held by its most capable and aspiring members or by its environmental constituencies.

One key thread in this question of organizational adaptiveness is the much debated and misunderstood controversy over the role of business vis-à-vis society. Usually cloaked under the self-righteous umbrella of social responsibilities of business, the combatants in this verbal battle are not so much divided for and against, but disagree on whether business is responsible to society on an economic or noneconomic basis. On one side are those who reason in terms of profit maximization of stockholder's wealth while the other extreme advocates philanthropy in the name of promoting the common good. How does this social issue bear on the subject of change management?

Economist Milton Friedman (1962) has long been the arch-proponent of the value of free, unrestricted markets as the most effective mechanism for optimal resource allocation. He views that managers are employees of the stockholders and are therefore responsible to this group of equity shareholders, who for all intents and purposes are unknown names or accounts. Friedman (1970) argues that if social responsibility is something more than empty rhetoric, it means that managers are acting in ways not in the best interests of the stockholders. Managers would be acting socially responsibly, but irresponsibly for shareholders, if they were to (a) hold back a price increase to help prevent inflation, when a price increase would be in the interests of the corporation, (b) spend more on pollution controls than required by law or in the best interests of the firm to help improve the environment, or (c) hire the less-productive hard-core unemployed in the spirit of reducing poverty when better qualified workers are available.

The question which Friedman and others from his school of thought repeatedly raise is how does the corporate executive really know what is the best interest of society? How also does he know his actions will further that end without reducing or destroying the real contributory economic power of the firm—to provide products and services for which it has capable expertise and a critical societal mission, as well as taxes on profit to support society in general?

The problem of identification of the overall function and role of the business firm is not one that can readily be answered simply with the response that it is

105

the production and distribution of goods and services. Henry Ford II (1970), chairman of Ford Motor Company, believes that the uniqueness of business is in managing and producing economic growth. One of the ways business can use such capabilities consistent with societal improvement is through providing and training people for more productive jobs which allow as much utilization as possible of human skills. Ford blasts business as being discriminatory in employment and selling practices because managers are preoccupied with traditional prejudices about race, sex, and ethnic background, when such prejudices are in themselves against the best economic interests of business. These prejudices artificially restrict the market for customers and employees. Urban deterioration is another social concern that will in the long run impact most heavily on firms dependent on the economic health of cities as a place of conducting business—retailers, banks, service agencies, and their suppliers.

Business has largely exhibited a forced-compliance attitude toward social issues that are directly related to the conduct of business. Discriminatory employment practices are but one example. The responsibilities for one's actions in the production or use of products and services is another to which managers are reluctantly becoming resigned. As vocal spokesmen for society urge legislative or judicial action, business managers gradually acknowledge the inevitable fact that they will be held responsible for cleaning up the messes that business has created.

But as Friedman pointed out, few businessmen, other than outright philanthropists, will feel economically compelled to improve their products' quality, safety, or performance, or to clean up their production processes to the fullest extent that is technologically possible, when their competitors lag in undertaking a comparable social investment. William C. Stolk (1968), chairman of the board for the Committee for Economic Development, believes that industry-wide approaches need to be undertaken to prevent delayed action by firms which create a social cost to other persons. But here the problem becomes more complex, since competition for most durable and semi-durable products is becoming internationalized, if not in manufacturing at least in distribution. Thus, voluntarily improving one's production processes, even if induced by government regulation, may create a competitive disadvantage domestically that would be upsetting to balance of payments and employment —in short, the cure may be worse than the disease. Exploitation, simply pollution by another name, in the short run may continue the effective practice until worldwide economically feasible solutions are negotiated and implemented.

Social responsibilities of business, as the concept has come to be popularized, connotes a value-laden stereotype imposed by a writer or a speaker on his audience. The substance of the issue cannot conceal the fact that priorities are being implied as if from some omnipotent source of truth and morality. While this may be all well and good in the interest of arousing concern and

106

debate about the problem, the real alternatives lie more in the direction of the degree to which business, or any institution, remains responsive to the environment on which it is dependent.

To speak of social responsibilities really clouds the issue that the impetus of concern should be more in the realm of achieving social responsiveness. This distinction is more one of substance than of semantics. As long as society remains divergent in its values, and as long as society continues to change, there can be no uniformly acceptable priority of societal objectives. Since business is not the forerunner of societal change, we should not expect that enterprise unilaterally attempt to promote its personal brand of social-consciousness doctrine.

Social responsiveness does not mean, however, that business delay action until there is a clear mandate by the public in the form of legislation or regulation. Strictly from a point of view of achieving economic viability, it is not in the best interest of business simply to react and bow to pressures once they become unavoidable. On the contrary, economic and social performance is more optimally achieved by responsive monitoring of trends and environmental changes in society and initiating appropriate strategies for survival. The longer business delays getting its own house in order to adapt to shifts in public sentiment, the more restricted its options become once government implements public policy to reflect such societal shifts.

Concerns about social responsiveness by managers and others is but one of the many complexities of change with which business must deal. The degree of responsiveness which can possibly be attained by any one organization is closely linked with the way in which the organizational structure, values, and communication are expressed. Central to this issue are the attitudes and behaviour of managers and executives who ultimately are responsible for the destiny of their organizations. As the force of change becomes greater outside and throughout organizations, the managerial role is forced to undergo profound reshaping.

5

Volatile
managerial roles

The managerial role in the 'seventies and 'eighties is tenuous and uncertain, faced with shifting managerial philosophies and the transition from the protestant to the social ethic. Managers are the potential change agents who initiate and nurture organizational renewal. Yet, the indicators of necessary or desirable change in organizational products, processes, or structure are unclear and often contradictory. Demands and expectations of events and groups inside and outside the organization vie for managerial attention and complicate the perceptual–diagnostic process.

Increasingly a manager finds himself having to work with mega-problems—those which are many-sided and have far-reaching ramifications—not simply with a highly defined problem to be solved by his own actions alone. One set of forces cries out for innovative design and novel organizational approaches. Claimants from society, customers, subordinates, and sometimes the manager's personal aspirations demand speedy and innovative approaches to improve products, the quality of work, or the quality of life itself. Other forces exert a dampening influence to hold things in place and prevent dilution of energy that comes from fragmented activities. Expectations from higher management, stockholders, and sometimes direct competition, tend to disquiet experimentation or hold it within controllable bounds.

Aggregative changes in technology and in the collective aspirations of human beings threaten to outstrip the capacity of institutions to cope with demands of their constituencies. The manager can no longer depend upon signposts of past experience to provide indicators of how to perform in his managerial role. In place of orderly experience and general predictability, the manager now experiences complexity, ambiguity, uncertainty, conflict, and incongruity. Increasing manifestations of such turbulence will greatly complicate the managerial mission of designing and operating an economically sound institution.

How does a manager behave in a shifting environment when the clues and expectations are contradictory or confusing? What are the types of demands he might expect in the coming years? How will his skill requirements be altered over the course of his career? Who shares responsibility for helping the manager to adapt and move towards greater responsiveness as a skilful agent of change? These are the issues explored as we build an inventory of the capabilities and limitations of the manager who faces a lifetime of guaranteed but unpredictable change.

Individual change confrontation

Management is rapidly becoming less the manipulation of things and people and more the manipulation of ideas and concepts. This means that organizational human resources—the principal input of knowledge—must change to keep pace with the requirements of a more complex management system. For the first time in history the advantage of experience—the equation of wisdom with longevity—is bowing to the mightier weight of formally learned knowledge. This shift, already consummated in several industries, means the annual obsolescence of millions of jobs—jobs which range from unskilled to the highest executive. Much of this obsolescence is the product of new technology, either through automation of organizational processes or through personal knowledge displacement. Containerized shipping, as one automation example, has eliminated dock jobs at the rate of some 4000–5000 per year in Britain alone. It is commonly expected that half of the knowledge received during an engineer's professional education is outdated within ten years.

Contrary to the past 800 generations of civilization, age and time work against the economic livelihood of large masses of individuals. The dynamics of massive change in the individual's trade or profession will result in earlier career peaks. It may become common practice for individuals to move laterally or even downward rather than the current system of upward promotions. Lifetime careers will yield more to serial careers as individuals make major occupational shifts two or more times during their working lifetimes.

Some of these shifts undoubtedly will be forced because of job obsolescence and total job elimination, the only resultant choice being retraining. Others will be motivated more by a desire for personal growth, a search for new challenges, or to deal directly with the boredom syndrome. Because of this greater forced or self-initiated mobility, organizations should expect higher turnover rates, especially within managerial ranks. Mobility under these circumstances can work to the advantage of the organization to initiate new ideas from a constantly renewed team of employees and managers.

Periodic career education to learn new skills must become more the rule than the exception. Most individuals will have ample time for formalized learning and skill development if they are motivated to use discretionary time in this manner. Except for scientific and professional personnel and their executive and political counterparts, more waking hours are now consumed

109

in leisure than work (Trist, 1970). For most career fields this educational process will be totally new learning, including purposefully forgetting or unlearning what may have been acquired in the past but is now untrue or inapplicable.

Acceptance of the life-change process, both career and personal, will come easier to those who can tolerate ambiguity, who can cope with temporary relationships, and who can break with tradition. The transition to learning new managerial skills will be smoothest for those who thrive on complexity and conflict. This adaptability will be more natural for those in the professional, academic, or upper managerial class than for the skilled or semi-skilled lower middle class (Duhl, 1963, p. 138). For the same reasons the professional–academic–managerial group will tend to be more experimental in varied life styles, not just in buying or trying new material things, but in radical shifts in the total style of living which may or may not coincide with shifts of career or employment.

But even for the advocates of change, that small minority of any society who not only seek change but are instrumental in its creation, there are upper thresholds to the amount of change the human organism can absorb. Toffler (1971) popularized the thesis of an upper limit of change stimuli and coined the term *future shock* as a symptomatic response to change over-stimulation. While all individuals routinize much of their behaviour to simplify the process of daily living, there are numerous changes in one's environment which fall outside the normal limits of conditioned behaviour—changes affecting one's job, family, finances, beliefs, and total system of life style. As clues are perceived for which there are no conventional responses, the human body undergoes a number of measurable physiological changes as it becomes oriented to the stimuli. The entire body becomes more energy charged and the senses sharpen to receive and process additional information much as occurs when a car driver sees another car abruptly pull into his path.

Medical research conducted in Britain, Japan, Sweden, and the United States links overdoses of change with physiological illnesses, some of which even result in death at a premature age. One group of researchers has developed a Life-Change Units Scale and Questionnaire by which forty-odd types of change, ranging from death of spouse to minor violations of the law, can be weighted and aggregated to determine if an individual is entering a potential danger level of change over-stimulation, one which will increase his probability of becoming physically ill (Rahe *et al.*, 1967; Holmes and Rahe, 1967). Even in the absence of physical illness, the symptoms of difficulty in assimilating uncommon change are found in mixed emotional stress: feelings of anxiety, depression, defensiveness, concern, or helplessness (Price, 1970).

Such stress is common for managers and professionals who repeatedly sense the need to make decisions affecting more than themselves, but who are aware of their limited knowledge or power to achieve optimum results. But the impact of emotional stress in the presence of change often strikes hardest

110

at the anti-change individual who resists with dogmatic determination the intrusion of innovation into his life space. The extreme change avoider believes that classes of people and events or ideas can be judged as either good or bad, and believes that his moral standards are correct. He subscribes to the myth of objectivity that it is possible to devise a set of rules and laws for every relationship and action and to apply this code impartially in unequivocally resolving conflict. To maintain a self-assured exterior, he emphasizes the autonomy of the individual in solving problems, usually to the denial of helpful inputs from others, as if contemporary man were independent rather than interdependent.

All individuals, whether pro- or anti-change, seek some personal balance between programmed and non-programmed decisions. The anti-change advocate naturally attempts to structure his life and environment to interdict frequent intrusion of non-routine problems. But even the innovative change-seeking person will adopt a certain amount of structured routine patterns to free him to concentrate on creative pursuits. The manager who boards a plane headed for an unfamiliar city and unthinkingly sits down, fastens his seat belt, then opens his brief case to continue his work has learned to adopt outwardly routine behaviours which allow him flexible immersion in cognitive activities.

Most individuals find deviations from the expected or programmed way of life disconcerting. Tannenbaum notes the dysfunctional behaviour frequently associated with rapid change:

> Most of us have not grown up accustomed to being open, rapidly adaptable, being able to 'roll with' the changing environments and the people who surround us. . . . We're often anxious and 'uptight' because of real doubt as to whether we're going to be able to make it. . . . In our organizations and in society, there's a lot of ferment going on, which thus far we've pretty well succeeded in repressing. [See Schmidt (1970, pp. 49–50)]

By repressing or withdrawing cognitively from change which is emotionally upsetting, it is possible to perceive incorrectly that predictability and certainty have been regained. Toffler (1971, pp. 358–64) synthesized the common first lines of defence against change into four basic strategies, all of which are maladaptive and eventually trap the change avoider.

1. Denial, or the perceptual blocking out of unwelcomed reality, is a way of attempting to live in an idealized, fantasized world. By closing one's mind to new information, a series of troublesome yet manageable problems are postponed until they develop a massive crisis.

2. Reversion back to previously programmed modes of behaviour or thoughts also serves to disquiet reality. For the unswerving traditionalist the old routines and standards of yesteryear serve as impractical solutions in the different context of today's problems.

111

3. *Super-simplification* is another remedy to handle the complexity of an environment beyond capability of understanding. Problems are narrowed to simplistic cause and effect and grossly over-generalized. In a search for a unitary solution numerous seemingly insolvable problems may be substituted for by one gigantic problem, such as the youth, when confused by the contradictory expectations of his parents, teachers, peers, and a fractionated society, simplifies and consolidates his existence by taking drugs.

4. *Extreme specialization* is used to handle change by filtering out all distracting informational inputs except those within a narrow band of interest. Specialization as a line of defence is doomed to failure. Although the individual apparently is able to cope adequately with change within his speciality, revolutionary advances elsewhere may dictate the elimination of his field. A business example is the extreme specialization of manufacturers of steam-locomotive engines. Although they produced a new and greatly improved model of steam locomotive, companies such as Baldwin Locomotive went into bankruptcy because they could not compete with the economies of the diesel and diesel-electric engines.

All of these defensive coping mechanisms may at one time or the other be used by all individuals. Used infrequently, they permit greater mental concentration and completion of tasks with higher payoffs. But used excessively or exclusively, they are not in keeping with reality and result in personal confusion and even trauma. Defensive behaviours to suppress or block the existence of change are encountered in all organizations. There is strong resistance to changes affecting income, status, health, and content of work. All individuals have difficulties accepting unconventional ideas or changes which they do not understand or are ill-prepared to accept. These idiosyncratic behaviours by individuals when confronted with change complicate and add a dimension of uncertainty to the managerial role.

Managerial role dilemma

Role ambiguity and role conflict are part of every manager's life. Role ambiguity is the uncertainty about decisions and actions when guidelines are lacking or inconsistent with situational demands. Role conflict results from opposing pressures on the manager. One set of forces suggests or expects one kind of behaviour and other forces have totally different expectations. Pro-change and goal-oriented managers can tolerate role ambiguity and conflict. They are inclined to capitalize on such uncertainty to turn the situation to both a personal and an institutional advantage. Anti-change, procedures-oriented managers expend their energies in fighting the conflict and ambiguity.

A case example of role ambiguity and conflict took place in a rapidly expanding district in a telephone company which was experiencing an increased incidence of work-completion delays by outside line crews, installation servicemen, and inside maintenance men. The delay was traced to the test section whose responsibility was to ensure that each work phase was operational before work was commenced on the next stage. The head of the test section was a veteran of 20 years' experience who solved a major crisis in service and maintenance some 10 years ago. His abilities, coupled with the vacuum created by the failure of higher-level managers to solve the service and maintenance crisis, resulted in his department's assumption of control over personnel from other departments. He even countermanded the orders of other foremen on matters such as use of overtime work. In practice, the chief test man became the *de facto* supervisor of the district because he filled a decision-making vacuum and was able to maintain his power because he controlled all the information necessary to coordinate inter-district activities (Lawrence and Seiler, 1965, pp. 552–7).

When asked for recommendations to improve the performance of this telephone district and dampen the dysfunctional interdepartmental conflict, many graduate students and managers provide exhortations that management should clarify lines of responsibilities and define levels of command. Unfortunately, the clichés of traditional management principles are of limited use in problems of this nature. The chief test man was performing a vital coordinating function, one that no one else apparently was willing or able to perform. And to his way of thinking, he was still functioning under the very ambiguous referendum of cleaning up the district and making it operational that had led to his assumption of power 10 years previously. Obviously here was an individual who had personal aspirations for power, was motivated to do a good job, and was decisive—even to the point of overstepping formal boundaries of authority. Left on his own, he turned an uncertain situation into a personal advantage and improved company performance. His unilateral decisions, however, were in conflict with the expectations of other managers and employees and no doubt caused departmental performance further below the optimum than was necessary.

This incident shows how managerial role behaviour is a function of the relationship between two major sets of variables: (a) the individual's personal characteristics; his abilities, expectations, fears, values, and ideals, and (b) an infinite number of environmental factors that are human, technical, and situational. Personal role behaviour requires assessment and balancing of these often ambiguous and conflicting role expectations. McGregor (1967, p. 46) emphasized the potential role dilemma when he wrote: 'The forces in the environment are by no means always explicit or consistent, and the forces within him are by no means purely rational or conscious'.

The role of any manager involves a set of relationships which are more highly complex than could possibly be suggested by a formal statement of job responsibilities and duties. The manager's role network includes superiors, subordinates, associates, secretaries, staff, suppliers, union representatives,

113

customers, government officials, and even consultants. And each of these constituents has different expectations from the manager's decisions and actions. When the manager's own role perception of personal aspirations and assessment of strengths and weaknesses, as well as his career and family expectations, are overlaid on his organizational role network, his role complexity becomes overwhelming. Clichés in the traditional literature about how to clarify and simplify authorities, responsibilities, and communication greatly over-simplify organizational realities.

Day-to-day problems and crises facing the manager present him with the constant dilemma of balancing the formal organizational needs against the informal personal needs of his constituents. For example, a simple cause-and-effect analysis of organizational needs may dictate reassignment of duties and the discharge of personnel. The manager is torn between such a dictate and his concern for his fellow employees, and may vacillate between these opposing forces. He may defer the decision because he fears union unrest, poor morale, and perhaps even overall lower efficiency, but the real reason is his concern for his fellow man.

Interestingly, both the results and the overall dimension of this dilemma between administrative logic and emotional involvement can be extremely complex. Countless examples of the almost bewildering consequences of decisions and actions involving human beings point to the need for more penetrating analyses and deeper understanding by managers of human behaviour. One interesting example took place in a subsidized housing development for the poor. A study of the development found that social workers collected the rent as well as counselled the tenants. Analysts concluded that the relative pay rate between rent collectors and social workers pointed to cost savings with the transfer of the rent collection function to newly hired rent collectors.

Administratively, the study's recommendations were logical and were implemented. But costs skyrocketed rather than declined. From a sociological and behavioural point of view, the monthly contact afforded by the task of rent collecting permitted the social workers opportunities for contact and counselling. Transfer of this task resulted in less contact, particularly with the more intractable tenants. Vandalism and general deterioration of the development resulted in much higher maintenance costs.

A critical aspect of human behaviour in organizations and managerial roles is role identity. Managers and all individuals attempt to codify their organizational roles to provide greater certainty in expectation interfaces. This simplification of prescribed role demands makes organizational interactions easier and more certain. But at the same time, as individuals become more secure in their official roles, they tend to change them. They seek to complicate their activities to make them personally more comfortable or satisfying. A secretary might refuse to do certain clerical activities, claiming they should be handled by somebody else; yet she may be quite willing to

114

undertake countless personal errands for managers because they provide her enjoyable opportunities for social interaction with people outside her office, even though performing personal courtesies is not an official part of her job. Ready (1967) explains the above phenomenon:

> The point is that any person's roles are an oversimplification of his being and his becoming. A fair amount of blind acquiescence goes with living at peace with one's assigned roles, and as enlightenment comes so likely does one's peace become troubled. (p. 28)

The young university graduate newly assigned to his first managerial role may initially rely quite heavily on official guidelines about his position as conveyed to him by his supervisor. If he is a bright and energetic person, this young manager quickly begins to expand his activities and relationships to increase his organizational space. By doing more things and getting to know more people, he learns more about the organization and becomes a more knowledgeable manager.

Much of his branching activity, however, may come as a result of finding that he could not get the job done by playing strictly according to game rules. Unconventional problems or changes in policies or procedures force him to modify his role, giving it an expansionary thrust which is all to the betterment of his performance and an asset to the organization. Another manager in similar circumstances who is more unsure of himself and wishes to obtain external superior reinforcement or guidance may attempt to restrict his duties. To protect his position he adapts his emergent behaviour to make his performance look good, even if it means intentionally creating problems for others with whom he has dealings.

Current managerial ambiguity results from a gap between the requirements for current and future skills or knowledge. Uncertainty and ambiguity develops a form of trauma, often resulting in a race between retirement and obsolescence. For example, many managers have deficiencies in understanding modern managerial tools such as computer programming, simulation models, systems analysis, or operations research. However, rather than recognize the deficiencies, many managers mistrust data processing, resulting in poor utilization of management-science techniques.

Should the experienced manager return to school to develop new managerial tools? How much time can he devote to learning and still keep up with the demands of the job? Will his skill weakness result in a lack of promotion? Such stressful thoughts cause a personal ambivalence about balancing dependence on the past with learning for the future. This uncertainty results in both personal and organizational costs. There seems little question that an adequate response to manage change requires both individual and institutional renewal and restructuring.

Experience–knowledge relevance

Managerial roles are beset by ambiguity, conflict, and interdependencies—these impact to make the task of managing more complex. Administrators and policy makers in all types of institutions are experiencing difficulty in utilizing the guidelines and theories of the past to solve today's ever-shifting problems. For example, there has been heavy dependence on Keynesian and neo-Keynesian economic theory in the post-Second World War period to utilize fiscal and monetary action to counteract independent economic disturbances. But these fiscal and monetary actions did not work in 1970–3, when advanced economies experienced recession and inflation simultaneously, which was unknown in conventional theory. Restricting the money supply, decreasing government spending, and increasing the effective tax rate to dampen inflation and reduce trade deficits seems to compound the problems of unemployment and recession. Even an overlay of incomes policies to affect the supply side of the equation by regulating prices and personal incomes is not fully effective in bringing relief on both fronts.

A similar complexity on the micro-level of understanding changes for initiating suitable action in organizations exists throughout the ranks of management. Depending on individual preparation and orientation for the unexpected, managers may display behaviour that is *active, ambivalent,* or *passive.* Consider active and passive behaviours as simply extremes along a continuum, with ambivalence as the midpoint, and it is easy to illustrate two contrasting portraits of the contemporary manager (Dalton, 1959).

The *active* manager holds up well under ambiguous dilemmas and even tends to make a game of them to spur his learning and creativity. He is undisturbed by conflicting official and unofficial pressures and uses the conflict to generate added information and round out his perceptual understanding of complex issues. Goal-oriented, he interprets the intent of organizational guidelines rather than follow the letter of the rule. He becomes a positive force of intervention, using his own ideas to invoke further change and shift the problem to a higher, more complex plane. This management of complexity produces greater resiliency. Tending to accept the challenge and responsibility for high risks, he does not become obsessed by failure but uses it to reorient himself and his subset of the organization.

By contrast, the *passive* manager hesitates to act. He attempts to escape in traditional methods or procedures even to the point of losing sight of goals. If the situation cannot be solved with existing systems, he pushes the problem to his superiors for resolution. Although he has a low tolerance for conflict, his blundering rule-bound behaviour frequently adds to the problems of others and creates even greater conflict. He sees the organization as a formal entity with strict rules of behaviour and suffers from not acquiring knowledge through experience. Behavioural adjustments to changes in policy, procedure, or organization are slow, as he feels lost without the security of a familiar footing.

By now, the reader is probably drawing a parallel between the passive manager and the traditional organization, and between the active manager and the proactive change-responsive organization. Naturally it is possible to find passive managers in change-responsive organizations and vice-versa. But it is no coincidence that managerial-role behaviour patterns tend to reflect organizational orientation. Upper management sets in motion a way of functioning within the organization, either explicitly by policy which filters down into specific rules and guidelines, or by example and expectation linked to the reward system. Whereas one or two decades ago the extensive use of formalized procedures and decision guidelines was a rational management practice in most organizations, the same practice today, if carried to extremes, may be more dysfunctional than helpful. Rather than simplify and standardize lower-level managerial decisions, over-restrictive rules create greater uncertainty if the problem encountered does not fit the predetermined model.

A narrow view of one's role is often a product of experience, especially if the past has a history of relative stability and a structural approach to managerial behaviour. This role rigidity results in organizational inflexibility and an inability to adjust to change. An example of role rigidity and passive management was a crisis in an overseas division of a large international company which resulted in the appointment of a new managing director. The new man in attempting to work through the managerial hierarchy found an inability and unwillingness to develop new strategies and actions to solve the crisis. Initially it seemed that the only solution was to dismiss the managers, but such a sweeping move would cause loss of operational knowledge and would probably traumatize the remaining managers.

The managing director decided to remove the hierarchical obstacle by regrouping his top managers into a series of task forces, making them assistants to him. With their positions of authority formally removed, they were forced to deal openly with one another and with former subordinates as equals to breach their traditional compartmentalized ways of thinking about problems. Although some failed to adjust to this unfamiliar state of ambiguity, the survivors, freed of all past policies other than an economic criterion, forged the collective output of the groups to provide the creative plans necessary to redirect the division.

Such problems of departures from experience and prediction bring forth one of three possible managerial behaviours.

1. **A tradition-based strategy** may be applied, assuming the problems are similar to past problems. A manager frequently sees this as a low-risk strategy since it conforms to what he thinks are higher management's expectations. An example here is the aforementioned case of the steam locomotive. Blind applications of past strategies are actually high risk, both personally and

117

organizationally, since failure to obtain results is unacceptable to either tradition-bound or change-responsive firms.

2. **A mixed strategy** would preserve the spirit of not defying tradition but clearly accept the problem as something requiring more than simply an extension of past thinking. The mixed strategy runs the risk of a failure to sharpen perceptions to identify a totally redefined problem or opportunity. This was the case in Eastman Kodak's refusal to purchase xerography technology but continue to develop a copier which eventually could not compete effectively with the dry-process xerography.

3. **A change-responsive strategy** would be to develop a totally new definition of the problem, perhaps seeing in the situation a benign condition for new opportunity, but one that may well render obsolete dimensions of the existing organization or strategies. In the case of Kodak, it might have been the concurrent development of xerography and traditional copying processes as contingency strategies.

The lesson to be learned is that structured job experiences confine managers to a narrow range of role behaviour, and as experiences become confined, so does the capacity for innovative thinking. Psychological research into the process of decision-centred thinking concludes that as a person reduces the level of complexity in his mental processing of information, he will actually experience a deterioration in the ability to perform complex problem solving in the future. Alternatively, with training that forces one to reach out mentally, it is possible to develop a greater capacity for perceiving highly differentiated informational inputs and integrating them for complex decision making (Driver and Streufert, 1969).

It may be that the old proverb 'a little knowledge is a dangerous thing' could be replaced by the organizational version that reads 'a lot of experience is a dangerous thing'. The type of experience we have in mind is where a manager with 20 years' service essentially repeats 1 year's worth of experience twenty times over.

Some organizations attempt to expand the knowledge and adaptability of their managers by periodically reassigning them to new positions or locations. Failure to develop mobility and adaptability has even been viewed as a deterrent to economic prosperity, a problem that Allan Skertchly (1968, p. 40) sees as particularly applicable to the United Kingdom. Yet while occasional job rotations are better at developing general management skills than traditional, long periods of specialization in the same function, they are by no means a panacea for overcoming role rigidity. They may make the manager adept at moving his family and household, but mere relocation will not develop flexibility in his thinking and problem-solving abilities.

One critic of corporate conformity described the traditional concept of the mobile manager as 'merely a piece on the corporate checkerboard, to be moved from place to place at the whim of corporate management' (Chandler,

1972, p. 126). What Chandler suggests is that while the manager outwardly appears to be flexible and adaptable to new situations, he is really learning to conform to a fairly rigid set of corporate values rather than becoming an *active* manager.

True, the reassigned manager is learning about different operations in the firm, but he may still not develop flexibility to deal with ambiguity and totally new problems. Emphasis on short-term performance alone and frequent reassignments both can greatly affect the outcomes of a current role and may stifle the reassigned manager in learning to develop self-initiative. And self-initiative is the all-critical personal resource necessary in higher levels of management, where frequent encounters with environmental change and surprises demand spontaneity and genuine flexibility (Ghiselli, 1963).

Dynamics of managerial skills

The erratic response to changing role demands raises questions about the mix of appropriate managerial skills. Development of the skills necessary to manage effectively during periods of turbulence as well as stability should be an integral part of the managerial learning process. Yet managers often concentrate too long on skills which they should be de-emphasizing, and neglect to develop those more germane to current and future demands.

Managerial skill dynamics should be considered along two time dimensions. The more apparent one is the shift in emphasis as an individual moves from lower to higher positions of managerial responsibility, or from the technical–professional ranks into management. Consideration should also be given to the consequences of time itself—to the ways in which shifting environments alter the pressures and requirements facing management. Exhibit 5.1 encapsulates the relative importance of managerial skills according to these twin dimensions. Until recently, managerial literature and teaching has focused on the acquisition of skills prevalent in the traditional and transitional phases. But the challenge of the future lies in developing additional new skills to manage ambiguity, conflict, and complexity—skills essential to a change-responsive managerial orientation.

Organizations enjoying relatively stable environments do not require the breadth of managerial skill development that is critical for managing in a state of turbulence. Traditionally oriented organizations concentrate heavily on technical, managerial-process, and human-relations skills. It is little coincidence that awareness of these three skills is an outgrowth of the early development of management thought and is a natural base for traditional management.

Concern for technical skill is the product of scientific management; managerial-process skills are the domain of the classical management school of thought; and human-relations skills are the result of the movement that bears this name. Technical skills in specialized functional areas continue to be necessary for most entry-level management positions, although within many types of industries the acquisition of these skill–knowledge bases is becoming more a function of education and less one of training and experience. Skills in managerial processes such as planning, organizing, coordinating, and controlling still remain essential to the everyday practice of management, although contemporary refinement has negated many of the simplistic principles originally associated with this school of thought.

From the research findings of early behavioural science investigations, management learned that an overlay of human relations or interpersonal skill

Exhibit 5.1

Shifting hierarchy of managerial skills

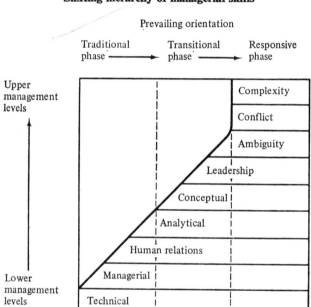

upon the technical–managerial process base could improve performance. Productivity came to be recognized as not simply an inevitable outcome of structuring activities and coercion or economic rewards alone, but also as dependent upon the willingness of the human resource to want to cooperate. Yet since many organizations consider that man is an instrument to be used by the organization, rather than view the organization as an instrument of man (Knowles and Saxberg, 1971, p. 7), the human-relations concept has often been used as a façade for the covert manipulation of individuals.

Management today continues to be heavily influenced by the teachings of the pioneer management theorists and researchers with the consequence that

120

these three foundational skills continue to be unduly emphasized and almost exclusively used in organizations bound by traditional philosophies of management. But a growing number of firms have come to focus more on the skills appropriate for the transitional phase. Especially within middle and upper management, the technical and to some degree management-process skills become augmented with the relatively more important analytical, conceptual, leadership skill areas (Basil, 1970, 1971).

The increased importance of problem solving and decision making has resulted in a coupling of the diagnostic ability of analytical skills with computer-based quantitative tools. As problems encompass a larger amount of organizational space, the conceptual skill to understand the interrelationships of all components of the organization becomes critical to hold suboptimization to the subsystem level and promote optimization at the system level, rather than the reverse. The interpersonal skill that emphasized one-to-one or manager-to-manager relationships is augmented by the leadership skill that spans multigroups, conveys deep understanding of human needs within the limitations of the organization, and provides a breadth rather than concentration of motivational appeal.

Managers in most contemporary organizations do relatively well if their behaviour evidences substantial qualitative attainment in these traditional and transitional phase skills. Such an accomplishment does not come by emphasizing one skill, such as analytical or leadership, to the absolute exclusion of all others, for the skills are interrelated and complementary with none being able to stand alone, regardless of managerial level.

Management is currently reaching the responsive frontier where the new skills of ambiguity resolution, conflict management, and complexity integration will become critical. Built on the skills of the transitional phase, these three additional skills will be keystones to guiding organizations and institutions through eras of increased uncertainty and turbulence. The skill to resolve and in some cases merely endure role, organizational, and environmental ambiguity or uncertainty calls for an uncommon capacity to be comfortable in limbo and open to environmental stimuli. Proficiency in scanning the internal and external environment enables the manager to guide his organization or sub-unit in one direction, yet remain flexible to reorient and redirect courses of action.

Conflict is inevitable within organizations and between organizations and their outside domain. Yet managers often feel uneasy when conflict is present, especially when it exists between individuals or subgroups of the organization, as if the existence of differences of opinion, policy, and objectives were pathological. As organizations become more complex, the level of conflict can only intensify, since greater contact will be made with individuals and groups whose perspectives and missions are dissimilar. Like ambiguity, conflict causes the manager and the organization to seek more information about external relationships and internal functioning. Conflict thus becomes a new link in the change-responsive process. Attempts to eliminate conflict and dissent and force conformity can only serve to reduce the relevant information flow needed for conceptual analysis and reform of obsolescent-prone managerial and corporate strategies.

Finally, the skill to integrate complexity subsumes the other skills, elevating conceptual skill to a new plane. Whereas conventionally recognized conceptual skill purports an understanding of the functioning of the system, the integration of complexity expands the scope to include all environmental elements as well. Based on the premise of reciprocal interdependencies, this skill enables the manager to fathom immense amounts of seemingly random bits of information, to piece data together into a meaningful conceptual scheme, and to derive decisions by manipulating the data within his mental scheme. This is human judgement pushed near the point of overload, surpassing man's ability simply to quantify conventional sources of information.

This perspective is intended to suggest relative changes in the priority of management skills over time and with advances in management level. By no means should this be considered an absolute hierarchical arrangement of skills, but rather a way of conceptualizing the dynamic skill requirements for the effective management of change.

Preparation for leadership

Leadership theories have concentrated on the narrow interpersonal dimension of the leader in his role as superior in a superior–subordinate relationship. They purport to describe or prescribe how the manager modifies the behaviour of others by coercing or encouraging them to perform, usually in the context of subverting or joining personal goals for the attainment of institutional goals. In the ideal view, the interpersonal leader is depicted as balancing the needs of individuals against the demands of the organization (Argyris, 1957; Bennis, 1961). Through the communication process, he gains the cooperation of others for the purpose of coordinating activities to achieve desired organizational goals (Knowles and Saxberg, 1971, pp. 87–93).

John Gardner (1969) had in mind a broader context of leadership when he wrote:

> Very few of our most prominent people take a really large view of the leadership assignment. Most of them are simply tending the machinery of that part of society to which they belong. (pp. 126–7)

This larger perspective sees leadership not simply as the terminal act of gaining cooperation to implement decisions. Rather, it incorporates the total process of decision making, both singularly and collectively, and synthesizes the full range of managerial skills appropriate to the responsive phase. The more complete connotation of leadership goes far beyond a manager responding to, manipulating, influencing, or guiding his subordinates by invoking his authority, personal charisma, or concern for development of the individual. Although important, these leadership acts are but a small part of the total weave of leadership in a change-responsive organization.

The current state of leadership theory is a far cry from the naïveté of the early efforts to find a universal set of personality traits and characteristics to select and promote personnel (Filley and House, 1969, pp. 393–416). But regardless of the advances of behavioural science theories on leadership, current management practices still advocate selection and promotion on the basis of selected traits (Fitzgerald and Carlson, 1971). Management has been given little specific help since the majority of current theories are situational in scope and design and offer little pragmatic advice to management.

The shift in the focus from traits to behaviour has muddied the waters even more. Douglas McGregor (1966, p. 73) noted that leadership behaviour is a complex relationship among four major categories of variables: '(1) the personal characteristics of the leaders; (2) the attitudes, needs, and other personal characteristics of the followers; (3) the characteristics of the organization, such as its purpose, its structure, the nature of the task to be performed; and (4) the social, economic, and political milieu'.

A popular explanation of leadership by some behavioural scientists identifies ideal styles or types of behaviour along a single continuum from autocratic, benevolent–authoritarian, consultative, democratic, participative, to *laissez faire*, in order to distinguish different styles of leadership (Basil and Cook, 1970).

Leadership behaviour is also differentiated according to role orientation ranging from *instrumental* (concern for task or getting the job done) to *expressive* (concern for people and member interaction). Bales *et al.* (1954) were among the first to recognize that these were not necessarily opposite-role orientations, but that some leaders behaved with high regard for both task and people—the so-called great-man theory of leadership. But equal regard for both task and people is an idealized myth, since it assumes that it is possible to maximize or even optimize both in every situation. Berelson and Steiner (1964) observed that superiors tend to evaluate as effective those managerial subordinates who are goal and task oriented and decisive in dealing with problems, while often the manager's subordinates have higher regard for the leader who is considerate and more participative oriented in his relationships. The notion that managers can be developed to have high regard for both instrumental and expressive behaviours has been popularized by the Blake and Mouton (1964) managerial grid approach to training.

Leadership in a turbulent environment is a critical factor in the development of a change-responsive organization. Task accomplishment and the development of a secure psychological environment to help subordinates live with complexity, uncertainty and ambiguity become equal and interrelated missions of leadership. The attainment of these two missions involves the integration of the following:

1. **Role orientation**—with its elements of instrumental and/or expressive behaviour.

2. **Supervisory distance**—which is the degree of freedom given to subordinates ranging from controlled participation and involvement to general and participative behaviour (sharing objectives with implementation at the discretion of the subordinate).

3. **Task environment**—ranging from highly structured, standardized, routine, to loosely structured, non-standardized, and non-routine.

4. **Expectations and abilities of subordinates**—for independence or participation in decisions.

Most managers like to think of themselves as more enlightened and humanistic than previous generations of managers. One of the outcomes of this is a fairly widespread belief that if a manager becomes more supportive, participative, and considerate in his relationships with other organizational members, he will be a more effective manager. This has led to many individual and organizational attempts to shift leadership styles towards expressive modes of behaviour. Leadership-training programmes in firms, hospitals, schools, and government have used behavioural-science learning methods to modify the attitudes and behaviour of the expressive ideal. Despite good intentions, such efforts frequently do not produce significant changes in managerial behaviour or performance and may in fact even be dysfunctional (House, 1968).

The failure of leadership-training programmes can generally be attributed to an incongruity between the substance of the training and the realities of the job. Removed and isolated from his regular tasks and co-workers, the manager–learner is involved in a new set of experiences—often drawing upon the power of group dynamics—in which participative, democratic, supportive relationships are rewarded. Unfortunately, the laboratory experience does not simulate the reality of organizational life.

The integration of role orientation, supervisory distance, task environment, and expectations and abilities of subordinates can rarely be simulated in the classroom. All too often the conventional leadership-effectiveness training course results in the trainee abandoning his past leadership styles and patterns for a new permissive set which will not work when he attempts to apply them in his organization. The course has not taught the manager to recognize situational factors, which have such a high input value in determining effective leadership behaviour.

Supportive and participative leadership behaviour may be appropriate in a non-routine, loosely structured environment, where subordinates have a high need for independence and are capable of working with general guidance. But it may not be effective in highly structured situations. Furthermore, research findings have failed to correlate productivity with greater job satisfaction under an expressively oriented and general style of supervision (Likert, 1967). Transitional theories and approaches to leadership have not provided clear-cut prescriptions for the management of change-responsive organizations.

The difficulties experienced in specific programmes of leadership training parallel problems encountered in the process of management development generally. Historically, the development of managerial potentials and skills can be viewed as occurring in three distinct but overlapping periods:

1. The era of the apprentice manager, with the grass-roots concept of learning the art of management through experience, hard work, and common sense.

2. The era of formalized management development, drawing upon established management concepts with periodic seminars to keep pace with relevant managerial knowledge.

3. The era of organization development (OD), which emerged in the 'sixties as the needs for group or system learning became more pronounced.

There have been several outstanding successes in reaping the payoffs from systematically thought-out investments in developing managerial resources. But, sadly, mediocrity is more prevalent than success, despite the billions of dollars expended on organization-sponsored educational and skill-building programmes. Attitudes towards management-development programmes vary, with many companies considering them a discretionary luxury, since these budgets are usually restricted during lean years when they may be most needed. Others consider management development as a fringe benefit for managers which implicitly assumes that it is simply an added employment inducement. Still others consider management development as somewhat of a status symbol to demonstrate that managers have been exposed to the latest development technique.

An extensive research study of management-development practices in the United States identified the following five weaknesses (Basil and Cook, 1969):

1. Failure to integrate the mission of management development—few organizations see management development as an integral component of corporate strategy and overall development of the organization. While few firms leave capital investments to chance, many overlook the responsibility to provide opportunities for the individual to develop his own potentials. Any organization that engages in forward planning of product development and capital investments should also be linking its plans to upgrading management skills.

2. Lack of management development objectives—related to the first shortcoming is the failure to develop measurable objectives. While target rates of return and performance standards are used for most tangible investments, few organizations develop more than a subjective feel for the evaluation of management-development investments. Few organizations engaged in formal development programmes have developed objectives, the strategies to achieve such objectives, and the standards of performance to measure achievement (Mager, 1968).

3. Inappropriate learning methodology—often there is a neglect of fundamentals of learning. Few management development programmes utilize behavioural change or adaptation processes available from the behavioural sciences. Management development does not sufficiently provide environments and opportunities for the learner to test his new knowledge, attitudes, or behaviour, reinforce his successes, and learn through failure.

4. Inadequate top management support—responsibilities for management development are frequently delegated to lower and often ill-trained management. Top management either abdicates its responsibility or assumes that line managers will develop subordinates. Yet, as McGregor (1966, p. 179) observed, many executives claim they are too busy with the task of managing to be burdened with the job of developing effective and progressive subordinates. Certainly development is a line responsibility, but it requires constant monitoring and support of specialized professional services. Management development, although it may be mandated as a responsibility of all managers, will not be an automatic by-product of day-to-day experience without formal recognition and reward.

5. Present, not future oriented—management development and organization development (OD) are primarily oriented to solving today's managerial problems. Rarely is management or OD correlated with the future mission of the organization to manage ambiguity and use conflict as a resource tool. It does not prepare the manager to function effectively with imperfect and uncertain information. Managers must be taught how to deal with complex situations without distorting information to oversimplify reality and minimize the impact of a hostile and turbulent environment.

Universities, change and turbulence

During a symposium on coping with change, Warren Schmidt (1970, p. 22) noted that even the transitional response of organizational development only builds 'organizational health and productivity in a climate of relative calm and affluence. O.D. methods have not yet clearly demonstrated their effectiveness in dealing with the strategy of confrontation—in which conflicting values and life styles meet head-on!'

It is in the university where the experience and knowledge of the past are most likely to meet head-on against conflicting values and life styles. Higher education is perhaps the most visible change-oriented institution. Because of its cosmopolitan, interdisciplinary character, the university interacts with more segments of society than any other single organization. With its intellec-

126

tual élite, critical and uncommitted thinkers, and idealistic youth, the university is the vortex of advanced ideas, concepts, and values ranging from nuclear fission to the nature of man. Contemporary universities serve both as a source of theoretical knowledge and professional education and as a major model for and initiator of social change.

This latter function—the university as a model of change—has not been utilized by those currently in positions of power and leadership. The greatest impetus to change has come not from the funding agencies or institutional clients, but from the forcing of confrontation by students. Non-university leaders may consider disturbances and outbursts on campus the work of a small cadre of radicals and anarchists who reject the establishment and today's society, and who offer few viable solutions to the issues they claim as problems. It is true that such small cadres create and lead demonstrations involving larger numbers of students (Sethi, 1971, pp. 236–66). But dissent and dissatisfaction run deep in today's youth, both in and out of the universities. The Lordstown syndrome of the younger work force of General Motors rejecting the work ethics of the company and even sabotaging the production of cars is further evidence of the widespread alienation of the younger generation. But it is the more volatile and articulate students who have led the revolt against the establishment.

The university has become the precursor of the general change model of society. University administrators have been caught between the radical demands of the students and sometimes the faculty, and the status quo demands of the fund-granting agencies. Perhaps in retrospect the fact that the universities survived such turbulence is evidence of adequate balancing of the conflicting demands.

As post-industrial societies become more dependent upon work performed by the mind rather than hands, firms, governmental agencies, and other organizations will take on more of the complexity characteristics of universities. Universities may become the prototype of organizations of the future. James Elden and associates (1970, p. 92) emphasize this modelling effect in their projection: 'As organizations function more on a knowledge base, they begin to function more like university organizations with shared power, highly mobile members, and non-operational goals'.

Although the university may provide a model of organizational form for the future, within the university there are many stresses as it attempts to cope with a changing role in society. Business schools within the university framework provide the primary interface between the university and the world of business. But even this reality relationship and orientation have not resulted in business schools providing leadership in change responsiveness. Kroos and Drucker (1969) emphasize this point:

Altogether the business schools in America have tended to react rather than to act. They have codified rather than initiated. The new concepts, ideas, and tools of business have originated largely outside the business school and practically without benefit of academicians. (pp. 21–2)

Levinson (1968) explains why business schools have not been change responsive:

Business schools are enmeshed in the same difficulties as the larger universities of which they are a part, and they are presently struggling to overcome the fractionation of diverse departments which prepare specialists. ... Even as the business schools work toward establishing programs for generalists, there are limits to what they can do, despite the major contributions they have made. They continue to face certain inherent limitations of academic institutions: they are often divorced from the daily reality problems of the subject matter they teach. No business school operates a business as a medical school operates a hospital; it is nearly impossible for them to teach those subtle elements which translate the subject matter into finished skill—the feel or artistry of the leadership role. (p. 113)

These authors feel that resistance to altering the scope of business education in the US comes largely from within the universities. In Britain and the European countries, cultural tradition both within and outside the university plays a heavy hand in holding back change in business education. Little if any prestige has been granted to higher education for business administration. The accent is still on economic or legal theory as the proper prerequisites for a career in business or government. The result has been a neglect of the administrative sciences in European universities. Until the 1963 *Report on Higher Education* under the chairmanship of Lord Robbins, British resources devoted to programmes of graduate business education were sparse. Despite the subsequent acceleration of postgraduate programmes, for several years after that report there was a continuing inertia to major change by predominately economics-minded faculty members and government and business leaders, which retarded revitalization of British business education (Skertchly, 1968; Central Training Council, 1969).

Universities are but microcosms of society in general and therefore face the same problems of change responsiveness. Within the university, faculty members spawn change and indoctrinate their students with the need for change. But they are unable to provide the intellectual leadership on the university-wide basis for change responsiveness. Reform is difficult where vestiges of power and goals held over from the past stubbornly withstand changing structures, constituencies, priorities, and responsibilities. Higher education is looked to as a resource in developing administrators, organizations, and strategies appropriate to solving problems caused by past decisions and the socio-economic tasks of the future. Universities have provided technological innovation and leadership in the physical sciences, and business and society with solutions to tangible technological problems. But in the social sciences and in human issues with complex societal interrelationships, progress has seriously lagged.

The social sciences have never received adequate support for research, and suffer from the complexity of open systems analytical methodologies. The inexact sciences lack interdisciplinary interaction with a resulting fragmentation of research activities. Business schools serve as the prime integrators and implementers of the social sciences in the realm of administration and management. And business school faculties' research is more applied and pragmatic, permitting faculties to be cognizant of the critical university–business–society interfacing role to be played by the business schools.

Business schools, however, have difficulty in defining their role and determining their constituencies. Michael Schiff (1969) enumerates four separate publics to be served by business education: (a) the traditional adolescent–adult seeking an education prior to work; (b) the working specialist who periodically needs to engage in continuing education to keep up with developments in his speciality; (c) the specialist–professional who is making the transition into the managerial ranks; and (d) the professional manager in need of a forum for exchanging ideas, concepts, and tools to hone and expand his existent skill–knowledge base.

Business schools have been unable to differentiate their programmes to satisfy these diverse groups of learners. Many business schools offering both undergraduate and graduate (MBA) degrees have not adequately identified different sets of objectives for each degree. However, leading business schools in Europe and the United States well recognize the need for such differentiation and for programme change. There is constant experimentation for new solutions, but unfortunately it is greatly hindered by the following factors:

1. Inadequate resources are provided either for research or for programme design.
2. The academic community of the rest of the university is suspicious of the role of the business school.
3. Reward systems are oriented to research for new knowledge but rarely to programme design and new teaching methodology.
4. Neither business nor government recognizes the pressing need for innovative administrative or managerial solutions, but rather accent support for technological breakthroughs with financial support primarily for the physical and medical sciences.

Self-criticism is rampant in business schools within universities, as exemplified by Professor Livingstone's (1971) comments:

How effectively a manager will perform on the job cannot be predicted by the number of degrees he holds, the grades he receives in school, or the formal management education programs he attends. . . . Managers are not

129

taught in formal education programs what they most need to know to build successful careers in management. Unless they acquire through their own experiences the knowledge and skills that are vital to their effectiveness, they are not likely to advance far up the organizational ladder. (p. 79)

There is, however, considerable dialogue about making business education more flexible and future-oriented, and there is some experimentation in programme content and pedagogy. Partially through their own motivation, students are becoming more involved in the process of education rather than being merely subjected to it. Some universities are attempting to produce graduates with judgemental skills as well as a background of conceptual and analytical tools. Many leaders and scholars alike are coming to realize that in an era of the leader–learner, the partnership between the campus and the firm must permit a freer interaction of faculty and businessmen (Schmidt, 1970). In Drucker's (1969c) words, there should be more of a 'circulation of the élites' among business, university, and government.

To develop change responsiveness in both the university and business firms, business leaders of the future will invest a year or two on campus involved in research and teaching, while faculty members assume temporary roles in business or government administration. The present structure of the university essentially interdicts such opportunities. University contact with the community will be more directed to working with people in their natural environments, rather than expecting clientele to come to the campus, where facilities are more convenient for the teacher. The business school will become more of a school without walls.

The university has a major role in assisting individuals, organizations, and institutions to adapt to future-oriented goal and role requirements. The universities contain the skills and human resources needed to adapt to and initiate change, and they can provide the arena for perpetual learning. They stand on the threshold of assuming a role as one of the major change agents of society.

The futuristic manager

The role of the manager has changed drastically in the past few decades, and will undergo even greater change in the next few. The manager of the 'seventies is in an imperfect and uncertain stage between the traditional and change-responsive behaviours, as shown in Exhibit 5.2.

Structural–institutional, technological, and social–behavioural change have not yet impacted severely on the manager and his role in the early 'seventies. Computer technology has created its own managerial cadre but has not yet resulted in major structural change in organizations. The encroachments of government have resulted in a greater awareness of environmental scanning needs, but little change in managerial philosophy. The shift away from the protestant ethic has been decried, but other than the growth of sensitivity programmes, and academic concern with organizational development, managerial role perception is unchanged.

'The essential task of modern management is to deal with change' (Ways, 1966, p. 539), and to do so will require a change in the managerial role itself as developed in Exhibit 5.2. The structural shift from manufacturing with its highly mechanized and therefore highly structured relationships of management and workers to service industries with loosely structured relationships

Exhibit 5.2
The managerial role in transition

Manager of the 'fifties and 'sixties	Manager of the 'seventies and 'eighties
1. Experience-based know-how, education as one-time activity	1. Managerial knowledge based on recurrent higher education
2. Technical, interpersonal, and analytical skills emphasized	2. Ambiguity, complexity, conflict skill management necessary
3. Expectation of continuity of organizational experiences	3. Adapts to incongruities in unpredictable new events
4. Standard operating procedures guide non-policy decisions	4. Decisions augmented by environmental scanning inputs
5. Inward perception emphasizes production, competition	5. Inward/outward perception includes societal problems
6. Relationships fairly stable	6. Relationships more temporary
7. Assumes rational organizational behaviour and common values	7. Rationality seen as subjective with heterogeneous values
8. Relies on formalized structure to clarify role	8. Accepts emergent behaviour as conveying role expectations
9. Task oriented	9. Goal oriented
10. Seeks commitment planning to perfect processes/products	10. Plans with contingencies to allow change of specification
11. Leadership styles compartmentalized into separate modes	11. Leadership as multi-dimensional situational–individual behaviours
12. Action oriented to keep physically busy	12. Combines periods of reflection with action
13. Individualistic approach to specialized problem solving	13. Interdisciplinary team approach to complex problem solving

will further accelerate the development of change-responsive managerial roles. The ratio of managers to workers will increase to handle the shift in the management orientation from the routine manipulation of material objects to the creation of ideas and the motivation of individuals to implement such ideas. Reflection and diagnosis will replace action as the prime activity of the manager. Cognitive team interaction, encouragement of dissent, tolerance of conflict, and acceptance of new ideas and methods of operation will mark the successful manager of the future.

Complexity of environmental change and the development of novel forms will create new sets of complexity for the manager. Turbulence in the manager's environment cannot but result in turbulence in his role. But recognition of the problem of volatility in the managerial role is an excellent prerequisite to solution. Organizations need to provide the appropriate climate to allow managerial growth and the development of change-responsive managers. And managers will have to change their perceptions of their roles and learn totally new sets of skills for future success.

6

The strategic gap

Environmental change has created a strategic gap—the shortfall between the actions of organizations and institutions and the objective of an orderly adaptation to change. The strategic gap has resulted in colossal failures in business firms and extravagant misallocations of resources by governments and other institutions. Before analysing these strategic blunders, it is necessary to establish by examination of the strategic feedback cycle why and how strategic gaps are created.

The strategic feedback cycle

The formulation of strategies is common to all forms of organizations and even to individuals. Exhibit 6.1 illustrates the five component steps in the process. Objectives, implicit or implied, are the beginning of the strategic feedback cycle. The literature on objectives is extensive, particularly on what are or

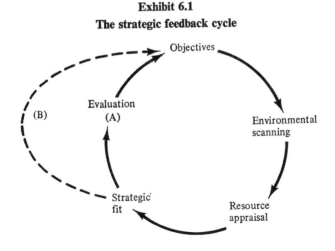

Exhibit 6.1
The strategic feedback cycle

should be the objectives of business firms. Basil (1970) defines the scope of the current controversies:

> On the theoretical plane, there has been considerable discussion as to whether the business firm has really only one objective—to maximize its profits. There is considerable evidence that, although firms still have an objective of making profits, they do not maximize profits in the traditional sense. The trend to professional management as the controlling element in business enterprise and away from the entrepreneur with his strong profit motive has led to a changing outlook on corporate objectives. (p. 24)

Ackoff (1970) develops a behavioural point of view on objectives:

> States or outcomes of behaviour that are desired are *objectives*. An organization may desire either to *obtain* something that it does not currently have (e.g., a dominant share of its market), or to *retain* something it already has (e.g., the dominant share in a particular area). Hence objectives may be either acquisitive or retentive. (p. 23)

Ansoff (1965) considers objectives more in terms of resource allocation:

> We define an *objective* as a measure of efficiency of the resource conversion process. An objective contains three elements: the particular *attribute* that is chosen as a measure of efficiency, the *yardstick*, or scale, by which the attribute is measured, and the *goal*—the particular value on the scale which the firm seeks to attain. (p. 40)

From the management-of-change point of view, objectives might best be considered in terms of the viability or survival of the organization. This means the development of a change responsiveness to permit adaptation to change without dysfunctional failures. Obviously this definition must be translated into specific objectives for the individual organization, stated in terms of the particular mission and environment of the organization.

In the strategic feedback cycle, objectives cannot be immutable but are subject to reappraisal and redevelopment as the organization moves through the environment-scanning, resource-appraisal, and strategic-fit steps. Track A in Exhibit 6.1 is that followed by the organization when the objectives pass the test of strategic fit. For example, suppose a business firm has developed the objective of overseas expansion and commences the step-by-step strategic feedback cycle. Environmental scanning signals that (a) a market exists, (b) competition is fragmented and vulnerable, (c) minor technological advances can be anticipated in the next five years. Resource appraisal substantiates that the company has the appropriate resources in the right mix. Strategic fit exists between the environment and the resources for the development of appropriate strategies. The strategic feedback cycle confirms the adequacy of the original objective of overseas expansion. The final step of evaluation is delayed until the strategies have been implemented, at which time there may be a reformulation of objectives based upon the experience of the company in the strategy-implementation phase. Track A is appropriate for this company.

An alternative scenario for a company with an objective of lowering unit costs by production automation illustrates why this company will follow track B. Environmental scanning signals that potential major technological change is imminent which would render obsolete the product for which production is being automated. Resource appraisal determines that sufficient resources exist for automation, but the strategic fit is inappropriate since the risk factor is too high to justify the investment. Track B shunts the strategic search to the reformulation of objectives to determine alternative ways for the company to manage the technological change.

Theories of strategy formulation

Development of theories of strategy formulation has not reached the sophistication of organizational design and individual–group behaviour theories. A simplified version of the relationships among basic components contained in various strategy-formulation theories is presented in Exhibit 6.2. Strategy theories have been considered primarily as a series of patterned relationships and a moving balance between organizational and environmental variables (Learned *et al.*, 1969, pp. 11–21). Although many of the strategy conceptual frameworks are relatively abstract, they contribute to an understanding of the strategic gap and the process of strategy formulation. Corporate strategy theories include equilibrium theory, strategy–structure relationships, long-range planning, contingency theory, and normative process models.

1. **Equilibrium theory.** The concept of equilibrium is central to general systems models of organizations and provides analytical means to distinguish between alternative strategy-response modes. Equilibrium theory has been derived from biological, ecological and economic sciences. Critics have questioned the appropriateness of borrowing concepts from other disciplines to explain organizational behaviour. But utilization of a concept such as the ecological adaptation of an organism or animal life to a changing environment provides one of the most powerful paradigms of strategy formulation. In fact, it can be considered as a major contribution to theories on the management of change.

Equilibrium models fall into two categories: homeostatic and morphogenic. The homeostatic or system-maintaining organism (firm) attempts to alter its behaviour or form of organization to counteract disruptive forces which threaten its perpetuation. Homeostatic organizations function in a relatively steady state, where strategy responses are exercised only to achieve a return to the pre-existing ideal state (Cannon, 1938; Zaleznick, 1964). Alternatively, a morphogenic or developmental model is one which seeks to grow through increases in size and/or complexity (Katz and Kahn, 1966; Buckley, 1967;

K

Olsen, 1968). Preservation of the basic integrity of the system is achieved through the process of growth and expansion strategies.

Equilibrium theory is more useful for describing variations in the objectives and strategies of organizations than in prescribing how to develop appropriate

Exhibit 6.2

Key variables in theories of strategy

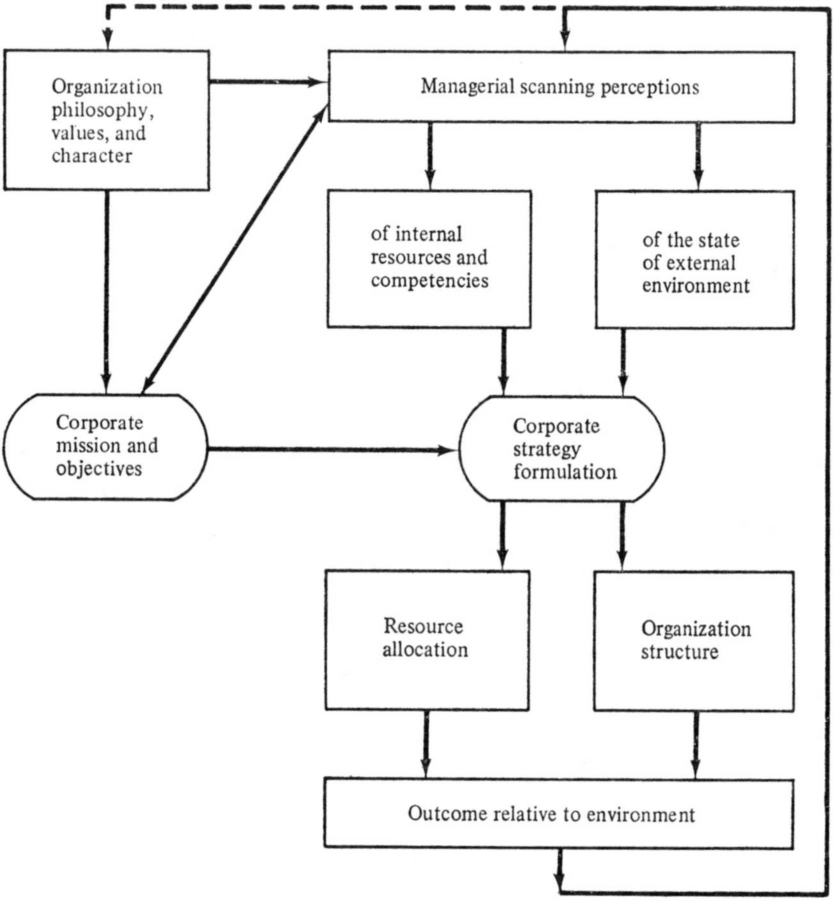

strategies to narrow the strategic gap. Yet it does point out the fallacies of some systems. Highly bureaucratic and tradition-bound organizations utilize predetermined strategies to effect automatic adjustment to disruptive forces by reliance upon a system of controls and standardized decision rules for correcting abnormal situations. But if the environment of a firm becomes unstable or turbulent, continued pursuit of stability-prone objectives and strategies will not return the firm to its previous equilibrium position.

136

Homeostatic strategies triggered automatically by crisis environmental change may temporarily dampen the extent of the disequilibrium, but they will seldom, if ever, bring about a resolution of the causes of the imbalance. Yet it is difficult for a firm to shift from a traditional, homeostatic posture toward a more transitional form without managerial change. Primarily such managerial change occurs in a crisis-change mould, creating uncertainty, confusion and resource misapplication before the new strategies can shift the firm toward a revitalizing turn-around.

2. Strategy–structure relationships. The analysis of the relationships between strategy and organization structure were pioneered by Alfred Chandler, Jr (1962):

> The comparison emphasizes that a company's strategy in time determined its structure and that the common denominator of structure and strategy has been the application of the enterprise's resources to market demand. Structure has been the design for integrating the enterprise's existing resources to current demand; strategy has been the plan for the allocation of resources to anticipated demand. (p. 383)

Chandler considers strategic decisions to be those concerned with the long-term health of the firm. By focusing on long-term actions rather than short-term reactions, he narrows the scope of strategies to changes 'in response to the opportunities and needs created by changing population and changing national income and by technological innovation' (p. 15). By restricting strategy to expansion in pursuit of opportunity, Chandler was able to identify three primary growth strategies which are linked to and limited by the form of structure appropriate to support each strategy:

> There seems to be no question that a new strategy created new administrative needs, for expansion through geographical dispersion, vertical integration, and product diversification added new resources, new activities, and an increasing number of entrepreneurial and operational actions and decisions. Nevertheless, executives still continue to administer both the old and new activities with the same personnel, using the same channels of communication and authority and the same types of information. Such administration, however, must become increasingly inefficient. (1962, pp. 14–15)

Both the strategy–structure research of Chandler and the theories of the homeostatic model conclude that the form of organization—and often the very staffing of top management—is a major obstacle that must be overcome if the firm is to grow or remain viable. Chandler was emphatic in recognizing the lag response of top executives as a severe limitation to advancing new growth strategies: 'This short survey not only stresses that expansion did cause administrative problems which led, in time, to organization change and readjustment, but it further suggests that the essential reshaping of administrative structure nearly always had to wait for a change in the top command' (p. 380).

3. Long-range planning. The pragmatic formulation of strategies by organizations and governments is considered the main function of long-range planning. Some planning theorists view planning as synonymous with the process of mission determination and strategy formulation (Steiner, 1969). Others equate strategic planning as encompassing both short- and long-range considerations to specify objectives and means (Anthony, 1965). Long-range planning relates strategies to change responsiveness as noted by Ackoff (1970, p. 1), 'planning is the wisdom to control change'.

Long-range planning considers the environment, characterizing it as predictable or unpredictable, and controllable or uncontrollable (Filley and House, 1969, p. 196). The assessment of these environmental states facilitates three appropriate forms of planning: commitment, contingency, and responsive. *Commitment planning* is most feasible where the environment is relatively certain and controllable. *Contingency planning* is appropriate where there is uncertainty in the environment but where change is limited. For example, car manufacturers recognize that pollution-control regulations will require progressive reductions in carbon monoxide and hydrocarbon emissions. But uncertainty about the appropriate technology results in motor car companies planning research in turbine, rotary, fuel cell, steam, electric, hydrogen cycle, and new versions of piston engines on a concurrent basis. However, it is unlikely that contingency planning would result in sufficient environment scanning by motor companies to avoid a strategic gap if a social and technological backlash embargoes the private car in favour of extensive public transportation.

Responsive planning is found where the future is unpredictable, as might be the case of a foreign company operating in a less-developed nation which is considering stringent foreign-investment restrictions. The best strategy posture is to develop elaborate and sophisticated early-warning scanning systems and restrict the allocation of resources in fixed commitments.

Most long-range planning is commitment planning, projecting that the future is reasonably certain. But strategy formulation in the management of change is more closely related to contingency and responsive planning with environments that are not stable. Research conclusions by Shank *et al.* (1973, p. 94) emphasize this necessary characteristic of planning: 'Future-oriented businesses will be best suited for loosely linked planning/budgeting systems'.

4. Contingency theory. The concept of contingency serves as the focal point for another variation of strategic theories. As advanced by Harvard researchers Lawrence and Lorsch (1969), contingency theory re-examines the structure–strategy relationship from a different perspective than that of Chandler. Contingency-theory research has examined primarily how the demands of various environmental sectors necessitate structural, managerial, and leadership differentiation among the major subsystems of an organization. At issue is the task of bringing about variation in organization and strategy 'to cope effectively with different environmental circumstances' (Lawrence and Lorsch, 1969, p. 187).

The Lawrence and Lorsch contingency model, substantiated by field research, examines strategies at one point in time and the structure for research, marketing, or production as dictated by such strategies:

> The environment with which a major department engages is decided by the key strategic choice, 'What business are we in?' *Once that decision is made*, whether explicitly or implicitly, the attributes of the chosen environment can be analyzed. (p. 209, italics added)

Despite the many insights generated by the Lawrence and Lorsch research, the static strategy assumption restricts its use as a general strategy-change model. The contingency approach has its greatest impact in the formulation

Exhibit 6.3

A sample of strategic-policy variables

Corporate mission	Product mix
Product research	Diversification
Market expansion	Customer service
Pricing	Promotion
Research and development	Supplier relations
Management controls	Physical facilities
Production volume	Channels of distribution
Sources of capital	Acquisition of facilities
Subsidiary management	Dividend policy
Organization	etc.

of substrategies (noted in Exhibit 6.3) and identification of integration requirements of major subsystems.

5. Normative process models. In contrast to research-based contingency theory, normative process models provide highly prescriptive and intuitive strategy models. Ansoff (1965, 1969) has developed a model typical of the normative process theories. He views strategy in a way similar to Chandler (1962) in terms of growth and diversification objectives, with a detailed framework for diversification–expansion alternatives. Ansoff considers that strategies are the output of a rational process of analysis which can be developed in a highly structured and logical fashion, utilizing managerial judgement and financial criteria.

Theoretical formulations of strategy range from highly abstract equilibrium to quasi-operational normative process models. Unfortunately the present state of the art in corporate-strategy theory has gaping omissions and shortcomings. However, it does provide a uniform pattern that strategy is a function of multiple interfaces between the firm, its subsystems, and the firm's various environmental sectors. These interfaces in turn are affected by

139

managerial goal orientations, philosophies, perceptions, and aspirations; the availability and kind of resources; and the degree of turbulence of the environment.

Identifying the strategic gap

The failures of strategy theories to provide guidelines for effective strategy formulation are compounded by managerial and institutional failures creating strategic gaps. Simple correlations are difficult if not impossible in the identification of the causes of strategic gaps. Errors in strategy formulation are often interrelated, with one mishap compounding others. Within these limitations, six major causes of strategic gaps can be identified:

1. Environmental scanning deficiencies
2. Organizational inflexibility
3. Insufficient environmental support
4. Resource inapplicability
5. Oversimplification of open-system complexity
6. Ignoring change signals.

These strategic-gap causes are related to the strategic feedback cycle. Exhibit 6.4 superimposes these six causes on the strategic cycle to indicate at what point in the feedback process they occur. Primarily they result from the lack of change responsiveness in the structuring and management of the organization.

Environmental scanning deficiencies

The potential impact of environmental change can be determined by environmental scanning. Such scanning is constantly done by all organizations in their interfaces with their environment. The salesman fills out call reports on his visits, in which he notes competitive trends and changes in the market. Purchasing agents are bombarded with new product intelligence, and all managers receive input from publications and business contacts. But rarely is all of this data organized well within any organization, and few have developed any managerial systems or special subsystems devoted to environmental scanning.

Long-range planning contains elements of environmental scanning and usually follows the steps outlined in the strategic feedback cycle. Rarely, however, have sophisticated techniques or intelligence systems been utilized to collect and categorize all environmental data that might impact on strategies. Technological forecasting, which may or may not be part of long-range planning, utilizes more sophisticated techniques for environmental scanning.

140

Exhibit 6.4
Identification of the strategic gap

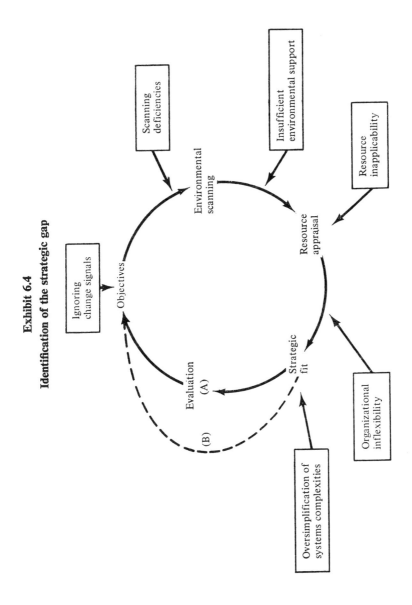

It has two methodologies, delphi and envelope forecasting (Kahn and Bruce-Briggs, 1972, pp. 186–91). Delphi utilizes multiple iterations of a questionnaire completed by a panel of experts, usually to predict the dates when certain technological events will occur. Delphi forecasts are summarized in medians and ranges within a time horizon. Envelope curves are a form of extrapolation in the sense that they predict technological inventions, using trends and past experiences in a particular field. Envelope curves have predicted such trends as computer capacity advances with amazing accuracy.

Technological forecasting using such techniques as delphi and envelope curves can provide useful environmental scanning, recognizing that specific individual technological inventions are unpredictable (Boettinger, 1969). But technology is not the only origin of change. Scanning forecasts should include social–behavioural and structural–institutional changes as well. The delphi technique in particular has a potential for being an exercise in a self-fulfilling prophecy (Kahn and Bruce-Briggs, 1972, p. 187). Furthermore, it is difficult to design and implement the appropriate utilization of an expert panel.

The best models for successful environmental scanning are civilian and military intelligence systems, but the cost is beyond the capabilities of all but the largest organizations. The present state of the art in environmental scan is primitive at most, with the result that business firms, governments, and other institutions are committing major resources without an effective scanning of the environment. Some current successes and failures illustrate the value and the difficulties of environmental scanning.

1. **Corporate farming.** The farming revolution in Western Europe and notably the United States has applied the techniques of business and mass production to farming with spectacular results. Yields have increased, employee productivity skyrocketed, and scientific farming has become widespread. This attracted newcomers into farming with disastrous results: Gates Rubber Company sold 10 000 acres in Colorado after three years of losses; CBK Agronomics planted diversified crops for four years on 80 000 acres, then abandoned farming for coal mining; Multiponics went bankrupt after two crops on 35 000 acres in the Southern US; and Great Western Ranches also went bankrupt after farming 4 000 000 acres in the West (Cordtz, 1972b).

The environmental scanning of these companies and others who have made little or no profits was totally inadequate. Corporate farming is not widespread, with slightly over 1 per cent of commercial farms in the US incorporated, of which 90 per cent are merely family-owned businesses operating in a corporate shell. Only 1800 farms, less than 0·1 per cent of the total, cultivating 15 million acres, are operated by corporations with more than 10 shareholders. The premise that modern managers and economies of scale could provide greater efficiencies than the independent farmer was never thoroughly investigated or researched by the big corporations. Economies of scale in farming are accomplished by discount buying, keeping hired workers productively busy,

142

and fully utilizing expensive equipment. But the independent farmer can achieve these through cooperatives and effective managerial practices.

Even large companies were not immune to errors in environmental scanning. S. S. Pierce Co. has abandoned farming; Purex and United Brands had major setbacks; and giant Tenneco has sold off 70 000 acres. United Brands, with virtual control of the banana market with 42 per cent of the US market, decided to enter the lettuce business with disastrous results. Its strategies were to sell directly to major supermarket chains and utilize its well-established Chiquita brand name. But the lettuce brokers successfully fought off the direct sales. United Brands was unable to maintain its premium quality in lettuce and saw its banana sales suffer because of consumer discontent with lettuce. Purex found its shareholders unwilling to accept loss years in agricultural products even if good years would more than compensate for the loss years. Tenneco, a company highly integrated with its ownership of J. I. Case (a manufacturer of farm implement equipment), packaging, and even petroleum, decided that large holdings of farmland were not worth the effort and sold all but 20 000 acres.

2. Mazda and the Wankel Engine. The Wankel engine, built by Dr Felix Wankel in 1957 in conjunction with NSU of Germany, may revolutionize the motor industry. It is light, powerful, relatively pollution free, has 40 per cent fewer parts, and is cheaper to build than the conventional internal combustion engine (Burck, 1972). In 1960, Toyo Kogyo (Mazda) was a relatively small manufacturer of trucks, machine tools, and minicars. Its president, Tsuneji Matsuda, considered it impossible to compete effectively with Toyota and Nissan, but recognized the potential for the Wankel engine. However, the Wankel was not yet a commercial reality and Mazda had to spend over 11 million dollars to develop the engine, with a total expenditure of over 36 million dollars for licensing, development and testing. Between 1967 and 1972 Mazda sold over 250 000 Wankel-powered cars and plans to double its production.

General Motors negotiated with Curtiss-Wright, which holds the US rights, for an outright purchase of rights for 50 million dollars, and expects to offer the Wankel as an option in the 1974 Vega. Environmental scanning was successfully performed in Japan by a machinery manufacturer, Toyo Kogyo, and shrewdly in the US by an aviation firm, Curtiss-Wright, but not by any of the car manufacturers.

Longer time horizons find Bendix developing electronic fuel injection to eliminate the carburettor; Ford and Japan's Honda working on a stratified charge to increase combustion; Chrysler researching turbine engines (turned down Wankel in favour of the turbine in 1962); Ford purchasing rights from Holland's Philips for the Stirling engine using hydrogen as the working medium; and General Electric, Dow Chemical, and Rockwell International researching rechargeable lithium or sodium batteries for the electric car (*Business Week*, 7 December 1972, pp. 60–70).

3. Packaging and pollution.—Packaging is one of the modern miracles of man to make his life easier, more convenient, and even reduce his cost of living. But there is another side to packaging with its proliferation, its litter and pollution, and its consumption of resources. The growth in packaging has been increasing at over 5 per cent a year in the US, of which over 50 per cent is paper (Alexander, 1972). Packaging companies promoted non-returnable containers in the 'sixties, resulting in a growth to nearly 70 per cent of beer and beverage sales. These throwaways annually use 3·8 million tons of glass, 2·5 million tons of steel, and over 300 thousand tons of aluminium, all of which have been extracted and formed at a cost of 12·5 million tons of coal or its energy equivalent.

Major consumer concern and potential government action are in the offing because the packaging industry has not done an adequate job of environmental scanning. Major technological breakthroughs on recycling can be achieved, but little cooperative and concerted action has been taken by the industry until the 'seventies, when a nonprofit National Center for Resource Recovery was established in the United States, with an operating budget of 2 million dollars. By that time, however, over 350 restrictive bills had been introduced at federal, state, and local levels. It may be too late for orderly action to be taken to solve the problem effectively. The effect of simple cause-and-effect regulation could be disastrous, not only to the packaging industry but also to society as a whole.

Organizational inflexibility

In some instances, organizations have recognized opportunity by effective environmental scanning, but have a strategic gap through internal inability to capitalize on the opportunity. It is primarily larger firms with past successes and complex organization structures which have the syndrome of organizational inflexibility. Organizational inflexibility results in a lack of change responsiveness, primarily internal to the firm or organization.

Some defence-industry-oriented firms exemplify organizational inflexibility when they attempt to convert to consumer or commercial markets. One large computer manufacturer received a contract from one of the major airlines to convert a computer system it had built for military purposes to a commercial reservation system. Because of internal inflexibility, engineers were unable to change their thinking from military to commercial specifications. Military specifications were far more exact and demanding than commercial, and the redesign of the commercial version had to be abandoned because the company was unable to adjust its thinking to the needs and cost limitations of commercial systems.

One of the major difficulties contributing to organizational inflexibility is the philosophy and attitude of the top management of a company. In the past there were problems of production-oriented companies which were unable to adjust to a marketing orientation; and there are innumerable examples of companies which have had a myopic view of their mission and opportunities (Levitt, 1960). Perhaps the most dramatic examples are the oil companies who pioneered the credit card but saw it solely as a means to sell petroleum products, and who failed to recognize the need for motel chains to service car travel. Other successes and failures illustrate this organizational inflexibility.

1. **RCA and computers.** RCA and General Electric (US) decided to challenge IBM in the building of computers, but both companies sold out their interests in computers in 1971-2. RCA took one of the biggest losses in business history in 1971, writing off 490 million dollars in computers (Demaree, 1972), and the estimates of General Electric's losses were from 200 to 500 million dollars. Both companies suffered from organizational inflexibility, even though in their traditional businesses they were considered outstanding performers.

RCA and General Electric were both highly successful in electronics, and foresaw the fantastic growth in computers. But both were traditionally oriented companies with organizational inflexibility. In 1968, when Robert W. Sarnoff assumed control of RCA from his father, great sums of money had been spent on computer development, but extraordinary profits from television obscured the lack of results from computer investments. The new chairman of the board decided that computers would become RCA's first priority, to offset the expected decline in profits from colour television as that market matured, even though RCA ranked fifth or sixth in computers and had a market share of no more than 4 per cent. A consulting study concluded that RCA would have to deliver a new line of computers within one year to gain 10 per cent of the market, but the company had no such line available and merely reconditioned its existing line. The company had inadequate systems for controlling computer manufacture and sales:

> Speaking of the inadequacy of RCA's financial controls, Donegan (ex-IBM divisional vice-president, now in charge of computer sales) recalls: 'I hadn't seen what was happening. The group financial staff hadn't seen it. The outside accountants who were in our skivvies hadn't seen it. The trouble was they were all used to seeing a cash sales business.' (Demaree, 1972, p. 131)

This is a condemnation of the lack of organizational flexibility when the company did not even adjust its financial record keeping to the requirements of a different type of business.

In October 1970, Robert Sarnoff assured his directors that the computer business would break even in 1972 and earn 50 million dollars a year by 1975. In September 1971, the board was advised that the computer division's 5 year cash needs would be 700 million dollars, 1971 would incur a loss of 70 million dollars, and no profits would be generated until 1976. It took the board less than three hours to abort RCA's computer business.

2. United Airlines and bureaucracy. In 1972 United Airlines, the largest airline in the non-communist world, had 47 000 full-time employees and 380 jet aircraft flying 1·2 million miles every day of the year. As noted in chapter 4, United Airlines' solution to the problem of size was centralization, with few decisions permitted at lower levels of management. A series of events starting in 1969 culminated in the resignation of George Keck as chief executive officer, and indicated the organizational inflexibility at United Airlines. The first was the failure of the company to lobby in Washington to prevent the proliferation of competition on the highly profitable Hawaii route, which resulted in United moving from a 14 million dollar profit to a 17 million dollar loss on the Hawaii run (Loving, 1972). The second was the lack of effective strategies to interdict a union demand for a flight engineer on the short-haul Boeing 737 aircraft which will cost United 100 million dollars in extra crew costs over the life of this aircraft. The third was the failure to monitor a massive on-line computer reservation contract with Sperry-Rand, with the result that considerable time and money were lost in reassigning the contract to IBM. The fourth was the slow response by United Airlines to the airline volume slump of 1969 and the failure to cut costs severely during 1969 and 1970. This organizational inflexibility led to the Board of Directors recruiting a new chief executive officer, and to a subsequent reorganization.

3. IBM and the Peripherals. IBM has been recognized as one of the truly great companies of the second half of the twentieth century, and has effectively controlled the computer-manufacturing industry since its first incursion into computers. Yet if it were not for IBM World-Trade's contributions of 53 per cent of total profit from its overseas sales, and the interest and dividend income from the company's 1800 million dollars in cash and securities, IBM would have recorded no year-to-year increases in net profits in recent years. Since 1968, the growth rate overall has halved from the historic rate it had maintained for the previous 57 consecutive years:

> This state of affairs has led some people, including former IBM executives, to the conclusion that IBM may be turning into just another big company, like GM or GE. (Bylinsky, 1972, p. 55)

The environment facing IBM has undergone major changes, transforming IBM and the computer industry and calling for innovative organizational and strategic changes. Computer-hardware sales have reached a saturation or maturity point. Technological advances have slowed after the development of three component generations from vacuum tubes to transistors to integrated circuits in less than 20 years. Existing equipment, although technically obsolete, is still serving the major needs of many users of computers. Peri-

146

pherals manufacturers have doubled their penetration from 150 million dollars in 1969 to over 300 million dollars by the end of 1970, and resulted in the displacement and reduction of IBM revenues by as much as 100 million dollars a year. Emerging nationalism in Europe may result in the merger of Siemens of Germany, ICL of the United Kingdom, and CII of France, threatening IBM's overseas sales and profits.

A new industry, computer leasing, purchased 3000 million dollars of system/ 360 computers, about 12 per cent of the total market, greatly reducing future revenues of IBM from leasing income. The strategy of introducing the system/ 370 to interdict the leasing companies backfired, with customers eliminating two or three 360's by substituting one 370. Leasing companies had by this time recovered much of their original investment in 360's and cut leasing prices. Thomas J. Watson, Jr, noted the effect of the strategic gap:

> We had invested a few hundred million dollars in the 370. Actually, we could stop any product a month before we plan to announce it. But we were reckoning that the economy was going to resume its growth, and it took us a long time to recognize that we were in a serious recession. We thought the leasing companies were responsible for our difficulties in making net sales, not the economy. (Quoted in Bylinsky, 1972, p. 58)

In summary, even the glamour company, IBM, created its strategic gap through organizational inflexibility. The overselling of the 360 computer creating an overcapacity in computing power, the overpricing of peripheral equipment creating new competitors, and 'unbundling' to price hardware and software separately were strategic errors of arrogance creating organizational inflexibility.

Insufficient environmental support

Structural–institutional change has been identified as one of the three major origins of change. The failure of an institution or government to anticipate other environmental changes and adjust its posture accordingly creates strategic gaps. The US government did not change its posture as its budget deficits and the role of the US dollar as the world's reserve currency created excessive external charges against its own gold reserves. Equally, the world monetary agreements were not changed to accommodate the deterioration of the dollar in overseas markets. The resulting crisis and subsequent devaluation of the dollar in 1971 created confusion and dysfunctions which could have been avoided by change-responsive strategies in the 'sixties.

1. **Pan American World Airways and a deteriorating environment.** Pan Am's strategic gap has primarily resulted from the lack of environmental support by the United States federal government. By 1972, the company had suffered losses of 100 million dollars in the last three years. The United States, unlike

147

a number of other nations, has no national government-owned airline or a quasi-public one, but allows Trans World Airlines and Pan Am to be its flag carriers. It provides no direct cash subsidies and even allows other United States airlines overseas routings in competition with TWA and Pan Am. The deteriorating environment has primarily been caused by the failure of the United States government and agencies to recognize the unique problems faced by Pan Am and TWA operating in competition with government-sponsored or subsidized airlines.

Pan Am has not been allowed to fly domestic flights, although TWA has been given extensive domestic routings. Lucrative overseas routings have brought new competition both from foreign airlines and from new routes given to other US airlines. Charter airlines have been allowed to siphon traffic from popular routings on which Pan Am could have used its new 747's which have a 32 per cent lower seat cost than 707's with the same load factor. Pan Am's revenue per passenger mile fell to 4·99 cents compared with 6·01 for domestic airlines. Nationalistic actions by foreign governments have curbed Pan Am's share of market on a number of overseas routings. Government has prevented any attempt by Pan Am to merge with a complementary domestic airline, even though such a merger would result in lower overall costs and perhaps even lower fares.

Even the Penn-Central railway merger fiasco and its resulting bankruptcy, with the potential that the United States government might have to follow the disastrous examples of France, Germany, and the United Kingdom in nationalizing railways, have not resulted in environmental support for Pan Am. And as Chairman Najeeb E. Halaby noted 'Getting Washington to change is like saddling a rhinoceros' (Cordtz, 1972a, p. 79). Unfortunately, Pan Am also made managerial errors such as buying 33 747's, making large terminal construction expenditures, and following fads in managerial organization and development with sensitivity training programmes rather than concentrating on developing more effective strategies.

2. Communication satellites and government indecision. Although a domestic satellite became technically feasible as early as 1965 with the launching of the international satellite system by the Communications Satellite Corporation, lack of environmental support by the United States government has stalled any domestic version (Lessing, 1972). The Federal Communications Commission originally planned a single conglomerate entity and then in 1970 indicated that private competitors would be eligible. A number of major companies like American Telephone and Telegraph, RCA, and Western Union have presented proposals, but there is no indication that a government decision is in the offing. In the meantime the more advanced direct-broadcasting type of satellite which could eliminate ground network and stations to beam directly to homes is also being stalled. The lack of environmental support by government analysis and decision is very costly both to the economy and to the individual.

Resource inapplicability

An obviously critical step in the strategic feedback cycle is resource appraisal to determine the applicability of resources to manage environmental change. A strategic gap is created by resource inapplicability and its companion, inappropriate allocation of resources, making it difficult for business firms and governments to achieve predetermined objectives. The United Kingdom's over-commitment to a government health scheme is now being repeated in the United States, where the Medicare programme for persons over 65 is costing two or three times the originally estimated costs in some states; and Russia and China have had massive failures in agriculture and industry from inadequate resource applicability.

1. **United States Machinery Company (USMC) and acquisition disaster.** Until the 'fifties USMC dominated the US shoe industry with 85 per cent of all shoe machines in the US, and over 75 per cent in the UK. The company permitted only leasing of its machines until an anti-trust suit in 1953 resulted in an order to sell as well as lease. The leasing strategy and the company's domination of the shoe-machinery industry made possible the realization of very high profits, resulting in no debt.

In 1956, after failures to grow through internal research and development, USMC started a series of 52 acquisitions, 31 in the United States and 21 overseas. But the company was particularly inept at resource appraisal, resulting in a 25 million dollar write-off in 1970 and 1971 alone. There was no long-range plan of acquisitions to match resources against the environmental scan, which was confirmed in the first acquisition as noted by President Herbert W. Jarvis:

> We found that the selling of machinery for department stores and the type of service organization needed to back it up were completely different from the shoe industry. (Quoted in Vanderwicken, 1972b, pp. 126–7)

The company overextended its finances, resulting in 97 million dollars of long-term debt and 49 million dollars of short-term debt in 1972. The company lacked the special marketing and product knowledge to make its acquisitions mesh with its current product lines. USMC further lacked the managerial capabilities to manage the new acquisitions as stated by Chairman William S. Brewster:

> We might have brought in new management and strengthened some of our management team before we acquired. This is the fundamental thing we did wrong. Having bought a company, we expected it to operate automatically, and do a good job. Some didn't. (Quoted in Vanderwicken, 1972b, p. 130)

2. **The brewing industry and economies of scale.** Small brewers have inadequate resources to compete against larger brewers, as environmental

149

conditions have changed. In 1972, ten companies controlled 70 per cent of the US beer market with 60 others sharing the remaining 30 per cent. This is all that remains from 735 in the 'thirties and 170 in 1960 (Burck, 1972).

The basic parameters of the industry are such that massive resources are required. The product is bulky, has a relatively short shelf life, and distribution is expensive. Labour costs are high, exceeded only by the construction industry. Beer is produced in capital-intensive plants with a construction cost of 25 to 40 dollars per barrel and a minimum capacity of 1·5 million barrels. Technological obsolescence requires high volume utilization to permit new investment. Canning lines have increased from capacities of 800 cans a minute in 1965 to 1200 in 1972, and bottling from 500 to 900 per minute.

Economies of scale plus technological advances have abruptly changed costs and productivity. For example, Schlitz, one of the largest companies, produces 4·4 million barrels with 483 production workers, while Falstaff, the seventh largest, produces 4·1 million with 1800 workers. The cost comparison is $1·08 per barrel for Schlitz and $4·39 for Falstaff. Vertical integration by the big brewers further reduces costs, and advertising and pricing strategies favour the large brewers, who have massive TV campaigns and are able to charge premium prices. Finally, beer consumption is growing slowly, so that volume increases by the major companies must come from the market share of the smaller firms.

Such industry examples illustrate the unwise and inapplicable use of organizational resources. This contributor to the strategic gap often is compounded by yet another weakness, that of over-simplification.

Over-simplification of open-systems complexity

Part of the strategic gap results from the formulation of strategies using simple correlation of cause and effect. A firm sets its objective to capture an increased share of a market and formulates strategies of price, advertising and promotion to attain the objective. But all too often it fails to realize that these strategies trigger counter strategies by competitors which constrain, interdict, and may totally defeat the initial strategies. Equally, man's reasoning abilities are not unlike those of his creation, the computer. Although the ultimate effect may be a ranking of alternatives, the process of elimination is by simple comparison of two alternatives, eventually resulting in a ranking and decision of the most appropriate of the choices developed.

Computers are of little use except in the extension process, since strategies are basically a one-time phenomenon for which programming would be too expensive and take too long to develop. Complexity plays an increasingly important part, since strategies are open system rather than closed system in their formulation and impact. The aspiration level of an Iranian dissident may trigger a rebellion which results in oil shortages and income loss for a

150

major oil company. Eventually this could result in a change in oil quotas in the United States, and major shifts in domestic and international strategies of oil companies around the world. Such is the concept of open-systems theory or its further extension of general systems theory.

Failures to predict complexity and open-systems impact and develop the appropriate change-responsive strategies include the following examples.

1. **Currency realignments impacts.** Although the evidence had been accumulating for years and was readily available for environmental scanning, the major currency realignments of 1971 resulted in strategic gaps around the world. Shipbuilders in Japan wrote all contracts in United States dollars and will lose over 1000 million dollars in outstanding orders. Bulova found its strategies on watch production—low priced in Japan, medium priced in Switzerland, and high priced electronic in the US—no longer totally valid with the yen up 17 per cent and Swiss francs increased 14 per cent over the US dollar. A US drug company shifted its production of drugs for the Italian market from Germany to France with the revaluation of the mark. These are but a few examples of the over-simplification of open-systems complexities.

2. **Japan's myopia.** A national commitment in Japan to trade surpluses totalling 20 000 million dollars in foreign reserves by 1972 almost regardless of the consequences, blinded Japan to the complexity and open-system impact of such a strategy.

The most obvious result was a 17 per cent revaluation of the yen in 1971 and a predicted additional revaluation of 10 to 12 per cent in 1973. It also caused restrictions in imports, since the Japanese sell 8500 million dollars of goods to, but import only 5000 million dollars from the United States. Major markets other than the US are not going to be available. The Common Market has insisted on the right to restrict any Japanese import that disturbs European markets.

There has been a neglect of Japan's infrastructure. Air and water pollution alienate the Japanese from their government; and the cumulative effect of this neglect will result in greatly increased taxes with fewer resources to build business and further exports. The lack of alternative strategies has resulted in Japan having only 4000 million dollars invested abroad compared to the 80 000 million by the United States. Furthermore, there has been a failure to develop multinational company capabilities and adjust the Japanese management system:

> . . . a special government study group returned to Japan convinced that multinational corporations need lots of capital, a technological edge, superior marketing and nimble management. . . . That's bad news for Japan . . . to this day Japanese business still buys far more technology than it develops, and finds marketing as fathomable as alchemy. Japan's management system has worked well up to now. However, it's a unique approach, marked by unabashed paternalism, near lifetime employment, promotion

L

by seniority, decisions by group consensus and mandatory retirement at fifty-five except for a few at the top. Can this odd system be transplanted around the world? (*Forbes*, 1 October 1972, p. 32)

Japanese industry has a growth syndrome with little strategy development to handle stagnation. For example, car manufacturing grew at a compound rate of 22 per cent from 1965 to 1971, but the lack of adequate roads and market saturation has slowed the growth rate to but 4 to 6 per cent for the home market, and export increases will cease due to import restrictions in the United States, Europe and elsewhere. Colour-television manufacturers have similar problems, with market saturation in Japan, since some 40 per cent of Tokyo homes already own two colour sets, and exports to the United States where 9 out of 10 of their colour sets are sold will drop by 15 to 20 per cent. Furthermore, American firms have started to manufacture colour television in Taiwan and other lower labour cost countries to offset Japanese imports.

Japan will have to 'suffer' revaluation, a rising tide of imports, greater leisure, a higher national propensity to consume, increased public spending and investment to improve the quality and equality of Japanese life, and acceptance of the obligations in world finance, trade and aid that go with rising economic power. Eventually, Japan can even look forward to joining more mature countries in 'enjoying' slower growth, high taxes, rising costs, and occasional devaluations. Progress, anyone? (Heller, 1972, p. 18)

3. European Common Market: promise and reality. Complexity and open-system impacts have been intensified in the EEC by political and economic issues. *The Economist's* (1 January 1971) commentary on progress of the EEC notes the Community's strategic gap:

British entry, the consequences of the Nixon package, the Franco-German argument have combined to make a busily ineffectual shambles of the common market at the very moment when everyone had expected the E.E.C. would be allowed to go into a sort of collective chrysalis, inside which might be generated the European butterfly everyone has been waiting for. Instead, that chrysalis is being smashed open before the metamorphosis of the creature inside has had time to take place.... Europe has the resources to become an actual superpower but its people are increasingly unwilling to allow this to happen. Why? Rightly or wrongly Europe's people do not fear invasion from the outside. Rightly or wrongly they lose little sleep over the notion of being won to communism by Moscow-financed subversion. Rightly or wrongly west Europeans, though they may cordially detest many of one another's policies, no longer expect to go to war with one another. (pp. 10, 13)

A major hurdle facing the EEC in its effort to establish a common currency is the necessity that the economies of all members advance at the same rate. This requires that Germany's demand for price stability be reconciled with

152

France's and Italy's demand for growth and the United Kingdom's attempt to reduce unemployment (Ball, 1971). No true single market exists, except perhaps in agricultural products, which are heavily subsidized, and farmers have a commitment by the EEC to buy whatever they produce at a predetermined price. The EEC has suspended the law of supply and demand for agricultural products.

The elimination of tariff barriers on manufactured goods still does not result in truly free internal trade. Indirect taxation, differing efficiencies in distribution systems, and many non-tariff barriers strangle trade, which may account for Volkswagen being able to sell twice as many cars in Britain in 1970 over a 13 per cent tariff barrier as it sold in either Italy or France. Until 1971, France would not allow the importation of blankets of sizes other than those used by French manufacturers, and 99 per cent of all government procurement contracts are still awarded locally. Even the creation of multinational companies within the EEC has lagged, the majority of such companies being American. A unified European company law 'promises to be a political mouse, of little practical use as a vehicle for industrial rationalization across European frontiers' (*The Economist*, 1 January 1972, p. 22).

4. Housing subsidies and higher costs. The intent of housing subsidies in affluent nations is to permit the less fortunate to have homes equivalent to those of their lower middle class. The theory is that such subsidies will create work for the construction industry and end the alienation that the poor have from the establishment and society in general. But the systems effect impacts to create new problems, often exceeding the magnitude and severity of the problems apparently solved by the action. The actions by the United States government to provide housing subsidies have boomeranged: 'In many ways, our housing subsidies demonstrate the truth of Forrester's law, propounded by Jay W. Forrester, professor of Management at MIT, who maintains that intuitive plans to solve complex urban problems often produce results opposite from those intended' (Breckenfeld, 1972, p. 137).

Housing subsidies in the United States in 1972 covered 1 American in 23, and are projected to cover 1 in 8 by 1978. They are so complex that George Romney, Secretary of Housing and Urban Development, noted in 1972 that, 'These housing-subsidy programs are so complicated that they are practically impossible of administration'.

The overall effect of the housing-subsidy programme has created a series of crises of catastrophic proportions. Subsidized housing as a percentage of total housing has risen from less than 9 per cent in 1967 to more than 25 per cent in 1971. By 1978, the annual cost will be 7500 million dollars, with a total subsidy cost amounting to 200 000 million dollars on subsidized housing for the total payments before the loans are retired, if no further subsidies are granted after 1978. This is almost equivalent to the total US federal budget in 1973. Secretary Romney has calculated that a 17 500 dollar apartment built under the housing subsidy Section 236 would cost taxpayers over 100 000 dollars and perhaps as much as 140 000 dollars over the 40-year payment life.

The systems effect has been predicted by the government, but no actions to remedy the problem have been taken: 'Under present law, as many as twenty-five million American households—forty per cent of the total population—are eligible for the major subsidy programs. . . . Yet unless major changes are made, as these programs continue to gain production momentum, it will be difficult to continue favoring a select few in the population while the rest of the nation is left to seek decent housing completely on its own' (Breckenfeld, 1972, p. 138).

The subsidy system has created economic dysfunctions, because easy terms and outright gifts have permitted concealment of overpricing and avoidance, of market discipline, so that the average price of a subsidized house has risen 40 per cent from 1965 to 1970, and monthly payments 84 per cent. In addition, in many instances, the subsidized housing programme 'has created an environment that promotes social disorder', according to the executive director of the National Capital Housing Authority in Washington, DC.

> St. Louis' Pruitt-Igoe project, which won an architectural award from the American Institute of Architects when it opened in 1956, became a socio-logical and financial disaster that bankrupted the local housing authority. All but 3,000 of the 12,000 residents have departed. Twenty-five of the project's thirty-three buildings stand empty, their windows smashed, their salable innards—plumbing, wiring, and hardware—stripped by thieves, their hallways hideouts for junkies. Last month city officials won Secretary Romney's permission to begin leveling some of the ruins, even though thirty-three million dollars of Pruitt-Igoe's original thirty-six million dollars cost has not yet been repaid to bondholders. The federal government will have to make good the enormous loss. (Breckenfeld, 1972, p. 163)

The complexity of the intertwined social and economic issues involved in subsidized housing has been greatly underestimated:

> . . . the gritty problem that underlies so much of the present trouble with housing subsidies: inherited poverty and dependency. Perhaps the most important lesson of the Sixties is that we have underestimated the complexity of social problems, and overestimated the effectiveness of conventional remedies. (Breckenfeld, 1972, p. 171)

Ignoring change signals

Effective environmental scanning generates a series of change signals. But all too often little if any attention is paid to such change signals by institutions, organizations, or individuals. In some cases, the environmental scanning is at fault in its failure to read such signals correctly. In others the change signal may come through very strongly, but it is ignored by those responsible for effecting change. The resulting strategic gap is difficult to remedy because it creates a crisis-change model adaptation which is wasteful of resources, and action may be too late to be effective.

1. **Volkswagen and Beetle immortality.** By 1972 Volkswagen had sold over 15 million Beetles, 5 million in the United States alone. It was West Germany's largest industrial company, third largest outside of the US, and the fourth largest car manufacturer in the world—and made a loss on selling cars. Success blinded Volkswagen to the change signals of rising affluence and changing taste, of new Japanese competition, as well as to world geopolitical changes from imbalance in payments resulting in major currency revaluations and devaluations. Volkswagen's strategic gap has many dimensions.

Volkswagen's profitability is dependent on the sale of Beetles in the United States, where dollar devaluation, new American-made small cars, and Japanese competition have drastically threatened VW's position. Toyota and Datsun sales in 1971 were 30 per cent of imports compared to 4 per cent in 1965, while VW slipped from 67 per cent in 1965 to 38 per cent in 1971. VW built its empire on the basis of the export of one car, the Beetle, with only 15 per cent of it assembled or manufactured outside of Germany. Overseas manufacture is primarily in Brazil, where VW produces 300 000 cars a year, but this market was not open to Germany's exports, and therefore the produce-in-Brazil strategy was dictated by external forces.

Acquisitions have not been appropriately developed in light of rather obvious signals. Heinrich Nordhoff, VW's great leader until 1968, acquired Auto Union solely to utilize its facilities for the production of Beetles. Auto Union's successful Audi was a by-product of the independence of its newly appointed manager, Rudolp Leiding, rather than a conscious effort to develop a new model. The 1969 acquisition of NSU Motorenwerke AG, manufacturer of sub-compact Prinz cars, was to gain contol of additional production facilities and, rather incidentally, the Wankel engine. But primarily it was seen as a financial manipulation to obtain additional production without any outlay of cash. German laws protecting the rights of minority shareholders and the general unprofitability of NSU resulted in two years' litigation, the loss of Auto Union Audi's earnings to subsidize NSU losses, and the outlay of 120 million dollars. The joint venture with Porsche to produce the VW Porsche 914 has yet to show a profit.

The result of these strategic gaps has been an acceleration of capital investment from a total of 177 million dollars in 1968 to 279 million dollars in 1969, 421 million dollars in 1970, 574 million dollars in 1971, 745 million dollars in 1972, and projections to 1975 of 2600 million dollars (Ball, 1972). VW has followed a crisis-change model, developing new cars without the model monoculture factors of its unbelievably successful Beetle. By 1973 VW manufactured a dozen very different models with variations of air-cooled motors in the rear, water-cooled motors in the front, one with a motor in

155

the middle, and with both front and rear wheel drive. And not one of the new models was an unqualified success.

2. Caterpillar Tractor Co. and saturated markets. Caterpillar Tractor received half of its 2200 million dollars sales in 1972 from overseas, 400 million dollars of which is manufactured or assembled overseas. Its exports totalling 700 million dollars are the largest of any United States company. Its compounded annual earnings exceeded 10 per cent from 1960 to 1971, and its return on equity ranged from 15 to 20 per cent. But Caterpillar faces a strategic gap, with change signals growing stronger over the last decade.

Caterpillar dominates the big earth-moving equipment field, gaining much of its growth from the major road-building activities in the United States during the 'sixties. But the priorities in the United States in the 'seventies and 'eighties will be on urban renewal, requiring smaller equipment, where Caterpillar has little or no competitive advantage. Technological superiority had permitted Caterpillar to dominate world markets during the 'sixties, but now many countries, and especially Japan, have the technical capability to challenge the technological leadership (Rose, 1972).

Earnings and margins have declined in the last six years and would have declined at a greater rate, had it not been for expanded international business. But this expanded business has been exports to less-developed nations, which account for 60 per cent of Caterpillar exports. The less-developed nations are increasingly having balance-of-payment problems, and US aid is expected to decrease sharply in the 'seventies. All of this adds up to increasing competition and loss of markets for Caterpillar. Its product strategies have been high quality and high price. But these strategies cannot be applied to the smaller equipment, where farm-equipment companies like Deere can produce a variant of a farm tractor and absorb costs over larger volumes. It will be difficult for Caterpillar to change its production systems, dealer organizations, and even its financing strategies in a short time to capture new markets for smaller equipment to offset its loss of foreign markets and big equipment sales.

Change responsiveness and the strategic gap

Strategic gaps, whether caused by environmental scanning failures, organizational inflexibility, or the other major reasons identified above, create change-responsiveness crises. The commitment of major resources over time decreases the ability of any organization to respond to change. The strategic gap widens, and its impact intensifies the difficulties to reallocate resources and develop and implement appropriate strategies.

The degree of change responsiveness required for viability is dependent on the stability or turbulence of the environment. This assessment of the environment and the development of change responsiveness lies within the domain of strategy formulation, the subject of the final chapter.

Part 3
Strategies for change responsiveness

The case for change responsiveness is one that society, organizations, and individuals cannot ignore. The massive costs of the traditional crisis-change model can no longer be afforded by society.

How can society, organizations, and individuals become change responsive? This is perhaps one of the most difficult issues facing society as a whole in the last few decades of the twentieth century. The answers are not simple ones and demand reforms of such staggering magnitude that they will be difficult and perhaps even impossible to institute.

Twentieth-century man, the obsolete generation, carries with him all his prejudices and conditionings. A separate set of strategies must be evolved to motivate him to accept and institute change by removing the economic and psychological threats associated with such change. The hope is great that twenty-first-century man can be educated to accept and manage ambiguity, uncertainty, and complexity. But this requires a series of proactive strategies that need to be instituted now.

Organizations' strategies for change involve new organizational forms and the development of change-conducive organizational climates. The transitional solutions have been in the right direction but need far more development of such concepts as task force management and modular structures to create the change responsiveness needed for the future.

Strategies for change must also involve institutional reform to create the conditions under which man can become a truly independent rather than dependent creature. This requires new techniques as yet relatively virgin in development such as environmental scanning and vector analysis.

7

The individual as change agent

How does the individual learn to cope with change? How does he participate as a change agent in initiating and controlling change? One can neither completely escape from his past nor live permanently in it. Peter Drucker (1969a) advocates the need for getting rid of yesterday and John Gardner (1965) urges developing the capacity for self-renewal. Both scholars address a similar requirement: human adaptability begins with a commitment to diminish dependence upon past learning and conditions that contradict the realities of the present and the problems of the future.

Consciously or unconsciously, each person decides how he is to face an unpredictable and changing future. Will he cling to his past and steadfastly resist changes he finds unpleasant and threatening? Will he reluctantly or passively accept whatever comes along as if fate were his destiny? Or, will he purposively act to shape his future? The decision will depend upon the individual's perception and preparation for change responsiveness.

Change agents are needed at every level of society. Some may emulate great reformers like Cervantes who satirized the bankrupt medieval Spanish society through the deeds and misadventures of Don Quixote. Others may only influence their own lives by learning to respond to change and initiate improvements in their own lives and careers so that they become more effective contributors to society.

This chapter focuses on the conditions, values, and strategies by which individuals can become change responsive and manage change. The individual is not and should not be solely responsible for developing these capabilities. Institutional change is a necessary prerequisite to provide the environmental support to permit individuals and organizations to become change responsive. This requires an integrated thrust of institutional, organizational, and individual change, to prevent large masses of twentieth-century man from becoming prematurely obsolete. Equally, such a thrust must design and implement appropriate programmes to permit twenty-first-century man to become more change responsive than his progenitor.

Career roles in transition

Individuals are faced with the necessity of adjusting to many types of changes throughout their lifetimes, both in work-related and in non-work roles. Our emphasis in this chapter is on examining the change dimensions of career or organizational behaviour of individuals. Much of this will equally condition the personal dimension of the whole person, but our focus is limited to the organizational interface. It seems unlikely that the next three decades will produce a largely workless society, with cybernation so advanced that machines will replace individuals in producing an economy's goods and services, although prestigious groups have forecast workless future scenarios (Ad Hoc Committee on the Triple Revolution, 1964). Work will therefore continue into the twenty-first century as a necessary contributor to individual mental health and economic well-being.

Exhibit 7.1

Balancing multiple career role needs

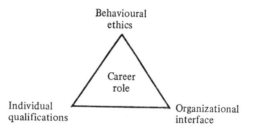

There is, however, no mistaking the profound changes which are, and will be, reshaping or revolutionizing the nature of jobs and work (Gooding, 1972). The protestant-ethic value that work is good in and of itself is being rapidly displaced by values of the social ethic that require more out of a job or career, and challenge the traditional motivational aspects of organizational life. Job roles are becoming more highly specialized, a natural consequence of coupling technological acceleration with large-size organizations. With job specialization and a fast turnover in technology and knowledge, a speed-up in career obsolescence is inevitable.

Most career roles are moving toward a restructuring of both personal needs and organizational job qualifications. The concept of motivation according to a need hierarchy, as first explained by Maslow (1954) and later applied to business firms by McGregor (1957), may soon reach the point where it is no longer a predominant explanation of behaviour in organizations. Rather than a scalar concept of needs as motivational influences, a more realistic explanation may involve a multiple balancing of more-or-less simultaneous needs that are all important to career and organizational performance (see Exhibit 7.1).

An individual learns through interaction with his environment, and the way

160

he perceives his actions to affect that environment. Some behaviours, such as language, he learns through operant conditioning, where selective reinforcement by outside forces conditions his behavioural response (Skinner, 1968). While stimulus–response–reinforcement patterns are appropriate for learning of tangible behaviours, abstract concepts and reasoning are learned more by a structural rearrangement of thought patterns (Bruner, 1960). Reinforcement is more muted; the individual is attracted toward those behaviours which hold positive or pleasurable outcomes and learns to avoid those that are negative. Over time, the individual shifts from a relatively passive to highly active involvement in his learning process. He becomes more reliant on himself for setting standards and evaluating his performance, whether the objectives relate to achievement tasks (Weiner, 1972) or moral development (Kohlberg, 1972).

Advancement of man's conditioning or learning process produces two potentially contradictory results. First, as an individual increases his body of knowledge, he is able to process more complex and abstract phenomena, to use past learning as a basis for insight into novel problems and for additional learning. But at the same time, usually there is a dampening of the spontaneity to experiment and to find excitement in new conditions and in frequent change. A few individuals remain innovators and seem to thrive on change, but for most the scope of allowable change is narrowed to very few interests. Any changes that fall outside that narrow band are ignored, denied, or considered disruptive.

Conditioned or patterned approaches to problem definition and solution simplify behaviour, and on the surface make the environment appear more predictable. But such conditioned behaviour is not always in the best interests of the individual, as it forces an extrapolation of the past into the future. This behaviour is frequently labelled with terms such as 'set in one's ways', 'myopic', or simply 'old fashioned'. When there is conflict between the individual's established values and behaviours and a changing environment, it is upsetting to his political, religious, or family life. But it is likely to be traumatic and dysfunctional when the conflict affects his job or career.

There is strong evidence that in the future an individual can no longer expect that acquired professional, craft, or trade skills and knowledge will suffice for a lifetime. Few individuals in the future will escape career obsolescence without continual, periodic, or redirected new learning. The primary strategy to cope with increased job complexity and need for knowledge has been reliance upon even greater specialization. Specialization can be expected to accelerate, but even with specialization there is an urgent necessity to keep abreast of the latest skills and knowledge required in one's job.

In medicine, like many other professions, new knowledge and techniques are becoming available so quickly that the practising physician is often critically behind the times professionally. When the half life of medical knowledge is about 10 years, doctors several years beyond medical school, internship, and residency are likely to be incompetent in providing their patients with the best and most modern medical care. Simply scanning the medical journals is not sufficient in a profession where skill requires observation and practice. Morton Rubenstein (1972), a practising neurologist, suggests the magnitude of this failure to keep pace with career change:

> Professionals who have worked in the postgraduate medical field estimate that between one-quarter and one-third of all practicing physicians in California (which is probably among the better states in this regard) do not, have not, and will not keep up with the newer medical developments. (p. J-6)

This problem is undoubtedly found, not only in California, but also in the rest of the world. Rubenstein supports the need for continuing education and retraining. His remedy for overcoming the medical obsolescence problem is 'to provide for and insist upon postgraduate medical education'.

Career development cannot be limited to one concentrated period of formal education, coupled with personal experience over the following 30 or 40 years. One solution for the firm to maintain necessary levels of competence is to hire new employees with up-to-date skills. The consequence of this strategy is catastrophic for society—the displacement of obsolete workers who become dependent on society. Even if the obsolete worker is not discharged, he loses the opportunity to assume greater responsibilities. The organization also loses, since it is unable to capitalize on its past development and the learning of the individual, who has acquired an intuitive feel for the organization and its environment.

Obviously the more turbulent the environment, the greater the need to acquire and/or develop newer knowledge and skills. But even firms in relatively stable environments experience obsolescence in some market segments. The demise of mature market segments in turn renders obsolete workers and managers whose skills and livelihood have been linked to that dying market.

Individuals attempt to protect themselves from the threat of career obsolescence either (a) through career learning and self-development or (b) by economic power applied through craft unions and professional associations. These two means do not have to be mutually exclusive as often the union or association insures that candidates meet strict qualification standards through testing and/or educational–apprenticeship programmes before acceptance as full members. But seldom do craft unions or licensing associations, such as the medical profession, insure that members' qualifications progress with the advancing state of the art.

Economic power to protect and raise member income is often substituted as a more important goal than periodic updating of skills or knowledge. The legal profession in many countries tends to be flooded with members; so bar associations may resort to price-fixing the minimum fee which attorneys can charge for specific services, thus bolstering the income of less-skilled members by inflating the price of legal services. Craft unions, such as plumbers or electricians in the construction industry, use a different strategy of arbitrarily restricting membership and additionally pressing for the enactment of building codes. This is ostensibly done to enhance health and safety, but its result is the perpetuation by law of the use of existing skills and the retardation of the implementation of more innovative methods, which may be less labour intensive, or may be performed by firms and persons outside the union.

Protective measures for preventing obsolescence, however they may be implemented, are at best temporary delaying tactics. Any profession, craft, or job skill—just as any firm's product-marketing effort—must continue to interface with and relate to the changing conditions and needs of society. The need for house painters may be diminished by new technology, such as building materials which need no painting. Para-professionals may replace or relieve the work load of professionals in some career fields, since they can be trained faster, and at less expense. Obsolescence can only be avoided through retraining and redevelopment, not by the use of power to delay and resist change.

Twentieth- versus twenty-first-century man

Between now and the beginning of the twenty-first century, the environment of man and his institutions will have changed noticeably if not radically. Post-industrialism for the primary nations of the world will become more advanced and many of the underdeveloped nations will have moved into a stronger footing of industrialism (Kahn and Bruce-Briggs, 1972). Many of the currently urgent social problems—pollution, discrimination, poverty, urban decay, mass transportation, resource use—will either have been solved or major steps taken toward their resolution. Inevitably other social problems will become recognized and priorities will shift. World population and technological products will continue to grow, exerting additional pressures on resources and generating more and often pessimistic questions about man's control of his environment and life (Maddox, 1972). To adjust to these changes and evolving pressures, values will continue to shift and the social ethic will become an integral frame of reference for a substantial portion of Western societies in the twenty-first century.

These brief projections sketch an important difference between those whose conditioning has been primarily in the first three quarters of the twentieth century and those whose experience is in the last few decades of this century. The former we shall call twentieth-century man, the latter, twenty-first-century man. Although these two groups coexist in contemporary society, the problems and decisions they face as individuals now and in the future are substantially different. Exhibit 7.2 highlights some of the differences which affect these separate problems by contrasting the basic conditioning, motivation, and ethic of these two groups. Generally individuals representative of twentieth-century man consider their formal education as completed; many do not even entertain the idea of the need for future systematic learning. They are presently working or seeking work and feel that their lives are fairly well established, that their personal futures will not be too different from the present. Society's problem with twentieth-century man will be one of maintaining him as a fully productive member of society.

As suggested by Exhibit 7.2, the gap between twentieth- and twenty-first-century man is not so much one of age or generation-gap differences as it is

Exhibit 7.2
Characteristics of twentieth- versus twenty-first-century man

Twentieth-century man	Twenty-first-century man
Conditioning and experiences	
Self sacrifice and struggle	Raised in affluence
Experience as best teacher	Emphasize formal education
Face-to-face learning	TV and automated learning
Repression of hostility	Expression of dissent
Localized frame of reference	Cosmopolitan, worldly
Fixed base of skills	Lifelong learning process
Motivations and expectations	
Stability, security concerns	Self-determination concerns
Acceptance of authority	Respond to actions not symbols
Status, in relation to others	Seek intrinsic satisfaction
Tolerate prolonged hardship	Demand immediate redress
Personal risk avoidance	Personal risk acceptance
Tangible objectives, rewards	Intangible, complex objectives
Values and ethic	
Compromise values for success	Honesty in acts and relations
Acquiesce in prejudices	Correct social injustice
Competition and conflict	Cooperation and collaboration
Power and authority are right	Truth, justice make right
Materialistic work ethic	Individual human dignity
Pessimism, provincialism	Optimistic dynamism

one of different sets of conditions and experiences. The individual who experienced the Great Depression, the urgencies of the Second World War and the social–economic–technological environments surrounding events of the 'fifties to the 'seventies has been conditioned by these vivid input factors. Contrast this to the twenty-first-century man who has always lived in the presence of television, computers, jets, men in space, supermarkets and shopping centres, and easy access to a car.

Twentieth-century man received most of his formative educational-experience conditioning directly—by family, teachers, and friends. Today's youth receives substantial conditioning through that ubiquitous and impersonal picture tube that has become a necessity even for the poor. With its immediacy and dramatization, television presents the full range of contradictions that exist within and among societies, between wealthy and impoverished, between healthy and ill, between the happy and the despondent, between youth and aged, between the informed and the ignorant. Television also suggests a wide range of plausible behaviours for coping with any problem: deceit, violence, power, dissent, education, love, drugs, religion, crime, sex, war, money, government—today's youth have seen it all!

The electronic world of computers and telecommunications gives the young person who will mature into the twenty-first-century man an instant awareness of worldly problems and the methods others have chosen for solutions. Television currently is the greatest teaching machine regardless of programme content, which for the most part is a vicarious, redundant, and simplistic form of conditioning—one that condenses highly complex social–behavioural problems into neat, understandable 30–60 minute segments. The greatest danger of constant exposure to television by early twenty-first-century man is that he is probably being conditioned to some behaviours which are socially violent, aggressive and destructive. Today's children typically are exposed to 20 or 30 hours of television viewing per week, yet social scientists still do not fully understand or agree upon the behavioural impact of this audiovisual medium (Davidson *et al.*, 1972; Liebert and Poulos, 1972).

Early twenty-first-century man is now in his formative years and is learning from experiences, both vicariously and directly, the behavioural tendencies which will condition his responses to his world of the future. For the individual who has not yet reached his majority, society will have to make major alterations in the conditioning processes—education and experiences—to prepare him adequately for positive rather than defensive responses to future changes. At the same time society must also alter structural conditions which constrain greater adaptability to change by the twentieth-century man who was conditioned and educated for a different set of events—those of stability and continuity.

Society's institutions and organizations must begin now to provide two separate sets of strategies for individuals to become more change responsive: one set for the generation tending toward obsolescence, and another for the generation that has yet to attain their most productive stage of development.

Strategies for the obsolete generation

Obsolescence can occur in two different ways. The first is failure of the individual to provide new sets of qualifications as his job is phased out by structural–institutional, technological, or social–behavioural change. This is the critical problem of the future. The second is caused primarily by a lack of mobility.

Lack of mobility can occur along any one of three dimensions: (a) among different jobs within a single organization, (b) geographically within an organization, or (c) between different organizations, which may also

165

involve geographical relocation (Veiga, 1973). The first two dimensions of blocked mobility are a combination of restrictive organizational practices, the personal life stage of the individual, and outdated or inadequate job abilities. Drucker (1969a, p. 254) attributes the obstacles to increased mobility between organizations to fettering devices such as 'pension plans, stock option plans, delayed compensation, and so on, with which we tie managers, professionals, and skilled people to a particular employer'.

Both categories of obsolescence result in varying degrees of trauma for the displaced individual. The professional manager, scientist, or skilled technician who has invested considerable time and money in his education, training, and experience will experience emotional letdown and even more serious psychological ills as he perceives his impending obsolescence (Rogers, 1973).

A blocked career, disinterest in work, and alienation toward the organization and society are symptoms of the twentieth-century man in the throes of obsolescence. The problem as summed up by a US Department of Labor report is one where workers' 'occupational achievements do not equal their original aspirations'. To the individual it is recognition that personal career investments do not have the desired payoff. For higher-level professionals and managers, the options for a career change are severely limited.

To make twentieth-century man more change responsive within his working life requires actions in three primary strategy areas:

1. The threat of change should be reduced and the built-in rigidities eliminated to permit twentieth-century man to adjust to occupational or organizational change.

2. Greater opportunity and challenge need to be created through job restructuring.

3. A change-supportive environment is required to permit individuals to acquire new job skills and even prepare for totally new careers.

No society can afford to wait for a new generation of managers, professionals, technicians, craftsmen, and factory and service workers, but must effectively utilize its current resources. The basic personality and motivation of twentieth-century man will not change perceptibly. Society in the free world cannot recondition or brainwash individuals to make them less rigid, more tolerant, or change-seeking. The only effective strategy is to change twentieth-century man's environmental constraints. This requires incentives and special institutional support to change the individual's perceptions of change by removing its economic and psychological threats.

Major economic and psychological threats occur when man is faced with profound change:

1. Inadequacy, both psychologically and economically, in terms of the lack of appropriate skills to retain his job or find a new one.

2. Lack of growth opportunities as doors close because of the individual's lack of qualifications.

3. Loss of employment, which is both economic and psychological in its impact.

4. A feeling of loss of self-esteem, producing depressions and apathy.

Several types of institutional support can be implemented to minimize the threat of change to the individual.

1. **Internal conditioning in the firm.** There has been a transitional response within firms to condition managers and less often employees to some degree of change responsiveness. Primarily, this has been in the form of job or geographical rotation. But the objective has been to develop specific job skills for a predetermined job, not to condition for change. Such reassignments have been at the discretion of the firm to satisfy its needs, not necessarily those of the individual.

Internal conditioning could be designed to create change responsiveness through special assignments, task-force membership, and changing the job structure to permit greater interface with environmental realities. Management and organization development can be restructured to permit individuals to acquire the new skills of managing complexity, uncertainty, and ambiguity. Much of the following chapter describes in detail how these organizational changes can be made.

2. **Job security.** Basically, this is the Japanese model of security for life. The Japanese practice of lifetime employment with a single firm mandates that the firm accept the responsibility for improving the skill–knowledge levels of its employees. In other countries such a policy has been at the discretion of management, and many firms have adopted such a retention–retraining philosophy in so far as this is possible and practicable. Universal enforcement of such a policy, however, would probably impose severe constraints on organizational flexibility, as not all firms will continue to grow or maintain comparable output levels. Displacement of entire industries because of technical and marketing changes cannot be ignored, and a fixed system would have to assume the ideal capability of all firms to diversify.

3. **Environmental scanning and job training.** Despite the previous criticism that unions and professional groups can ignore the need for skills development or resist job-content changes, there are notable exceptions. Sweden for some 20 years has promoted labour upgrading and mobility through an autonomous agency working with unions, firms, and government. Central to the programme is environmental scanning to anticipate job redundancies and opportunities in the near future. By systematically inducing new training and shifting workers from one type of skill to another, often with physical relocation of families, Sweden has transformed its industry and improved efficiency through reduced unemployment (Drucker, 1969, p. 60).

It is doubtful if the Swedish example will be followed widely in other, larger economies where the problems of political acceptance and administrative complexity might frown upon this as further intensification of the managed-economy concept and one encumbered with bureaucratic slowness to change. Difficult though the solution may be in the context of the political and cultural milieu of most of the Western democracies, the need is great for institutional reform that may ease the career-adjustment–redirection problem of twentieth-century man.

4. An education–training fund and independent redevelopment. Creation of an education–training fund system would provide the opportunity for every one to redevelop his skills and redirect his career by drawing on a government-spawned fund to which he has contributed. Its desirability is based on the premise that few individuals will be able to escape from the need for periodic or occasional career-related development in the face of declining skills and job-knowledge over a 40- or 50-year working period. Educational resources currently are provided by taxpayers through government to underwrite the cost of basic education for a specified number of years. They are primarily for those who have not yet entered the labour force. Few resources are available to the general public for education or formalized training after completion of this basic required education. The most notable exception is the plan for training military personnel after discharge, or sometimes before discharge, so they acquire appropriate skills for a civilian career or job.

The purpose of the education–training fund would be to make every individual largely self-sufficient for maintaining job-related skills throughout his lifetime. Such a fund could be initiated by legislative act to require mandatory contributions by all employees, and possibly employers. An individual could utilize his contribution at any time for training, education, and general redevelopment or self-improvement. It would provide sufficient funds for his living costs as well as tuition, but the payout could not exceed his contributions plus those of his employer, except during an initial stage of contribution into the fund. An individual need not pursue full-time education or training to qualify for his benefits. He could draw upon the fund while still employed to develop his skills on a part-time basis.

The government could very well make more use of the private sector (Etzioni, 1971) and the education–training fund could be administered by competitive private firms in the financial or insurance industries with regulatory safeguards prescribed by government, but with mandatory contributions. The individual or his employer could then have a choice as to which agency would administer their investment.

To operationalize the initial fund, two stages would be necessary:

Stage 1. As an interim step, individuals who immediately had need of additional education or job training could use an amount up to a limited proportion of past income taxes paid as a credit for receiving a loan. This loan would be repaid by a slightly higher rate of taxes in the future until the loan plus interest had been repaid. The government tax agency would act as the collection centre for loan repayment, with the funds provided by one of the private firms operating in a fiduciary-agency capacity to administer part of the fund.

Stage 2. Under the main provisions of the programme, the employee would begin paying into his funded account at a prescribed per cent of gross income up to an annual upper limit. The fund could be limited in its accumulation to a figure of three times the employee's annual gross income. At the discretion of the individual, he could tap into this reserve for enhancing his employment-related skills, including career counselling–testing services and/or a living allowance for full-time learning. In case of death of the employee, accumulated contributions plus interest earnings would be paid to the individual's beneficiaries, therefore serving as an additional insurance policy.

This proposed institutional change would permit the individual the security and flexibility necessary to maintain his employability at optimal levels throughout his lifetime. Unlike retirement programmes which provide only a nominal level of income beyond age 60 or 65, the education–training fund is aimed at improving quality of working life before retirement by making options available. Whatever credit balance has been accumulated at time of retirement could be used for retirement learning programmes (Cole, 1973) or as additional annuity income.

An educational–training fund would allow an individual who previously considered his formal education to be completed the opportunity to undertake his own advanced career development or retraining, thus giving him greater self-determination and independence. The fund is not intended to substitute for continued efforts by business and other institutions to provide for internal training and development programmes. It is conceivable, however, that the fund could be used to augment an individual's skill development through a programme designed and operated by his employer. Company-sponsored programmes could be eligible for subsidy by the individual's fund account where the internal programme was as cost effective as outside alternatives. Such provisions would give an individual the capacity to have greater involvement in shaping his career path with an employer since the full cost of shifting him from a fully productive position into one for growth and learning would not be borne by the organization alone. Coupled with certain changes in the structure and climate of organizations (as proposed in the next chapter), the individual becomes freer of the dictates and whims of his organizational superiors in shaping his personal career future.

The above proposal sketches the rudiments of an institutional change which would improve the likelihood that twentieth-century man could adjust to career change. Adoption of the education–training fund would remove a major structural blockage which locks millions of individuals into a single career and causes the economic and psychological trauma of the all too familiar mid-career crisis (Rogers, 1973). Modifications of the fund certainly could be localized to individual organizations or industries, possibly through joint management–union action, although the degree undoubtedly would be less than for a nation-wide programme.

Higher education is highly subsidized today either by public taxes for state-supported institutions or by philanthropic endowments for the private schools. If the education–training fund were adopted and available to all, higher education could be priced to the individual user on a full-cost basis. Under Stage 1 of the fund, a student would draw against future income to pay for the full cost of his education, not for only one-fifth to one-half of it. Ideally, if society really values personal independence, all young people would be encouraged to participate in the fund in lieu of expecting parents to pay for this privilege.

A higher rate of income tax upon beginning work would be a means of repaying the loan and would also act as an incentive against excessive time devoted to higher education early in one's life. The same terms would also apply to those individuals choosing to enter a technical school or job-training programme rather than college or university. By making the opportunity for some form of post-basic education or training a right available to all, society should expect that a much greater proportion of young people would choose the less expensive and quicker payoff of technical-skills training.

Society may be particularly concerned about disadvantaged groups such as the handicapped or minorities who do not gain adequate language and numerical skills during basic education to be fully employable. For such cases, society might prefer to extend them additional subsidies for a sufficient number of years to break the poverty cycle and give them the means by which to become more independent.

The twenty-first-century man

Questions still remain about societal changes or provisions for youth and future generations who have not yet completed their basic conditioning and ventured into the world of employment. Society, teachers, parents, and employers cannot ignore the consequences of education and pre-employment experiences upon the ways in which the twenty-first-century man adapts to and reshapes his changing environment.

1. Are his learning conditions really developing in him the skills and attitudes necessary to cope with complexity, ambiguity and change; or are most of his tough decisions being made for him?

2. Is he receiving balanced experiences; or is he forced to remain in unbroken education or pleasure-oriented activities where he is prevented from intermittently or concomitantly contributing to society?

3. Is society providing sufficient exposure and guidance in the critical task

170

of evaluating and selecting vital and rewarding career fields; or does chance and limited knowledge of career alternatives still prevail?

The world in which the twenty-first-century man works and behaves will be largely one of abstract concepts. The days in which most people produced tangible products or performed a job that could be observed and understood by their children is largely a thing of the past. The future modelling effect of a parent's work upon his children's learning will be reduced. How many working fathers or mothers even today can convey to their children a precise explanation or demonstration of the nature of their work and its output?

Jobs which involve abstract concepts and whose products are processes or functions rather than physical products are subject to much greater job-content change because they are comprised of knowledge and cognitive–interpersonal skills. In just the past two decades jobs which are part of the 'knowledge organization' (Zand, 1969) or what Gross (1968) calls the 'learning force' have increased to where they now outnumber tangible and production-oriented jobs within the more highly developed societies. What must the prospects for abstract and conceptual work be in the year 2000?

With this trend in the nature of work, the major challenge for society is to change the educational process for the twenty-first-century man. Educational and other conditioning institutions must design and implement different sets of experiences to accentuate the abstract, the ambiguous, the uncertain, and the complex—conditions of work that are certain to prevail in the twenty-first century. Youth will have to be given more responsibility, not less, for making decisions which affect their daily and future lives. This includes the critical decision on higher education or technical training beyond completion of whatever minimal education society considers necessary for every citizen.

Most affluent societies, through parental influence and/or wealth coupled with taxpayer support of higher education, encourage young people to remain as students or recipients of the educational system until well into their twenties or even thirties. Has the widespread availability of low-cost education to the student made him more flexible, more willing to make risky decisions, and more accepting of the consequences of his own decisions? Or has it made him more dependent, more willing to accept the easy route, and more concerned with his personal edification rather than contributing to the society that has been his benefactor for so many years?

There is no straightforward unqualified answer to the above questions. They are complex and unanswerable in yes or no alternatives. There is little doubt that education for the twenty-first-century man will become increasingly more essential because of the more conceptual–abstract nature of career skills. But the concentration of formal education into the first third of an individual's life is a practice that has tenuous value even for the mature twentieth-century man. And the custom of accumulating hundreds of credit hours in college or university before putting one's skills, knowledge, and

171

interest to the pragmatic test of a productive job may not be wise use of educational resources, much less the time and energy of youth.

The need to create a more independent man through earlier decision making responsibility creates a new dilemma. How can an individual at age 18 know that he really wants to invest 6–8 years in higher education before he has had any work experience? How many educational resources are ill-spent on the person who after one or more years on the job decides that he is not suited to the profession or job category he has chosen? These questions are symptomatic of the problems facing education, and particularly universities in the training of twenty-first-century man.

1. **New roles for the university.** The creation of Renaissance man in the twenty-first century is an anachronism. In the sixteenth century some 520 000 book titles were published; currently more than 500 000 titles are published in a single year (Hauser, 1973). The knowledge explosion is so great that even doctoral seminars in universities are unable to impart the knowledge required for most professions today.

The humanist–specialist function will require further lengthening of the number of years to be spent in a university prior to any contribution to society. The specialist, and perhaps humanist knowledge as well, can only be expected to be relevant for a decade, or two decades at the most. This points to a restructuring of the university in either of two directions. The first is to shorten the first experience to two to three years, emphasizing general, humanist knowledge coupled with the development of skills appropriate to handling uncertainty, ambiguity, and complexity. This will require new learning–teaching methodology and pedagogy.

The second direction is that of extreme specialization for two to three years in new smaller modules of learning disciplines. Both directions lead to the same basic point—reduce the first learning experiences. Both would be followed by work experience. Mature individuals would return to the university or to other appropriate learning centres after some years of work experience, drawing upon their education–training fund reserves. As skills became obsolete, they would return once again after some further years of work experience.

The objective of such a system change is to begin early to condition the twenty-first-century man to become more responsible and responsive in preparing for his own future. By shortening the first exposure to the university or other educational centres, young people will no longer remain indefinitely within the confines of the educational system. They will be forced to manage a greater share of the complexities impacting on their lives. The majority of subsequent postgraduate training will be enhanced by the exposure to the practical rather than the theorized world. Certainly this will be true for the study of business, where the exposure to the reality of the business world will provide an experience base on which new skills can be built. Higher education and technical training will be viewed as life-long processes, which are expected to take place at age 40 or 50 just as much as at age 20 or 30.

Such changes would also force educational and training institutions to become more responsive to demand changes impacting both from the students and from organizational–employer needs. Development of this responsiveness capability would not necessitate a shift from public to private institutions or vice versa. But it would mean that all educational institutions and each department or discipline within them would have to become economically self-sufficient. If all state financial aid, other than for research grants, were channelled to universities, colleges, and technical-trade institutes on the basis of student choice rather than through the political bargaining process of legislatures as the fund-granting authority, such institutions of higher education would quickly have to become responsive to the needs for their services by students and other institutions. Placed on a profit-centre basis, each department would then have greater motivation to evaluate the marketability and effectiveness of its programmes and teaching.

2. Career counselling. Counselling is an integral part of most educational systems in the 'seventies. But all too often it is either based on inadequate data or directed to relatively narrow interests, such as the choice of curricula in the high schools and colleges. An independent agency, not unlike that established in Sweden, must provide sophisticated environmental scanning, psychological –aptitude testing, and highly specific career counselling. This service is provided to both the young seeking initial educational training, and the experienced seeking the updating of their skills.

More informative career counsellors undoubtedly would create greater change responsiveness in higher education since the independent agency would monitor the performance records of centres of education. Any individual or organization would be able to obtain selective information on such factors as the rate of growth or decline of new entrants into specific career fields, starting salaries, placement records of schools providing instruction in any career field, or progress advancements of each school's graduates in their jobs or professions. Such information could be compiled rather easily through a minimal number of additional classification questions that would be completed on income-tax returns. Conceivably it could revolutionize what currently is a very haphazard or random approach to career-related environmental scanning by both individuals and universities.

These recommended changes are not intended to be a unilateral condemnation of the process of higher education, nor should they be construed as a mandate that higher education should only involve career-related subjects. The main objectives are to (a) make individuals and institutions more knowledgeable about the market for environmental changes; (b) allow the individual to bear the full cost of his education; (c) enable every person access to higher education or training by providing loan support or later, self-contribution funding; (d) develop a change-responsive approach to education and

173

training; and (e) provide lifetime training to reduce and hopefully eliminate human obsolescence.

Such changes may well involve higher costs to society, but for the most part they will be borne in relationship to benefits received through the mechanism of the education–training fund. Higher costs may also accrue because of the smaller size of the work force as individuals return to school or to training centres for new skills development. But the cost of educationally displaced unemployment, unlike that of the worker made obsolete and involuntarily put out of work, is really an investment in continued career-change responsiveness.

Our emphasis upon making the twenty-first-century man more independent, or freer of the society-induced obstacles which deter career mobility, does not suggest an artificial return to the protestant ethic. But it does attempt to reverse the trend from independence to dependence, whether such a dependence be on organizations or governments in general. The education–training fund belongs to the individual. He has paid for it or will pay for it out of his own income. It is not a government handout. Rather it recognizes a combination of the protestant and the social ethics with an obligation on the part of the individual to put forth the effort for his own security and livelihood.

The truly mobile individual

The most common organizational role in the future will be even more intense specialization than we now know it. This predominance of specialists will add to the complexity of the generalists since it is they who must activate, coordinate, and capture the work of the specialists. Society will have a continuing and expanding need for generalists in the administration of firms, universities, governments and governmental agencies, and other institutions. Their job in the future as in the past will continue to involve defining objectives, formulating policies, directing strategies, and managerially integrating the output of specialists.

Rewards in the past, especially in business, have been for the generalist, the upward climbing manager. In other professions such as medicine and law, or in the craft or technical fields, the opposite has generally been true, the greatest recognition and reward going to the specialist. As the size and complexity of organizations increase, two separate tracks will have to be developed not just for motivating and administering rewards but for renewing, retreading, and redirecting career skills.

The specialist renews himself by keeping up with the advancing state of the profession, craft, or trade. In the professional and technical areas, this process of renewal cannot be satisfactorily attained simply by accumulating more experience, as was noted previously in the case of the physician. For some, keeping up will involve formalized and concentrated learning reinforced by

174

practical experience. For others, it will involve shifting away from the original line of specialization by branching into new areas.

The intensive training of the specialist will create new problems, since focusing intently on one narrow segment of a field or task will produce a brilliant idiot not unlike the *idiot savant* who can do sophisticated mathematical calculations in his head in seconds but does not even understand what he has done. How can the specialist acquire both an awareness of where his specialty fits into the larger weave of organizational decision making and an ability to relate to other specialists?

To survive in an organization and make effective contributions to the whole, specialists will have to develop some of the interpersonal, team-coordinative capabilities of the generalist, although to a lesser degree. Learning which concentrates simply on the technical skill dimension of even the specialist's job will prove inadequate if he is to function in an interacting organizational role.

By contrast, development of the skills of a generalist in management is largely different from the learning of the generalist in other professions. In most professional disciplines the individual first acquires a generalist's knowledge and then spends years concentrating upon developing superior skill and knowledge about a narrow segment of the whole. In management the process is reversed. From an original, specialized base, a variety of experiences and a broadening educational scope expands individual capacity toward more conceptual and analytical skills. These skills, plus the higher-level skills of managing ambiguity, uncertainty, and complexity permit the generalist to provide the leadership necessary to coordinate the contributions of specialists.

The truly mobile individual is the person who is able to cross the generalist–specialist track in zig-zag fashion if necessary or if he so desires. In the 'seventies it may appear that the easier cross-over within business is from the specialist to progressively more generalist positions. In the future the route from generalist to specialist may become the more expedient one. The return to the university or educational centre may be for specialized training where environmental scanning and career counselling have identified opportunities. Generalists can become as equally obsolete as specialists since education in the future will be required to develop generalists rather than the hit-or-miss experience route of the 'fifties and 'sixties. Education can provide systematic conditioning to enable individuals to expand the complexity of their mental information processing systems (Schroder *et al.*, 1967).

Flexibility between specialist and generalist routes will depend on internal changes in the structuring and reward systems of organization, which are described in the next chapter. But successful career mobility may also require that society restructure the value it attaches to different types of careers. Individuals who receive high incomes do so primarily because of a scarcity of individuals with specific abilities or willingness to perform a job. But in some cases, society could pay less for the same quality of service if more realistic qualifications could be defined. Obvious examples involve the use of technicians and para-professionals for many medical and dental services. But many professions have knowledge and skill requirements that seem unnecessary in a world with increasing needs and diminishing resources. For example, why does a medical degree make the psychiatrist a more prestigious clinical therapist than the psychologist, when in high probability the MD has received more limited education and training in the behavioural sciences?

Shortening the amount of time required in education and training before beginning to practise a career does have the advantage of encouraging more frequent or even redirectional training at a later stage in life. To compensate for the lack of breadth because of more intense specialization, greater team efforts will be required. Through complexity analysis and the systems

Exhibit 7.3

Specialist team replacement of generalists

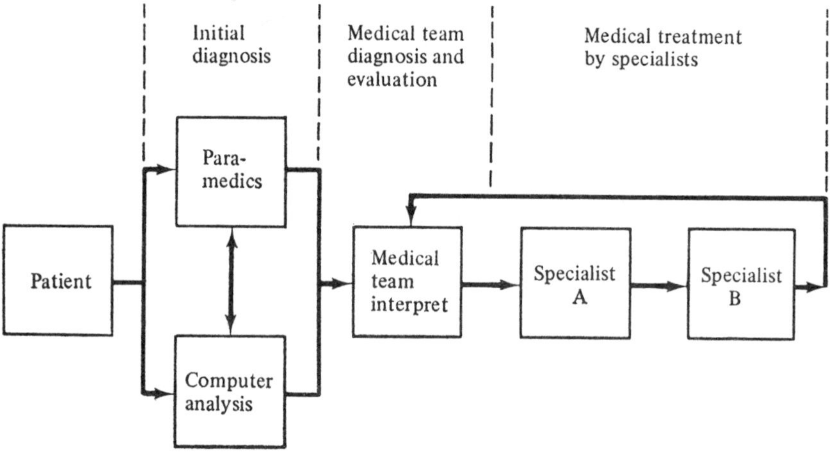

approach, it is possible to divide complex problems into smaller segments with each segment serviced by a specialist, perhaps invoking additional inter-face with machines. As illustrated in Exhibit 7.3, medical diagnosis and treatment could utilize a team of specialists to supplant the wisdom of a single generalist—wisdom which is impossible to find in any one person because of the advances of medical science. Individual para-professionals and medical specialists become linked elements of the entire patient-care process.

To promote greater mobility, institutional restrictions such as the loyalty contracts of company-pension plans will have to be de-emphasized or abandoned. From the viewpoint of society and, perhaps increasingly, the individual firm, vested pension plans which are common to all employers should be utilized to promote change responsiveness. Organizations must also de-emphasize the importance of formal qualifications as prerequisites to employment and promotion. Unfortunately the rapid rise in levels of education

176

which are interlinked inseparably with affluence have led to a degree syndrome in the 'sixties and 'seventies. This results in over-qualification early in a person's career, but leaves him unresponsive to shifts in future career demands, since on paper he has the necessary degree. In reality, academic degrees are highly temporal, with diminishing practical value unless augmented by additional learning.

Change and the need for individual change responsiveness are not limited to the educated managerial and professional élite. Not all individuals in either the twentieth or twenty-first century can be expected to achieve self-fulfilment through their job or career. While the professional often does not differentiate his career from his personal life, the technical or even unskilled worker may find great contentment in a job that mentally is not too demanding, but which allows him to work out-of-doors, in social contact with clients, or any number of conditions which provide motivational satisfaction for different people. The central point is that society through its institutions and organizations has to be oriented to provide the psychological support and the means for skill-knowledge acquisition to motivate all individuals to cope with change.

Change pathology and motivation

Twentieth-century man has been conditioned to perceive stability and continuity as normal and change as pathological. But in the 'seventies and 'eighties change is normal and resistance to change pathological. How can twentieth-century man learn to accept change and be insulated against its dysfunctional psychological and economic by-products?

Two interrelated factors affect man's ability to live with change. The first is the appropriate structural–institutional support to provide alternative courses of action to the individual faced with change. Dockworkers resist containerization since it directly affects their economic livelihood, and because no really viable alternative has been offered them to encourage a change to containerization. But support cannot be directed only to insulate the individual against economic harm. It must also consider the psychological effects associated with psychological security and a feeling of self-worth. Even if the dockworker were guaranteed for life against economic hardship from the impact of change on his job, he would have received inadequate structural–institutional support. Receipt of an early pension or make-work practices would not satisfy his need for a feeling of usefulness and contribution to society.

Educational opportunities are another aspect of structural–institutional support, not solely in its availability but also in its relevance and its return on investment. The shrinking of the differential income between those careers requiring long and difficult courses of study and those requiring far less learning effort will result in future generations being less willing to make sacrifices for long-term investments in education except for intrinsic reasons.

The failure of environmental scanning by educational institutions, individuals, and society results in over-supplies in some fields, resulting in obsolescence before the graduate even starts his career.

Countervailing power will have to be brought to bear on organizations which have successfully used power to minimize change. Unions and professional organizations like those of doctors and lawyers have used a power base to erode the ability of society to institute change which is best for society as a whole. Structural–institutional support would not eliminate such groups but reorient its own role to allow them to operate more effectively and in the best interests of society.

Existing support functions such as unemployment insurance need to be redirected toward training and counselling. The education–training fund and career counselling would be major steps in this direction to change the focus from a form of economic dole to a means for rehabilitating the individual to become a more productive, functioning member of society. Perhaps the civil servant syndrome—little interest and less concern for the individual, who becomes merely another person in a queue—is partially responsible for the present failures of governmental unemployment insurance–job relocation agencies. These activities could be subcontracted to a number of competing companies, allowing the individual greater choice with the private-enterprise system approach of greater self-interest resulting in greater interest in individual clients.

The second interrelated factor that affects man's ability to live with change is man's psychological motivation to accept and initiate change. One of the interesting aspects about man's behaviour is that as he becomes a more complex person, he develops greater ability to control or to respond to his environment. This has been recognized by behavioural scientists not only in the concept of man's motivational hierarchy of needs, but also in his development of moral values and overall mental or learning abilities (Piaget, 1952; Maslow, 1954; Kolhburg, 1972). These various theories of motivation or development have a similarity in that the individual progresses from a rather mechanistic or physical stage through a progression of levels that lead toward increasingly more complex or abstract stages.

As individuals shift more toward the values of the social ethic, they will also become more complex and diverse in their personal motivational hierarchy. The institutions and organizations of society must also reallocate their rewards and incentives which they provide to their constituencies. Although security in the form of a right to income or a job will still be retained under the social ethic, organizational rewards will have to expand beyond purely economic–security ones. Individuals under the social ethic are probably more receptive to change, but at the same time they are more critical and analytical of its meaning to themselves and to society.

Two extremes of motivation are possible under a social ethic. One is an intense desire to contribute to the common good of society and help one's

178

fellow man. The other is the hedonistic philosophy which results in man drifting from day to day in pursuit of pleasure. Past civilizations emphasizing hedonism have planted seeds of self-destruction. Society, even under a social ethic, must provide incentives and the structural mechanisms to permit its members to pursue objectives of contributing to society.

Twentieth Century Man cannot be remade. Society has no alternative but to accept his motivational patterns and his behavioural conditioning. China's effort to create a 'new Maoist man' is producing a paradox of success amid failure. The goal of this human-engineering experiment on one-fourth of the world's population is a citizenry dedicated to working only for the good of society and the state, not for personal material rewards or career gains. . . . While professing hope for the future, they are back-pedaling from idealism today. Material incentives are widely denounced—and just as widely employed. . . . And alongside the carrot there remains the stick: The political and social pressure for conformity to the 'Maoist man' vision is powerful and pervasive. (Phillips, 1972, p. 18)

To develop change-responsive individuals, it is necessary for twentieth-century man to build upon an existing psychological conditioning base. But at the same time the organizations and institutions of society need to super-impose upon him another set of conditions which will not cause him to perpetuate the difficulties of individual adjustment to change.

For the twenty-first-century man, the conditioning process can now be changed if society is willing to assign it the necessary priority so that he will be exposed to learning conditions that create challenge in meeting change and provide the tools to allow him to manage change.

Man, whether he be of the twentieth century or the twenty-first century, cannot act as a change agent without a reorientation and restructuring of organizations through which he can affect change. Such change-responsive organizations are the subject of the next chapter.

8

Organizational design for change

Organizations in crisis are forced to adapt both strategies and structure under the environmental pressures of change. But crisis-change adaptation results in dysfunctional and even traumatic adjustments in communication patterns, relationship networks, and even decision making. Organizational change and the further uncertainties of environmental change can create chaos, unless the organization has developed change responsiveness as its modus operandi. The inability to make accurate predictions demands that an organization design flexibility into its system if there is to be minimal disruption in change adaptation. Change-responsive organizations require a reshaping of organizational requirements and expectations both structurally and psychologically. Such a process of reassessment and adjustment begins with a re-evaluation of the concept of time itself. In an era when managers are attempting to extend their planning horizons, the more appropriate alternative may be to shorten time perspectives.

The time horizon and content of any forward planning activity should be a function of (a) the rate of environmental change and (b) the degree of predictability of the firm's environment. A mapping or vectoring of these two variables is the preliminary step in determining (a) whether the firm can afford to commit its resources more than two to five years into the future, and (b) the degree of structural flexibility that must be built into the organization. The process of environmental vector analysis is described in the following chapter as an input to strategy development. But our immediate concern is how the results of vector analysis provide the guidelines by which the psychological climate, configuration of tasks, and embodiment of role relationships must be altered to maintain harmony with the environment.

The upper half of Exhibit 8.1 identifies the four primary types of environmental states as diagnosed by the vectoring process. We are most concerned about the unstable and turbulent state as these contain a higher degree of uncertainty, complexity, and conflict. Firms facing the fast changing and unpredictable environment of turbulence require a modular or cluster organization. Such an organizational form can encourage and promote temporary yet highly specified missions for corporate sub-units. As change accelerates in the decades ahead, all but the smallest of firms will experience turbulent environments and need some application of the modular organizational form. This modular configuration will render obsolete to some degree the traditional assumptions about authority, control, incentives, and hierarchy.

Exhibit 8.1

Matching organization and environment

(1)	(2)	(3)	(4)
Environmental states			
Stable	Transitional	Unstable	Turbulent
Organizational states			
Directive	Delegative	Matrix	Modular
Organizational characteristics			
Functional standardization	Rational task segmentation, decentralization	Tasks combined in project or product group	Management by temporary teams
Authority-based leadership	Delegated decision authority	Dual technical administrative supervision	Problem-solving orientation
Formalized communication hierarchy	Profit centres for control, incentives	Emphasis on task coordination	Mission-directed technical and administrative coordination
Control via budgets and standards	Results-based leadership	Slight upward job mobility	Self-destruct criteria
Rewards for upward mobility	Infrequent downward communication, management by exception	Professional rewards sought, functional identity	Inter-team competition allowed
			Multiple channels of mobility

The intent of this chapter is not to prescribe or predict a single type of organization of the future. Rather we are concerned with developing a conceptual model of organizational design which can be adapted to fit specific enterprise contingencies. No complex change in either the structure or process of organization can become workable until the reasons for that change and the ways by which it is operationalized are understood and philosophically accepted. Thus, this chapter is more concerned with illustrating the underlying

181

conditions and means by which firms move towards change-responsive structures than with the prescription of uniform structural variables.

Organization is an intangible quality, more the product of a collective state of mind than of any documented body of rules and procedures, or at least it should be for the change-responsive-organization. To the twentieth-century man, the recommended changes and guidelines may appear to lie on the outer reaches of the frontier of innovative organizational practices. To the twenty-first-century man, they will be central to his way of thinking and behaving.

Interlinking organizational climate and structure

Only the most naïve practitioner or student of management believes that organizational charts and statements of job descriptions symbolically represent a firm's organization. Organizational realities are shaped not simply by the ideal physical division of tasks and reporting relationships but also by a firm's goals, remuneration policies, leadership behaviours, technology, and product–market environment. Encompassing all of these are the underlying managerial assumptions about the role of individuals vis-à-vis the organization. These assumptions or philosophies permeate the organization and convey to those within it a sense of man–organizational relationships with regard to what is and is not expected of individuals, and what they in turn can expect from the organization.

Organizational design does not end, and logically does not necessarily begin, with the physical or structural configuration of activities. Organization is essentially a pragmatic process for channelling behaviour within a firm. Although it would simplify the organizing process if man's behaviour were rational and the product of simple cause–effect relationships, such an assumption is pure fiction. Man's behaviour in organizations is not simply the product of cognitive rationality or of a logical and mechanistic mode of processing information. In addition to the structural properties which managers design as a mechanism for guiding behaviour, management also tacitly overlays a psychological–sociological climate that is equally powerful in affecting individual and group behaviour.

In tapping the psychological dimension of man, organizational climate infuses values, ideologies, and human motives into a gestalt of sentiment. Use of the word sentiment in this context is akin to feelings, motives, or affective concerns as explained in the theory of group behaviour by George Homans (1950). Sentiments in an organization result as individuals and groups carry out activities and interact with each other. Feelings are associated not only with what one does but also with the ways in which his activities interact with or limit interaction with others. Conceptually, the web of activities, interactions, and associative sentiments range from those required by the system to those which emerge independently, or as a consequence of the

182

intent of organizational design. Since it is unfathomable to anticipate all specific task requirements and interactions, actual organizational behaviour occurs as emergent factors amplify, elaborate, or constrain system requirements.

During the past forty years managers have expressed growing concern about the question of employee motivation and the meaning of organizational membership to the individual. As the behavioural sciences have produced more in the way of usable theory, firms have attempted to make the individual feel more a part of the organization and more committed to its mission. Notions of punishment and coercion-centred management have been substantially altered by variations of concepts such as management development, job enlargement, organization development, participative leadership, and management by objectives. Such techniques of the transitional era of management attest to the intent by corporations to create a more productive and hopefully more satisfying internal environment.

Undoubtedly such programmes will increase in the future and we advocate expanding their use as part of the effort to develop in individuals and organizations a capacity for self-renewal and adaptation to change. Yet seldom have these programmes or techniques been fully integrated into a concept of management that links the development of human resources and organization with environmental strategy requirements. Often these activities, despite the good intentions of management, are more of an add-on character intended to correct a current deficiency, to bring about some improvement in future performance, or simply to minimize employee frustrations by providing more individual benefits but with little expectation that the corporation will increase its level of performance for the social costs incurred.

A healthy organizational *esprit de corps* has been equated with corporate strength and health (Houston, 1972). But *esprit de corps* as a personification of organizational climate is not simply a product of charismatic leadership, or an identification with national loyalty and pride as the concept is applied to military organizations. Rather, it is more of a ratio between perceived expectations and corporate reality. Perception is a key word here since in a literal sense, truth or absolute reality in organizations is illusive. But man's perceptual limitations are real and it is his perceptions that condition his behaviour.

Human aspirations are increasing at a geometric rate. The critical issue in shaping organizational climate is whether employees' expectations are rising faster than the firm's capacity to satisfy these expectations. Organization structures and climates are one of the major motivating and dismotivating factors that condition employee attitudes and behaviour (Herzberg *et al.*, 1959).

These aspirations demand new power distributions, fewer unilateral actions, and opportunities for individuals at all levels to be heard and be influential. Such concepts are closely tied to the individual's feelings of whether he is dependent or can be independent and to some degree shape the environment in which he functions. New aspiration levels have caused firms to attempt to balance (a) hierarchical authority against professional expertise and (b) the utilization of group talent against individual contribution.

A basic ingredient in organizational climate is the reward and punishment system. It can result in innovation and attainment of objectives, or alternatively precipitate apathy and withdrawal. In many instances it forces managers into win–lose personal political competitions.

To understand organizational climate and its impact on organization survival and success, two questions need to be answered.

1. How does a firm assess the quality or nature of its organizational climate?
2. How can a firm develop a supportive organizational climate?

Towards a change-responsive climate

In broad dimensions a homogeneous organizational climate, particularly within major subsystems, is common to most organizations. Managers at all levels pick up cues of expected managerial behaviour and transmit that behaviour to their units while amplifying some attributes or modifying others because of personal idiosyncrasies. Thus, every manager has his own perception about the climate in which he and others work. But managers are prone to perceptional distortions or biases because of the many demands placed on them and their unique role in shaping organizational climate. Reliance upon an intuitive feel for assessing climate may therefore overlook or minimize the importance of some dimensions which are major concerns to others who view the organization from a different perspective.

For the above reasons, differences in climate are most accurately diagnosed when audited by formal behavioural studies. An example of one of the more widely used behavioural-science instruments for auditing the character of organizational climate is the Profile of Organizational Characteristics developed by Rensis Likert (1967) and colleagues at the Foundation for Research on Human Behaviour at Ann Arbor, Michigan. When administered to a cross-sectional sample of company employees, this questionnaire assesses individual perceptions of several major categories of organizational variables: leadership motivation, communication, interaction–influence, decision making, goal setting, control, and performance goals. Likert differentiates the central tendencies in organizational profiles by four ideal types of systems which generally move from unilateral and exploitive use of authority (System 1) to that which emphasizes participative team relationships and shared power to set goals, implement controls, and make decisions (System 4).

A less rigorous but conceptually easy-to-understand approach to differentiate the character of organizational climates is the classification scheme used by Roger Harrison (1972). Harrison divides organizational orientations into four general categories which he identifies as power, role, task, or person orientations. Each creates a type of organizational climate which has far-reaching effects on organizational performance.

1. **The power-oriented organization** tries to dominate its environment and suppress all opposition with strong controls over subordinates. Individual interests are sacrificed to attain organizational objectives generating subsequent dismotivation. Although this type of firm can quickly counter simple threats rapidly through unilateral decisions, it fares less well in dealing with complex environmental change, because communication channels to the decision centre are quickly overloaded.

2. **The role-oriented firm** personifies the bureaucratic model with an intense concern for legitimacy, rules, rights, hierarchy, and status to provide an orderly, rational procedure for regulating activities or abrogating conflict. The bureaucratic model provides for individual economic security, reinforcing its system of programmed coordination. But concern for procedure taxes flexibility, especially in adjusting to complex environmental changes and even in mobilizing forces against competitive threat. It is most suited to a stable environment.

3. **Task-oriented firms,** in contrast, emphasize achievement of superordinate or higher mega-level goals with no procedural or hierarchical constraint allowed to compromise task accomplishment. Moderate security and high opportunities for voluntary goal commitment are provided for the individual, but within the confines of the firm's goals. This type of firm copes well with threat, tending to favour effectiveness over speed, in contrast to power orientation. It is highly flexible in dealing with environmental change, and adjusts resources to meet the task. Coordination is only moderately successful, since some diversity in structure and subgoals may complicate integration of common efforts.

4. **The person-centred orientation** has been limited historically to small firms which are created to serve the interests of their members, such as professional partnerships of accountants, doctors, or lawyers, and possibly some think tanks or other technologically based smaller enterprises. Although concern for the individual ranks high, the firm may deal inadequately with threat and be slow to adjust. Integrating the efforts and objectives of individual members is difficult. But the organization is often able to adjust to environmental complexity if the change is compatible with members' personal interests.

Organizational climate and organizational structure must be able to balance conflicting objectives and demands. The task-directed firm probably has the optimal combination of adaptive characteristics in an unstable or turbulent environment. Some attributes of the power orientation are useful, especially in countering threat. But overall, the flexibility of the task-oriented firm will provide for the greatest effectiveness in dealing with change. An overlay of person-oriented attributes can provide a desirable balance to cope with uncertainty and complexity where sub-goals and strategies change quickly and where personal and corporate goals are positively correlated.

Harold Leavitt (1964, p. 376) suggests that the conventional concept of individuals being forced to adapt to organizations will be reversed, with organizations adapting to their members. This seems unlikely for twentieth-century man and contemporary organizations. Nevertheless, internal social–behavioural pressures and increasing external complexity will force greater adaptability of organizational climate to the particular capabilities and interests of organizational members.

What is really necessary is an unleashing and productive tapping of the latent value of human resources. The thought that managers should seek to change

Exhibit 8.2

Goal and need comparisons as a basis for constraints and potential conflict

Society	Organization	Individual
Uniform and equal rights	Organizational–strategy flexibility	Personal freedom and autonomy
Social-welfare priorities	Economic-based objectives	Meaningful personal goals
Consumer–public protection	Human-resource mobility	Self-determination with security
Environmental concern and action	Freedom to innovate	Satisfying life style and career
Economic growth and high standards of living		Higher standard of living

the attitudes and behaviour of their employees rather than the organization is recognized today as a potentially costly and ineffectual method of bringing about improved performance. Chapple and Sayles (1961, p. 202) emphasized this observation in their statement: 'To obtain lasting change, one does not try to change people, but rather to change the organizational constraints that operate upon them.'

For any firm to be in a position to reduce the constraints operating upon individual members to develop change responsiveness, a realistic examination must be made of the constraints placed upon the firm. From the viewpoint of the firm, the major constraints to achieving its own ends require some balancing of the demands of individuals with those of society and the basic economic mission of the firm. Just as individual and organizational aspirations may conflict on some points, so also may the concerns of society, as expressed by government, conflict with and reduce the options available to both organizations and individuals. Exhibit 8.2 presents a comparison of some of the goals and needs of these sectors. Throughout the past four decades the rights and freedoms of the individual have been shaped, increased or abrogated by government. Governmental concern for collective welfare usually but not always constrains organizational options.

One of the potential dangers of the 'seventies is that society's concern to solve social problems will result in a deterioration of living standards. Governments seem confused over the mission of business firms and their role for society. Are they to be economic tools or social pawns? Historically, business firms have provided the impetus and the means for constantly rising standards of living. If their mission is redefined to be correcting social ills, can they fulfil their economic mission? Certainly business firms cannot be allowed to pollute the air and water or to exploit labour or consumers. But if firms are forced to pursue social objectives that detract from or even constrain their basic function to provide goods and services, will society have sufficient resources to achieve its other goals? Present trends indicate that society may have to accept lower living standards, individuals probably will have less independence, and organizations will lose flexibility and adaptability options.

Society and its institutions, including business firms, must recognize and resolve the potential conflict of goals without crippling or destroying the ability of any one segment to accomplish its principal mission. Short-sighted perspectives can result in dysfunctional conflict. For example, management in business firms must guard against viewing the aspirations of the individual as hostile to the firm's flexibility. Personal goals need not be mutually exclusive of organizational goals but can be highly complementary. If organizations are to develop the necessary creative flexibility to cope with turbulent environments, changes in organizational climate must bring the totality of the individual's contribution into active involvement in the activities and missions of firms.

The development of a change-responsive climate and the organizational design and structure to support and create such a climate is a difficult task. The traditional managerial attitudes and philosophies greatly constrain the innovative spirit required for change responsiveness. Equally, the potential constraints imposed by a demanding environment, particularly government, in creating major mission confusion and conflict, may interdict the move toward change-responsive climates and structures. The conclusions are obvious—societies, institutions, organizations, and individuals need change-responsive climates and structures. The question is whether society through its instrument of government will provide a supportive or a restrictive environment for the business firm and for individuals.

Old and new organizational forms

Current models of organization, highly developed around concepts of centralization–decentralization and traditional hierarchical organization structures, provide few solutions to the challenge of organizational design. Their greatest limitation is the inability to cope effectively with complexity, ambiguity, and turbulence. Primarily this results in a management-by-crisis approach to change. Central to the crisis rigidities of contemporary modes of structure is the assumption that sub-units are created to be permanent, whether they be product divisions, line departments, or specialized staff services.

Currently most organizations are changed only because of (a) failure of the unit to perform satisfactorily, (b) technological displacement of the unit's products or processes, or (c) physically outgrowing the form of organization. It is a rare case when an organizational unit is created intentionally for a limited single mission, and accomplishment of that mission begins a self-destruct process for that organizational component. The construction, aerospace, and motion-picture industries are among the few where a specific project is known to be limited. But even then the construction and aerospace firms often assume that another project will come along and much of the work force will move relatively intact to the new task. As Sayles and Chandler (1971, p. 182) observe: 'A project office is established with a very explicit goal and an implicit life span, the time needed to complete the mission'.

However, as practised in the aerospace industry and in similar highly complex technological endeavours, where research and development is a major key to success, the project form of organization tends to be highly centralized and highly retentive of functional loyalties.

Today, most firms in established industries resist the philosophy of temporary organization on either of two principles. One is the locked-in effect caused by long-term commitments. Especially with high investments in capital assets, managers feel psychologically committed to stability of organization for decades at a time. So long as a factory, retail store or type of service covers more than variable costs, unprofitable operations are carried by the profitable ones and justified by their contribution to consolidated expenses, addition to capacity, or support of market extension.

A second reason to accept permanence is the belief that individuals cannot function well in a state of uncertainty where there is fear of losing familiar jobs and their accompanying status and power. This notion is linked to the impression that termination or phasing out of a particular organizational unit is a sign of failure rather than of success, either of which may be the real case. True, the unskilled worker or craftsman indoctrinated in the protestant ethic and a product of twentieth-century ways of thinking about job security and stability may have an insecure fear of changing jobs. But managers should not lose sight of the reality that a rising proportion of all corporate employees are highly educated and trained professionals and, as professionals, have a different career outlook from their craft or trade-minded counterparts.

Professionals are not noted adherents to the organization-man syndrome; their loyalties are divided between organization and profession. For many,

188

the contributions to the discipline and status accorded by peers carries higher priority than rewards bestowed by the corporation or institution. Given this outlook, many assumptions about the dangers and fears of temporary task assignments are erroneous. Accounting and consulting firms, the theatrical arts, universities, and research institutes are staffed by professionals who for the most part find challenge in a change of assignment. Furthermore, a growing number of professionals, such as those who accept positions in temporary agencies of government, recognize them as temporary assignments.

Realistically, however, even among the ranks of professionals, traditional motivations for security cause a rejection of temporary organizations. The acceptance of temporary assignments on a broad scale must await considerable changes in environmental support and the substitution of individual security for greater personal psychological independence, coupled with institutional changes to provide more favourable collective security.

Futuristic literature (Bennis, 1966) predicts that organizations of the future will be temporary and free-form. The transitional response is the project or matrix form of organization which allows some degree of temporariness in structural arrangements. Matrix organization balances the partially antagonistic needs of intense coordination of work flow with that of developing specialized technological capabilities (Galbraith, 1971). By combining functional and project or product forms, it is particularly applicable to the development of new products. Although the matrix organization provides excellent horizontal coordination (Basil, 1970), it is not designed for ease of entry and exit of temporary sub-organizations within a firm. The matrix organization requires extensive modification for firms to function in a turbulent environment where innovation is necessary. One answer to the need for flexible organizational sub-units is the modular form of organization which has some similarities to matrix management.

A concept of modular structure

A modular organization consists of a constellation of organizational sub-units that by design are mission oriented with limited life. Units are created to solve specific problems or to innovate towards specified objectives with either success or failure triggering the process of self-destruction of the unit. By this we do not necessarily mean that every component of an organization is temporary, although for some types of enterprise conceivably all units might be temporary. The ratio between temporary and more permanent organizational units will depend primarily upon the environment of the firm and the markets in which it functions.

As illustrated in Exhibit 8.3, the modular organization consists of a permanent set of functions: (a) environmental scanners who perceive the threats and opportunities in the environment; and (b) resource controllers who develop the strategic fit, define the mission, and allocate resources to an appropriate mission-control centre. Additionally it contains mission-control centres which are activated to exploit an opportunity and implement the strategies developed by the resource controllers.

Mission-control centres function largely as mission-directing, fund-granting, and evaluation centres. Staffed with functional specialists and

Exhibit 8.3

A modular concept of organization

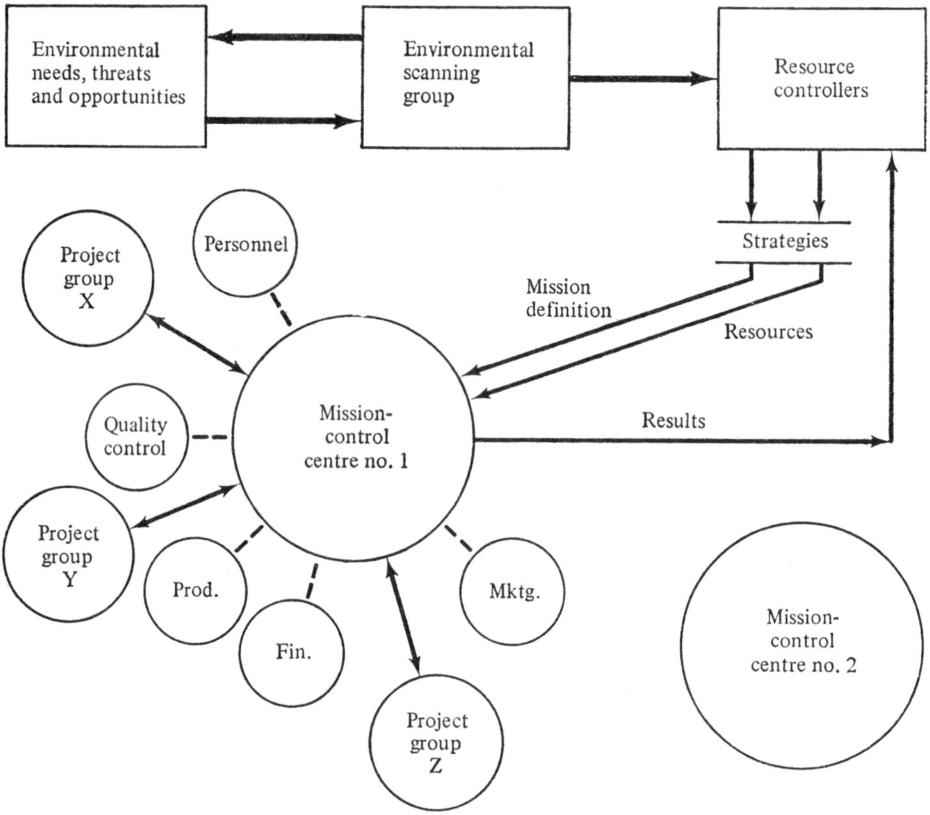

Environmental needs, threats and opportunities

Environmental scanning group

Resource controllers

Project group X

Personnel

Strategies

Mission definition

Resources

Quality control

Mission-control centre no. 1

Results

Project group Y

Prod.

Fin.

Mktg.

Project group Z

Mission-control centre no. 2

managers with a generalist's perspective, they act as the strategy and project-synthesizing body. New module sub-units are created either at the request of the mission-control centre or upon approval of proposals submitted by individuals or groups within the modular sub-units.

The mission-control centre does not act in a passive role to allow individuals complete freedom to follow their own dictates. Each centre has a superordinate mission which provides general guidelines for evaluating the merits of possible alternative actions. In addition to providing resources for approved member-

190

initiated proposals, the control group directs strategies by requesting proposals or forming new units to tackle specific missions supportive of the superordinate mission. Some might be very short-duration, low-budget projects to resolve problems faced by other operating units; others might be the development and production of specific product–service outputs compatible with or complementary to existing lines. This group might also create competitive sub-units to seek grants or to bid on proposals requested by governments or other funding–procurement organizations.

Mission-control centres play much the same organizational role as many not-for-profit foundations and governmental agencies. In this respect, the mission-control centre has flexible options much like those of a government procurement agency purchasing from independent private contractors. Prior to the Second World War, most of the defence material of the United States was produced in government-owned and operated arsenals and shipyards. But to prevent locking itself into self-perpetuating internal suppliers which might resist expanding state-of-the-art technologies rapidly enough to keep defence systems current with those of other powers, most purchases are now channelled through several quasi-private defence contractors. All of the drawbacks of the so-called military–industrial complex notwithstanding, the US Department of Defense certainly enjoys greater procurement flexibility than 30 years ago. This same type of flexibility can occur in modularly organized firms to encourage greater internal competition for resources and safeguard against locked-in, inappropriate, long-range programmes of action.

Modular sub-units can be used for launching new product ventures such as developing and test marketing a medical instrument, designing and securing approval of a car passenger safety restraint system, innovating a programme to upgrade the skills and income of a disadvantaged group, designing a means to improve reading skills of slow-learning children, or an infinite number of missions which cannot easily be achieved by permanent organizational processes. Timetables and provisions for evaluation are negotiated between the new module and the mission-control centre to spell out criteria for funding and performance assessment. The unit knows from the outset that it ceases to exist if it fails to progress according to scheduled check-points (within boundaries for reasonable uncertainty), and will be ready as a unit or have individual members ready for new projects when the mission is completed.

Firms with mass-produced, mass-marketed products, once a new product idea is developed, tested, and established on the market, would convert to a more traditional quasi-permanent production–marketing organization structure. Quite conceivably, one of the first experimental uses of a temporary module unit by such a firm would be to research the adequacies of existing product lines, to locate non-contributing products and new product–market potentials. An alternative to this modular approach, which may have greater immediate appeal to such firms, is the task-force management concept developed later in this chapter.

The mission-control centres and module units are staffed with professional functional specialists and managers. But unlike most current forms of project-based organization, the continuance of both mission-control centres and module units is dependent upon a predetermined performance evaluation of the degree of success of the unit. Individual members, however, would be reassigned if other mission-control centres or module units needed their services. Realistically, organizational slack with an excess of highly qualified people would exist to allow quick exploitation of environmental opportunities. This cost would be subject to a cost–benefit analysis for justification of resource allocation.

Conventional project units with joint control by project administrators and functional department heads tend to give the functional supervisor more say in performance evaluation and promotion of persons within his function. Such a system creates conflict and ambiguities as to whose word is final or what objectives really have top priority—those of the functional discipline or the project?

There is less conflict between administrators and technicians in the module unit because they are quasi-autonomous and have a common interest in the success of the mission from both a technological and an economic viewpoint. The emergent conflict between advancing the state of the art in the professional disciplines and the market-mindedness of the line managers becomes a stimulus to creativity and further search to resolve problems of mutual interest.

One of the unique advantages of the modular unit form of organization is that it offers a high potential for identification with the unit's mission by individuals within the group. Even in current decentralized organizations, there is limited opportunity for individuals to grasp the unit's total mission, unless they are in general management positions. Most individuals are forced to adhere to functional sub-goals, and fail to see how their activities integrate with the whole mission and task. For the non–professional worker, performance is linked simply to job standards and seldom to even a functional type of mission.

In the modular organization, particularly massive and complex missions might at different points in time spin off dozens of supportive units, each with its own special mission to be responsible for a component or sub-system. The mission-control centre in such a situation would have many of the characteristics of a project headquarters, and exert a high degree of coordination between units. Especially in projects which extend the state of the art in several disciplines, autonomy of innovation has to be balanced with integrating complex sub-system inputs into the total project. But, even so, the intent is to make each group responsible for a particular sub-mission and to evaluate everyone in that group on the basis of the unit's success or failure, not to leave this reward function to the discretion of functional staff managers who may be only remotely familiar with the specialized missions on which their subordinates are working.

Under the modular system, adaptability and flexibility would become a primary basis for competence. Linked to this would be the elevation of human resources as the primary asset behind competency. Rather than have a market or production capability dictating a narrow range of corporate competency and pushing individual contributions into that prescribed range, human resources would now become freer to pull the organization in the direction of their collective expertise.

Modular organizations would permit the generation of a number of innovative projects on an investment write-off, self-destruct set of criteria rather than the traditional ROI sensitivity analysis approach. Traditional organizations with such criteria and a high proportion of corporate resources locked into continuing programmes do not have the mechanisms to initiate and support potentially high-payoff ventures. Innovative firms attempting to expand state-of-the-art technology may over-commit to a few endeavours and thus consume a disproportionate share of resources. Such firms would fail both to hedge options and to exercise evaluation controls.

Where the unit is initiated by the proposal of a few individuals, the initiators would have a high degree of compatibility between personal objectives and corporate mission. In effect, they would be pursuing personal goals by the creation and design of the special mission. Competitive recruiting to enhance further the coordination of personal and organizational goals would be based on common guidelines for transfers, incentives, and promotion. Motivation would be enhanced through the psychological satisfaction of defining and attaining one's own goals. Friedlander's (1966) study of 1000 white-collar scientists, engineers, and managers substantiates the impact of intrinsic self-actualizing work as a stimulus to high performance:

> Comparisons among the three potential motivators for high performers only indicate a clear hierarchy: intrinsic work is of greatest importance, recognition is second, and the social environment is valued least. This motivational hierarchy contrasts with that of low performers, for whom the social environment is most important, intrinsic work second, and recognition least important. (p. 149)

Utilizing temporary organization structures

Modular organizations have major advantages over current organizational models:

1. They provide the motivational advantage of allowing members to define and attain highly identifiable goals.

2. They permit self-determination with an organizational form closest to the primary group (Barnard, 1938).

3. They contain a self-destruct element which promotes the effective allocation and utilization of resources.

But equally, modular organizations have major disadvantages, primarily those connected with temporary assignments for the traditionally motivated twentieth-century man. Modular organizations may promote élitism, a common phenomenon in organizations, regardless of institutional form (Mills, 1959; Domhoff, 1967). This élitism is reinforced by the separation of managers and employees into permanent and temporary classifications. Twentieth-century man places a high priority on a permanent assignment. This has been the experience in project organizations in aerospace and similar high-technology industries. This will continue until major institutional changes have been effected to provide the necessary economic and psychological security basic to the use of modular and other temporary organizational forms.

From a countervailing power point of view, the objectives of the resource controllers would be identical with the mission-control centres and their satellite project groups. From a conflict point of view between temporary and permanent assignments, there would be mobility between the control centre and project modular units, depending upon the personal goals of the individual and his desire for career development. Further, members of the control centre would have objectives identical to members of the modular units whom they advise and coordinate—success of the mission.

Organizational slack between reassignments is another possible disadvantage of modular organizations. Most organizations have some under-utilized resources to serve as a reserve against unpredictable environmental-organizational interfaces. But the modular organizational form identifies and funds these temporarily non-productive resources rather than covertly sanctioning a build-up of excess resources into entrenched bureaucratic subsystems.

Task-force management

Most organizations will be unable to implement the modular form until the supporting institutional changes have been effected. The strong dysfunctional and dismotivational effects of temporary organizations will make the majority of organizations reluctant to experiment with unfamiliar forms of organization.

Task-force management affords an intermediate step towards a temporary organization. Long used in an ad hoc way by government, universities, and other organizations, the task force serves as a quasi-modular approach that can readily be adapted to any type of organization. The normal utilization of task forces is an ad hoc team with cross-functional membership and a highly specific objective. It allows flexibility in problem solving and inter-functional coordination, as a task force can be quickly assembled and function within the existing structure.

Similar to the modular organization, although not requiring basic structural change, the task force helps overcome the problem of building functional and operational walls around departments and sub-units. Rather than the myopic view of one function, and the viewing of company problems through the perceptual blinders of a functional identity, task forces can break down these walls and broaden perspectives. Organizational effectiveness does not come about by a simple summing of the separate contributions, for seldom are the parts wholly unrelated. This limitation was noted in developing the concept of modular organizations which have at best only quasi-autonomous sub-units. Complete autonomy is both unreal and unnecessary and is most closely approximated only with financially linked subsidiaries. The advantage of the task force is the promotion of a holistic problem-solving perspective that forces consideration of constraints and advantages of alternative solutions from multiple perspectives.

A task force can be quasi-permanent if it is intended to function as a coordinating unit linking several departments or functions. More commonly, it is temporary and self-destructs at the completion of the assigned task. The task force is essentially a technique to bridge functions while at the same time utilizing the benefits of specialization to solve complex problems.

Task forces are especially useful where informal or authoritarian channels of communication do not work, or are too limited in scope to do anything more than reduce symptoms without solving problems. Under a decentralized philosophy, decisions frequently are too local in scope. Under centralization there may be a tendency to over-simplify because of a global perspective. The cross-functional task force can utilize both sets of opposing advantages by allowing representation of both higher-level policy-making managers and lower-level technically oriented managers or staff within the same small group.

Any form of problem solving in organizations has at least two dimensions, the technical aspects and the psychological or behavioural implications of the process itself. The more firms channel the solution of problems into functional pigeonholes with each specialty attempting to effect its separate resolution, the more each sub-unit will function as a part unto itself. This even occurs to the extent of a denial of interrelationships with other functions, which often intensifies problems by increasing inter-group conflict. As changes in the use of materials, processes, technologies, or markets are interjected into an organization the extent of interrelated problems is accentuated. One consequence is an upward referral of problems for decision which overloads higher-level managers with day-to-day concerns. Another may be that individuals feel less motivated to relate the problem to the total organization. Sub-unit goals become either splintered or overly narrow, to the point that the unit fails to perform adequately on activities necessary for the total organization.

An example of functional pigeonholes took place in an air force transport command. A unit of air-traffic controllers was responsible for scheduling the point of origin and time departure of all sorties a month at a time. Since the individual base air-traffic control units were evaluated on the basis of on-time departures, and because there was competition between bases to have the best record for the month, these units would launch aircraft at the designated time so long as they had a craft that was acceptable by the crew as reasonably safe to fly. But as a result of this narrow functional viewpoint for on-time departures, aircraft would be cleared for take-off when only fractionally loaded or in the midst of a maintenance job not sufficiently critical to abort the flight. Consequently loading crews were unable to reach their criterion of capacity utilization, and maintenance crews were unable to adhere to a standardized service schedule.

Here is a case where a small group task force with representation from at least the four directly involved parties—traffic controllers, maintenance, flight crews, and load crews—could have been used to approach the problem more from a perspective of the total transport command mission rather than a local functional view. If the task force is held responsible not only for developing a solution, but also implementing it, individual members are forced to see their relationship to the larger mission.

Task-force membership forces the understanding of the constraints faced by other parties and the interworkings of the organization. Often for the first time, an individual becomes exposed to a larger diagonal slice of the organization. Through his temporary assignment he should learn why the solution that helps him may complicate the problems of others.

Task forces are not without problems. In a climate where temporary assignments are unprecedented, or at least rare, individuals may feel insecure and hostile about being selected for such a group. This is particularly true if the assignment is to be full-time for a month or more rather than as a part-time addition to regular duties. A member may believe that his security and power are threatened. There is also the real possibility that a basic lack of capabilities may be exposed to those outside his functional clan. But even where the use of task forces is more established, there is an initial seemingly non-productive period of establishing working relationships with new team members. If the leadership position is not assigned, and individuals from different backgrounds and levels within the corporation are thrust together as equals, there is the trauma and uncertainty of the jousting for positions of emergent leadership.

Task-force members can be taught to move towards an acceptance of collaboration and power equalization rather than the more typical judgemental reliance on authority as a basis of decision making (Prince, 1972). Despite all the popularized criticisms of the use of committees, the decision-making, action-oriented task force will consistently come up with better problem solutions than the sum total of individual decisions (Hall, 1971). This is especially true where group members are trained in group dynamics and the process of consensus decision making. Where the task force is responsible for implementing its own decisions rather than merely offering recommendations, the individual members will be more committed to the implementation phase.

Strategic organization development

In an article on approaches to dealing with conflict in organizations, Daniel Katz (1964) noted three basic strategies: (a) assume the structure is sound and make it work either by force or by readjusting, re-educating, or reassigning personnel; (b) set up additional machinery to minimize the problem, such as adding one or more coordinating links; or (c) change the institutional structure to eliminate the causes of the problems. The principal organizational strategies suggested in this chapter, while not limited to conflict concerns, have been more of the third order—change the structure and institutional climate to allow a redesigned system to function more effectively.

However, it is not always enough simply to free the structural and environmental constraints that limit change-responsive behaviour. Individuals not experienced at working in temporary task groups need guidance in learning how to benefit from such freedoms. This is a learning task with two primary considerations: (a) changing or altering behaviour for the present job assignment, and (b) developing in the individual the capacity for continuing adaptability. In tackling these dual learning objectives, the means to modify behaviour can be sought (a) on the job or within the job setting, or (b) cognitively, emotionally, and physically removed from the job and organizational environment.

The process of management development traditionally has emphasized job-related methods to handle the tasks of acquiring current job skills, knowledge, and attitudes. Development of adaptive capacity more typically has turned away from job settings to formal seminars, schools, and workshops. However, in this latter case, if the job climate or structure does not allow a testing and experimentation with new concepts and skills (other than direct, job-related information), there is low probability that the manager's formal learning will be reinforced and become a part of his behaviour repertoire (Basil and Cook, 1973).

The past 15 years have seen increased use of the organizational setting as a laboratory for learning human relations and decision skills, partly because of the suspected low transfer effect of traditional management-development programmes and partly because of growing knowledge about experience-based learning. As an application of group-dynamics techniques, various modes of laboratory training have been used by an increasing number of firms in the United States, England, Japan, Holland and elsewhere. These therapeutic group processes, using techniques variously referred to as encounter groups, sensitivity training, and T-groups, while not originally job-related, have now become linked with organizational settings. Collectively, this form of group learning or team learning has come to be known as organization development or simply OD. Two advocates of OD, Burke and Schmidt (1970), offer this definition:

> Using knowledge and techniques from the behavioural sciences, organization development (OD) is a *process* which attempts to increase organizational effectiveness by integrating individual desires for growth and development with organizational goals. Typically, this process is a planned change effort which involves a total system over a period of time, and these change efforts are related to the organization's mission. (p. 153)

Although the attributes in the above description are highly desirable, in reality they represent more of an ideal than prevailing practice has achieved. Few OD change efforts have genuinely tackled the total system, except in small firms. The Tavistock Institute, National Training Laboratories, and other consulting groups have been relatively successful in the first corrective strategy mentioned by Katz, of making existing sub-systems work by using group problem-solving sessions to clarify roles and increase empathy in accepting the viewpoints and constraints of individuals in other positions.

There are many variations of OD and the concerned reader can find articles on the subject in almost any current management journal, or more in-depth coverage in books such as those by Bennis (1969), Beckhard (1969), Blake and Mouton (1964), Argyris (1970), and others. A typical OD effort involves the following steps:

1. A higher-level manager notices symptoms of organizational problems: falling behind schedule, excessive design or production changes, hostilities and attribution of problems to other groups, etc.

2. He consults a trainer-change agent from the outside or possibly from an internal psychological–personnel staff.

3. The trainer and manager meet initially to explore possible problems and organizational needs.

4. The trainer then investigates the perceptions of several of the individuals concerned with the problems through interviews, and possibly written instruments such as the Likert Profile.

5. A one- or two-day meeting away from the business facility brings together the key individuals for feedback by the trainer about most frequently mentioned problems; and the team-building process begins with discussion, elaboration, and analysis of perceived problems and contributing factors.

6. The group begins to define objectives and priorities of actions within the group's capabilities as the beginning of an awareness and intent to change attitudes and behaviour (French, 1969).

198

7. With several sub-groups, similar techniques are applied at the local levels, with former participants playing prominent roles in providing feedback and facilitating openness of discussion.

OD efforts that attempt to work within the existing structure base much of their intended change upon the premise that, through human-relations skill-training and team-building processes, individuals will undergo changes in attitudes which will lead to changes in behaviour (Wohlking, 1970). While substantial results are possible by relying on process techniques alone, the potentials for change are more limited than if structural or task changes are also included. In some cases, quicker results are gained by changing the structure of work flow or interactions and/or altering the tasks performed by one or more groups (Greiner, 1972a).

Strategic organizational development (SOD) is developed here as a further refinement of OD, to utilize an integrated attempt to change behaviour within organizations and thus organizational output by combining changes in (a) structure, (b) task, and/or (c) process. This allows multiple routes or combinations of routes to permit quicker and more effective formulation and implementation of strategies. SOD is not confined to a single path of change running from process to attitudes to behaviour, since it (a) changes structure or task to (b) change behaviour directly, which then (c) leads to changes in group norms, values, attitudes, and aspirations (Greiner, 1972a; Leavitt, 1964; Miller *et al.*, 1972; Raia, 1972; Wohlking, 1970).

This integrated type of strategic organizational development is both desirable and most easily applied when firms move into more temporary organizations via task forces and modular structures. Under such conditions, there are minimal built-in organizational constraints and established norms that have to be diminished or made impotent before infusing a new set of values and processes. Because of the spontaneous creation of a new unit under the modular structure and the quick assembly of individuals, team-building activities speed up the process of (a) developing task and mission direction, (b) linking highly specialized knowledge resources, (c) bringing about the ordering of leadership, and (d) evolving decision guidelines and procedures necessary to pull the group together as a functioning unit.

As described by Normann (1971), when an organizational sub-unit is involved in a basic reorientation or new type of innovation, rather than merely some variation of current objectives, there will be widespread changes in the task, political, and cognitive systems of the individuals involved. The SOD process supports major change efforts, by highly tailoring the organization to the uniqueness of the situational mission and to the cognitive–emotional structures of individuals within the unit. The diagnostic–analytical–action processes of the SOD intervention serve to elaborate necessary roles, establish patterns of interaction, and promote a higher degree of consensus decision making through power sharing.

O

This integrated approach to strategic organization development increases the probability of success in managing temporary mission-directed groups. Furthermore, through the experience of success in managing this type of change, individuals develop greater capacity for continuing to adapt.

Motivational reward systems

Most organizations develop a high degree of dependence for organizational members, and there is often a lack of congruence between the needs of aspiring individuals and the demands of formal organization (Argyris, 1957, 1964). To develop change responsiveness, organizations should pursue courses of action which allow the individual to be more independent in his thoughts, values, and actions. But what happens to the time-tested need for well-defined structures, limited role prescriptions, and the exercise of controls to assure conformity to corporate character and orderly and predictable behaviour?

No one can successfully argue against the need to have an underlying basis of goal direction and orderliness of linked human and material resources. By definition, organization means an interrelationship of parts toward collective objectives, not just a random collection of resources. But any organization facing a potentially turbulent environment needs to be pliant and to expand the latitude and depth of its human resources if it is to adapt rather than stagnate. Simply because those in positions of power feel insecure about loosening control, or because tradition has perpetuated the ideal of running a tightly controlled and highly defined operation, it does not follow that this is the most effective practice.

With the recognition that effective management of change is the most critical dimension for organizational survival, how can independence and the development of self-esteem and self-fulfilment for individual employees be enhanced? Or more simply, how are change agents to be developed?

The previous chapter was concerned with the problem of making the twentieth- and twenty-first-century man more change responsive. As noted there, the problem is not one that lies completely within the control of individuals alone. It requires changes within institutions to bring about the conditions and support necessary to (a) allow those who aspire to greater freedom and self-determination the opportunity for achieving their objectives, and (b) reduce the threat of change for those who need help in overcoming pending obsolescence. Much of the responsibility lies within organizations in moving away from the impersonal–standardized conditions created by bigness to a renaissance of accepting employee individuality. A major change within reach of most firms is to give the employee greater responsibility for determining how he would like to benefit from and contribute to the organization.

Obviously there are many individuals who because of past failures, traumas, insecurities, and conditioning do not seek independence but acquiesce in accepting a life of dependence. No amount of organizational change will alter the personalities and behaviour of these people to the point where the firm will discontinue treating and using them much as it would any other purchased machine or supply input. But the majority will respond to opportunities for self-determination (McGregor, 1966).

Organizations for years have functioned as political systems with bargaining and negotiation (Cyert and March, 1963). Such bargaining is ostensibly for purposes of furthering the firm's objectives, although individuals may receive status or even pecuniary rewards through reciprocal deals as incentives to negotiate. Can organizations set up a formal system for the individual to negotiate his future within the firm?

An individual's career typically unfolds at the dictates or whims of managers above him. Career development is usually interpreted as synonymous with hierarchical advancement, and to negotiate that ladder may mean yielding on many of one's aspirations or principles in order to follow the prescribed career path. Even the experience of management by objectives (MBO), the closest proximate to date of participating in shaping one's future, has not been too successful in breaking out of this pattern. The negotiations between subordinate and superior in MBO systems are focused largely on the current job task, although exceptions can be found in academic institutions where personal and organizational objectives are less separable. But in a system of open career negotiation, individuals are not limited to thinking solely in terms of current job demands or objectives.

To implement such a motivational system, it is necessary that a person's source of advice not remain limited to his immediate superior. If a modular organization is used, the mission-control centre of the firm can serve as a consultant base for career counselling–negotiating. An individual and his supervisor consult with representatives of this group to determine feasible alternatives to correlate the individual's qualifications, aspirations, and the current and expected needs of the firm. However, it must be recognized that the predictability of manpower needs will vary inversely with the stability of the environment and the permanence of the organization. In a stable and largely permanent organization, the possible career options will be more limited and more certain. The more temporary organizations will offer greater opportunity but with far less certainty. However, both permit career negotiation and the use of a cross-functional ad hoc group to act as a consulting body.

The critical factor is to provide feedback on the qualities required for success in successive career stages. Greater self-determination also requires complex, less standardized reward–motivational processes. The transitional approach of substituting psychological and sociological rewards for economic rewards provides the correct direction for future reward systems. The upper levels of Maslow's (1954) need hierarchy, McGregor's theory Y, and Herzberg's (1959) exposure of the lack of motivation in hygienic–extrinsic factors are steps in the direction of realistic motivation. Twentieth-century man will still be motivated by status needs and both economic and psychological security. But he will increasingly expect and respond to opportunities for greater self-determination. This requires tolerance for mistakes, because navigation in uncharted territory may result in foundering in unknown shoals. Innovative action needs positive support, including psychological reinforcement. The bureaucratic philosophy of preventing mistakes through highly standardized procedures stifles creativity and innovation. Change-responsive organizations cannot afford the inflexibility of hierarchical sifting of information through multiple managerial levels before a decision can be made. The change-responsive organization must permit not only decentralized decision making but also reward such behaviour.

Managerial hierarchies and change responsiveness

Flexibility to function effectively in turbulent environments requires greater reliance on temporary, task-oriented sub-systems coupled with a climate-and-reward system that promotes individual self-determination and motivation. Such flexibility does not mean the elimination of organizational hierarchies. Innovative organizational practices to maximize effective utilization of human resources can be practised within hierarchical authorities.

Without organizational hierarchies, civilization would not be able to function at the current level of complexity and allow leadership to function effectively. The perpetuation of leadership is essential to prevent dissipation of the system's resources and ultimate destruction of the system.

Unfortunately, traditional hierarchies with emphasis on vertical structure distort communication, increase uncertainty, and slow the process of decision making. The transitional solution of decentralization is a move toward flatter structures, but does not provide the integrative advantages of modular and task-force organizations. Change-responsive organizations still require hierarchies, direction and leadership. But greater reliance is placed on task forces, project groups, and other integrating devices.

Additionally, change-responsive systems must have flexibility in resource allocation. Resource flexibility is difficult to achieve, both for human and non-human resources. The decision criteria for non-human resources, as well as for the degree of change responsiveness required, involve a number of factors:

1. The state of the environment—is the organization vectoring from stable to unstable or turbulent states?

2. The time horizon—the state of the environment will determine appropriate guidelines for a short or long time horizon.

3. Technological change—are there potential breakthroughs that may affect the firm's technological capabilities in the near future?

4. Structural–institutional change—will world geopolitical or institutional change constrain or aid potential strategies?

5. Social–behavioural change—will life styles, ethics, or other behavioural changes place new demands on the organization?

Human resources must be managed and allocated equally on the decision criteria for non-human resources, but their allocation is complicated by additional factors:

1. Is there a strategic fit between the current reservoir of human resources and the strategic mission dictated by the environmental scan?

2. Has the organizational design developed a change-responsive climate to attract and hold the appropriate human resources?

3. Has there been sufficient organizational and individual development and learning to permit quick strategy adaptation and implementation?

Change-responsive resource allocation does not always demand that the fixed-asset base be relatively low or convertible to multiple uses. In some cases the most workable strategy may be high commitment to fixed assets to reduce the idiosyncrasies of the human variable, complicated in part because of the inability of many production-type jobs to have meaningful rewards in themselves. In maturing or mature industries, repetitive physical labour jobs will gradually be replaced by machine, spurred by technological improvements and dysfunctional worker behaviour.

It is ironical that behavioural scientists, concerned with humanistic values, have been studying and worrying about the conditions of the worker on the assembly line and prescribing alternatives to make his job more enriching. Although this contribution has been impressive, perhaps society would have benefited more if the focus of research had been directed towards how to effect more meaningful change throughout the organization. The acceptance of change and how to retrain and redirect the obsolete worker are still unresolved problems. Furthermore, the relative proportion of repetitive, machine-paced jobs is decreasing, and there is evidence that some workers prefer the mindless repetitiveness of such jobs, seeking their fulfilment outside the job.

Humanistic or social–behavioural change impacts on the business firm in economic terms of productivity, costs, and markets. Some firms, such as those mass producing goods, may have to pay for inflexibility in the short run, since the trade-off between a rigid and a flexible structure is too costly to permit flexibility. But even a decision to create production and organizational rigidity is a move toward greater environmental sensitivity, if management recognizes this as a short-run decision, whose economics will not permit more provisions for change-responsive behaviour.

In the case of mass-produced consumer goods or highly standardized industrial products, the current trade-off may favour absolute rigidity and

203

permanent entrenchment in a fixed-asset resource base to permit cost efficiencies. From the managerial viewpoint, there may have to be a strategic trade-off between efficiency and effectiveness. Perhaps it is not possible to sustain both, and for some organizations societal demands may make efficiency in the short run a more desirable alternative. As environment and organization limit strategy, so does strategy shape the structure and character of the organization.

9

Strategies
for change

Change spawns new change. The Protestant reformation spawned the counter-reformation by the Catholic church. The new freedoms of the French revolution spawned the dictatorship of Napoleon. The major question facing society is how to manage change to develop more effective governments, institutions, organizations and individuals. Strategies for change must have the highest priority if society is not to encounter chaos and create an uncontrollable turbulence for its institutions and its members.

The complexity of the world in the last decades of the twentieth century is staggering. Independent nation states artificially attempt to control their economic and social destinies at a time when none can exist without some interaction with other countries. Technology has a thousand fathers, each almost unknown to the other. Technology creates system effects ranging from pollution in affluent nations to economic obsolescence for a one-export product country. The unleashing of social–behavioural change like the Red Guards movement of Communist China can almost destroy a society. With complexity and with the almost stone-age state of systems and complexity analysis and prediction, strategies for change must have great flexibility to manage the ambiguity and uncertainty of the environment of the last decades of the twentieth century.

Environmental states

The categorization of environmental states is a prerequisite to developing strategies for change. Each agency, whether it be a nation or an individual, faces a unique environment. Each environment is in a stage of change, affected by its interaction with and interdependence on more global environmental change. For example, a coffee grower in Colombia defines his environment in terms of the general economic–political–social conditions within Colombia. Wage laws, increasing industrialization, and the aspiration level of his employees drastically affect the availability and cost of his labour. Each of the components of his environment, including such things as labour-saving machinery utilized by his competitors, and the comparative productivity of his farm, could be considered as sub-environments which can be categorized in a similar way to his total environment.

Four states of environment as depicted in Exhibit 9.1 provide a means of identification and categorization as a prerequisite to the development of appropriate strategies for change: stable, transition, unstable, and turbulent. The environmental states are differentiated primarily by two conditioning factors—the rate of change and the magnitude of change. The impact of both

Exhibit 9.1

Environmental states

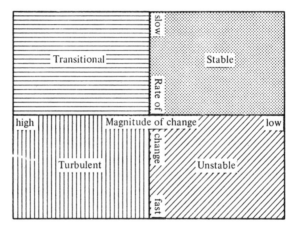

of these change factors is determined through environmental scanning by the agency potentially affected by the change.

In the example of the Colombian coffee grower, he examines each segment of his environment in terms of current and future changes to project their rate and magnitude. If he were considering increasing the acreage he allocates to coffee plants, he would aggregate the rate and magnitude of change of all of the environmental components to determine the overall state of his environment as stable, transitional, unstable, or turbulent. Most likely his environmental scanning would be incomplete, since he would not have intelligence about technological possibilities such as the research activities of a food-processing company to synthesize a coffee substitute from petroleum products or safflower seeds. Such research activities, while potentially severe in their change impact, are in the nature of a global environmental change. They would be beyond the forecasting capabilities of an individual such as the Colombian coffee grower or even of most organizations.

206

Definitive descriptions of the stable, transitional, unstable and turbulent environmental states are arbitrary and difficult to develop in specific terms for the two factors of rate and magnitude of change. They are most readily defined in terms of types of strategies required for each, and the appropriate time horizons for such strategies. Planning horizons are drastically shortened in the turbulent state, with strategies of immediate investment payback and limited fixed-resource commitment, as depicted in Exhibit 9.2. The turbulent environmental state is one where the impact of change as well as the changes themselves become unpredictable. Obviously this greatly shortens planning-time horizons and interdicts longer-term strategies.

Exhibit 9.2

Planning time horizons and strategies

Environmental states	Planning horizons (years)	Strategies
Turbulent	1–2	Immediate investment payback Moratorium on fixed-resource commitment
Unstable	2–3	Liquidation of fixed-asset positions Limited fixed-resource commitment
Transitional	3–5	Cautious fixed-resource commitment Strict new-venture appraisal
Stable	5–20	Longer-term fixed-resource commitments Search for incremental-investment opportunities

The unstable and transitional environmental states introduce similar, but progressively less drastic, constraints on strategy formulation. It is only in the stable environmental state, which will become less and less common in the decades ahead, where longer-term commitments and the search for incremental longer-term opportunities can be instituted.

Environmental scanning by any agency would follow a series of steps.

1. **Definition of environmental segments.** What are the segments that constitute the environment facing any agency? A broad classification of segments is similar to those of the origins of change: structural–institutional would include such factors as political, economic and geopolitical change; social–behavioural—work-force productivity and availability of appropriately skilled labour; and technological—new product breakthroughs and alteration of markets. Each of these segments and even sub-segments are scanned separately.

2. **Rate and magnitude of change in segments.** The determination of the type of change with the estimates of rate and magnitude is completed separately for each environmental sub-segment. Time and cost constraints on environmental scanning will limit the accuracy of these estimates and projections, making it difficult for the individual and all but the largest of organizations to have a high confidence level in such estimates. This will be particularly true for global environmental-change impact. Complexity produces such a plethora of effects that it is almost impossible to forecast global environmental-change impact. New institutions will emerge in the late 'seventies and 'eighties whose sole function will be systematic environmental scanning for other agencies. But it is unlikely that by, say, 1975, there will be adequate environmental scanning to permit good projections of global environmental-change impact. Reliability will be much more accurate in scanning the more familiar environmental sectors, yet there is danger in failing to probe beyond established boundaries.

3. **Categorization of environmental state by segment.** Each segment, and perhaps each sub-segment, will be classified as stable, transitional, unstable, or turbulent. The current state of the art in environmental scanning requires the use of qualitative judgements rather than quantitative precision in such classifications. Primarily, this judgement will be tempered by the perceptions of the degree of impact that the change will have on the environmental segment or sub-segment.

4. **Determination of environmental state.** Each segment and sub-segment has been subjected to environmental scanning and classified as stable, transitional, unstable, or turbulent. Since the state of the environment in any one segment or sub-segment impacts on the overall planning time horizons and strategies of the agency, possibly negating either the benign effects of the stable state or the hostile effects of the turbulent state, there must be an aggregation of the segment states into one overall environmental state. It may be possible to overcome the turbulent effect of one sub-segment without major effect on the agency. This is why the environmental scanning is done separately for each segment and sub-segment. But as each segment is analysed in turn, a pattern will emerge of the environmental state of the agency as a whole. It is this pattern which will condition the planning time horizons and the strategies of the agency.

Vector analysis

The determination of environmental states needs the injection of the time element to permit strategic planning. The determination of environmental states at any point in time is in itself inadequate, since the most critical element is for an agency to determine its future planning horizons. Vector analysis is the further sophistication of environmental scanning to project future environmental states over a period of time, as depicted in Exhibit 9.3. The vector analysis is represented by an arrow which indicates that the agency for which this vector analysis has been prepared is currently in a stable environmental state until 1976. In 1977 it is expected to move into a transitional environmental state, and in 1980, into a turbulent one.

Vector analysis in effect shows the direction of change over a time period among the four environmental states or vectors. The time period depends on the original state for which the agency starts, and on the ability of the agency to do accurate and reliable environmental scanning. Sophisticated utilization of vector analysis with environmental scanning to determine environmental states must await the design and utilization of more effective means of data collection and forecasting techniques. Today's crude techniques of delphi and envelope curve forecasting are not adequate, and much research and conceptualization remains to be done before vector analysis will be fully utilized in the management of change.

Exhibit 9.3
Vector analysis

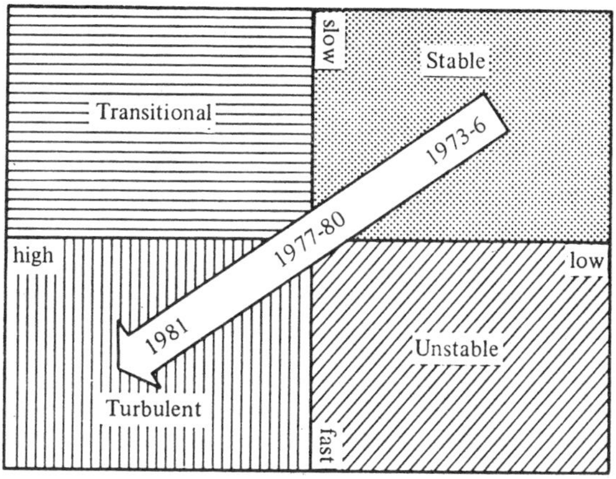

Strategic consequences of accelerating change

Change has major strategic consequences, ranging from the creation of turbulent environments to the need for new organizational forms and missions.

1. Turbulent environments. Systems effects on an international scale have created turbulent environments ranging from skyjacking to potential blackmail of the world by the backward oil-producing nations (*Wall Street Journal,* 5 January 1973, p. 1). The EEC is entering a new phase which will create sets of new relationships as yet undefined.

Now that the Common Market embraces more people and greater monetary reserves, produces more automobiles, has a higher sustained growth rate and bigger portion of world trade than the United States, a major confrontation seems inevitable. . . . For example, a complete overhaul and renegotiation of the Common Market's agricultural policy is inevitable, and the British will have some very strong ideas about what has to be done. . . . Along with Pompidou, Heath set the tone and the goal when he told the summit meeting: 'The Community is now coming to take its place as a major power in the world'. (Cook, 1973, p. 18 and p. 25)

The impacts from structural–institutional, technological, and social–behavioural change will certainly create environmental states of turbulence in segments and sub-segments, and for many agencies such turbulence will be pervasive.

2. Disequilibrium. The effect of turbulent environmental states will be to create disequilibrium obsoleting individual careers, firms, institutions, and even countries. Such disequilibrium might be corrected by greater reliance on freer market systems but the tendency will be for some form of governmental action, most likely through managed economies, to compensate for the effect of some major change. This is likely to treat only the symptoms, further aggravating the underlying problems, creating even greater disequilibrium.

3. Uncertainty. Man and his creation, society, abhor uncertainty. But change creates uncertainty—often great uncertainty. This makes it difficult for governments to develop strategic actions, restricts new investments, and causes all forms of trauma for individuals.

4. Prediction difficulties. Change and resulting turbulent environmental states make prediction difficult, if not impossible. Vector analysis provides the conceptual framework for prediction from a strategic point of view, but currently can only really predict the direction of the impact of change.

5. Obsolescence of organizational and institutional forms. Change has outpaced the ability of man and society to provide the appropriate organizational and institutional forms to cope with and manage such change. Governmental obsolescence is widespread, and few institutions are equipped for change responsiveness. Moreover, few individuals have developed a tolerance for change.

A change-responsive model

The strategic consequences of accelerating change are such that the more traditional crisis-change model will no longer work. Time, which has been the ally of the crisis-change model to allow accommodation to change, has now become its enemy. Not only is the impact of change greater, but also time has been telescoped, with new waves of change occurring before agencies have even reacted to the initial change.

A change-responsive agency is one that anticipates and scans the environ-

210

ment to identify change. But the inability to predict specific changes and their consequences, with at most a vector analysis indicating direction of change, requires the change-responsive agency to develop organizational forms and processes to manage any change. The goals become organizational and individual longer-range survival and viability. The means involve primarily the redesign of organizational forms, redefinition of institutional roles and mission, and the reorientation of the individual.

1. **Redesign of organizational forms.** The accent on hierarchy, on formal control systems, and even on permanent organization structures must give way to task force or modular organization structures, shared decision making, and a reward system to orient organizational members towards innovation and creativity rather than conformity.

Organizational form can either hinder or support the actions of organizational members. A supportive organizational climate, with appropriate rewards for change-responsive behaviour, provides a conditioning process for twentieth-century man to compensate for his prior conformity conditioning. Openness and willingness to encourage constructive conflict are integral parts of a change-responsive organization. Finally, the change-responsive organizational form must be able to deal with change, not in a confrontation-crisis mode, but in an accommodating fashion, to minimize dysfunctions and maximize the advantages associated with change.

2. **Redefinition of institutional roles and missions.** The primary role of institutions in a change-responsive model is to encourage and support independent rather than dependent behaviour. This applies equally to individuals and to organizations, to create greater opportunity for independent action. What is the ultimate mission for institutions charged with the regulation of business? It would seem that the present perception of this mission and the actions of such institutions is to create a higher dependence on government both for the consumer and for business firms. In many countries, there can be no collaboration between competing companies for fear of anti-trust action on the part of the government. This results in separate rather than combined research and development activities, and overall a much higher cost to society. An excellent example of this is the development of reduced pollution engines for cars, where one major research and development effort could provide more massive resources and produce a lower cost device for the consumer.

The redefinition of institutional roles and missions is long overdue to reform a veritable patchwork quilt of regulations and conflicting actions. There is need, even great need, to regulate the business firm and to protect the consumer. But the end objective of such protection seems to be lost. The role of such institutions in the last decades of the 20th century is clear—to create change responsiveness in all of the institutions of society, including the business firm, and to provide the environment which can permit the individual to survive and manage change for himself.

3. **Reorientation of the individual.** It is the reorientation of the twentieth-century man to accept and encourage change which is society's greatest challenge. Hopefully, change-responsive institutions, and particularly educational institutions, will provide the appropriate experiences and training for the twenty-first-century man. The motivational pattern of twentieth-century man is fixed in place, and what is required is to provide the appropriate environmental support which can permit him to satisfy his needs while surrounded and engulfed by change. The majority of such support must come within the organizations where man fulfils his work destiny. Supportive organizational climates and longer-term re-education programmes can reduce the trauma of change, recognizing that changed behaviour is not within the realm of possibility.

Institutional support in the form of economic back-up systems such as the education–training fund is also required for individual reorientation to permit the development of personal independence. Society has moved more and more towards fostering dependence rather than independence in its members. Business firms have created conformity through strong hierarchies and elaborate systems and then decried the lack of initiative and decision-making ability of managers. The re-orientation of the individual towards change-responsive behaviour is particularly dependent on organizational climate and forms. Without active guidance and support from the organizational entity, twentieth-century man in particular will resist rather than adapt to change.

Individuals will have to assume considerable responsibility for their own destiny and be willing to reorient themselves to change-responsive conditions through training and education. It will be difficult for twentieth-century man to change his role from dependent to independent. And for many, such a transition is not possible. Society cannot abandon its members, as the Eskimo family used to abandon its elders to allow them to die in the snow when they could no longer contribute to the well-being of the family. A transition strategy may very well have to permit society to continue its role as father to those members who cannot face the trauma of independent action.

Change-responsive strategies and actions

The change-responsive model provides organizational and institutional support to create the appropriate means for adapting to and managing change. It creates and encourages the evolution of individuals as change agents to effect change. What are the strategic factors involved in the change-responsive organization's management of change?

1. **Environmental scanning.** This becomes one of the most important aspects of change-responsive future strategy development since, without knowledge about environmental states, no effective strategies can be developed. But environmental scanning is severely limited by the failure of managers or managerial scholars to develop effective means and tools for such scanning. Governments do a great deal of sub-system environmental scanning, but rarely develop and disseminate the results in a way that can be used by organizations and individuals to determine environmental states.

New agencies are required for effective environmental scanning, with the granting of major research grants to universities and 'think tanks' to provide new methodology and techniques. The career-counselling function to provide environmental scanning help for individuals should result in much more effective change-responsive strategies and actions by individuals. The acceptance of this need by large, sophisticated organizations will spur further developments as firms see this initially as a means to provide them with competitive advantages.

2. Vector analysis. The direction, rate, and magnitude of change are critical dimensions in the determination of change-responsive strategies. Vector analysis, like its companion, environmental scanning, is not sufficiently well developed to be more than a rough approximation to the progressive ordering of environmental states over a future period of time. But conceptually it forces the strategists to recognize the temporal measures involved in strategy formulation. How is the organization to deal with uncertain change in an undetermined time period? When strategists are faced with such uncertainties, they are likely to be ostrich-like in their response. No one knows what is going to happen and therefore it is better to assume that change will be benign and at worst will affect only non-critical factors.

Vector analysis forces a recognition of change and provides a framework for analysis. Over time, more sophisticated methods will be developed to permit vector analysis to be more precise, but even in its current primitive state it permits more effective change-responsive strategy formulation.

3. Resource flexibility. One of the major lessons involved in the in-depth examination of management of change is that resource flexibility is imperative in developing change-responsive strategies. The commitment of resources to long-range projects without the ability to redirect such resources denies change-responsive strategies. Yet an examination of current strategies in the 'seventies indicates that organizations, and particularly business firms, are making larger and larger commitments of fixed resources. Volkswagen is typical, increasing its fixed investment in car-producing plants and equipment some fivefold over a five-year period.

There is strong evidence that such longer-term commitments of fixed resources, based on a state of the environment a decade before, does lead to failure as the environmental state shifts. A classic example was the chemical industry's major investment in plastic-producing plants in the 'fifties, which were obsoleted or plagued by overcapacity by the 'sixties. Unless the environmental scanning and vector analysis can give assurance of a stable environmental state, the commitment of resources to a fixed base becomes particularly unresponsive to change. Change-responsive strategies require a high degree of resource flexibility, including both human and non-human resources.

4. Internal intelligence systems. Management information systems (MIS) have come under attack from all quarters as being oversold, inaccurate and inappropriate. Such criticisms of the current state of MIS are justified, but effective internal intelligence systems are mandatory for the development of change-responsive strategies. Environmental scanning and vector analysis will provide appraisal of the external environment and conditions. Resource flexibility will permit a quick redirection of resources as strategies become more change responsive. But internal evaluation of change-responsiveness abilities and successes is equally important in the development of change-responsive strategies.

Computers can provide the data collection and data analysis, and future generations of computers will solve the problem of raw-data access and direct reading of input without the need for key punching and magnetic punched tapes from typewriters. The problems lie in programming and the interface between the system designers and the data users. In addition, there is the problem of what information needs to be collected and in what form should the output be for effective internal intelligence systems. Intelligence systems must not only be for statistical and financial information but also for evaluating and understanding the human resource.

A veritable treasure house of competent management exists in every organization, but the system of identification of such potential and its capture is antiquated or non-existent. Human resources will become critical to the success of change-responsive strategies in the future. The highly conditioned, predictable, and conforming organization of the past will give way to the freer form, uncertain, and innovative one of the future. Human resources will move further and further from being standardized, interchangeable components to be plugged into the structure when a need arises. Initiative, creativity, and independence will be the mark of tomorrow's successful manager. But such qualities as these also make coordination difficult. The answer lies in a sophisticated internal intelligence system that can be used by all levels of management to bring order out of potential chaos.

5. Ruthless re-evaluation and appraisal. Flexibility in organization structure and in resource allocation requires constant re-evaluation of strategies and performance against the standards of survival and viability in uncertain and turbulent environments. The concept of a one-time strategic decision and internal follow-up to ensure its implementation will be replaced with periodic re-evaluation of the environment and the strategy that has been evolved for that environmental state. Such appraisals must be ruthless, like the surgeon who must amputate the gangrenous leg to save the patient. Organizations too must be ruthless to abort inappropriate strategies and the organizations which they may have created if they are to stay change responsive.

6. Technological maturity. The worship of technology has produced many disciples whose faith is never questioned. Technology has tended to be the master rather than the slave of society and of society's institutions. Accelerating obsolescence of technology has created conditions where one new invention invalidates another almost before it has been introduced. The case of the Vickers turboprop aircraft in the United Kingdom and Lockheed in the United States being made obsolete by the new jet aircraft are but two examples of the problem of managing technology. It could be argued that this was a failure of environmental scanning, but equally it was a lack of technological maturity.

Investments in technology must pass cost–feasibility tests like any other strategy. The need for resource flexibility could in some cases invalidate such investments, and in others demand them. A firm faced with a long pay-back cycle from technological research investments would require an assurance of a continued environmental state of stability. But a firm in a transition environmental state might decide to make a major commitment to technology to lessen the need for other fixed-resource commitments as it enters an unstable or turbulent environmental state. Technological maturity would examine technology not as a wizard but as any other strategic decision, the major goal being one of change responsiveness.

7. Philosophy of reform. Society must adopt a philosophy of reform for its institutions, its goals, and its members. Primarily such a philosophy is one of developing change responsiveness, which perhaps is no more than a willingness to institute reform without the need for crisis confrontations. Commitment to past decisions and strategies is dangerous, since changes in environmental states can invalidate the best of strategies. An example of such a commitment and its potential for disaster is the continuance of post offices as separate governmental institutions with very narrow perspectives and missions. The ubiquitousness of the telephone and its ability to be a computer terminal make it highly likely that post offices for the transmission of messages in written form are already obsolete. But without a philosophy of reform and the development of new institutions and institutional missions and goals, it is highly unlikely that the telephone can assume this new role.

The development of change-responsive strategies requires the willingness to break with tradition, to abandon inappropriate strategies and organizational forms, and to accept a philosophy of reform.

New institutional forms and national policy

The role of government to develop a change-responsive society differs substantially from the past. Some dimensions, like national planning, must be extended, and others, like massive civil service staffed agencies, must be reduced and eliminated.

P

1. **National planning commissions.** More global policy-making powers must be allowed national governments and even supragovernments like the EEC. This is not central planning like that of the Communist Bloc for massive resource allocation. Rather it is a form of management of change with extensive environmental scanning and recognition of the supportive function of government. One additional dimension is the management of complexity to project the systems effect of the introduction of a change into one element of society. Government has the role of ensuring aesthetic and psychologically supportive physical environments of cities. The role of the design of a network of cities would fall to a national planning commission.

To create a change-responsive set of strategies for implementation by national planning commissions, it is necessary to recognize the importance of creating the appropriate motivation for change-responsiveness among organizations and individuals. Returning to the example of the network of cities of the national planning commission, appropriate rewards must be built into the implementation phase to persuade individuals to move to such cities. The experience of the 'seventies has been that planned cities have not considered the motivation to attract inhabitants, but rather have attempted to force companies not to build in highly developed areas like London or Paris.

National planning commissions will be government–business–labour–university coalitions to draw upon the best possible resources available. Extensive use of task-force organizations and temporary assignments from other society groups will guard against traditional answers. Furthermore, the constant renewal of membership from constituencies will ensure a realistic appraisal of the planning needs. Staff would be kept to a minimum with the use of contractual relationships with experts to supply the environmental scanning and the detailed planning.

2. **Extended time horizons.** Environmental states of turbulence will result in a greatly shortened time horizon for organizations and individuals. But equally they must result in an extended time horizon for governments. There are many instances of long time horizons by governments, such as the planning of the water supply for water-short Southern California, where government has been one to two decades ahead of the increased demand in the building of aqueducts. But there are many more instances of poor time-horizon commitments by government, ranging from the severe world energy crisis in the 'seventies to failure of the United Kingdom to build supermotorways when all the evidence pointed to greatly increasing car ownership.

Unfortunately, government will have to underwrite those projects necessary for society's survival where private enterprise has scanned and found a longer-term turbulent environmental state. Such projects may be a joint private-enterprise–government project like communication satellites in the United States or the Concorde with France and the United Kingdom. The problem here is how to retain the initiative of private enterprise.

A further problem is the one of political parties, where it is difficult in a

216

Western democracy to obtain long-term commitments. Society may have to compromise on its ability to have the see-saw effect of changing national goals and commitments to obtain the fruits of extended time horizons. Of course, there must still be a change responsiveness to abort a programme which is no longer viable because of major environmental shifts.

3. Simplification of bureaucracy. Society's already complex weave is further complicated by the action of governments. There is scattered jurisdiction, multiple taxing agencies, and unbelievable wastes of resources through duplication of services. The advocates of a simple tax system note that a country like the United States could resort to one taxing base of perhaps 20 per cent of income for individuals by eliminating all forms of deductions. The present system of city, state, and federal income-tax authorities could be eliminated and some form of revenue sharing instituted. With strict control of withholding all taxes on all income, even the filing of income-tax returns could be eliminated.

Elaborate and wasteful bureaucratic methods would give way to simple, exception-controlled systems. Random audits rather than complex collection of massive amounts of information would greatly reduce the cost of government administration.

The business government interface would change to goal determination on a jointly negotiated basis with a high degree of self-regulation, perhaps by industry groups. The power of government is so great that after-the-fact audits with extensive fines would ensure attainment of the goals set by society for the business firm.

This simplification of bureaucracy is extremely difficult to institute because of the growth of the public sector, and the built-in resistance to change both on the part of the civil servants and of politicians. But without such simplification, society some day might just strangle to death in its own red tape.

4. Change-responsive institutions. The building up of elaborate bureaucratic institutions is the mark of the twentieth century and particularly of the post-Second World War period. Few, if any, of such institutions are change responsive. The normal course of action to introduce change into government bureaucracies is to create one more level of bureaucracy. How can society obtain change-responsive institutions?

The principal way to make government change responsive is to eliminate bureaucracy and its institutions. This is completely at odds with the practice of governments in the past, which have built up larger and larger bureaucracies with more and more civil servants.

But how can bureaucratic institutions be eliminated? The major means is to reverse the process of hiring civil servants and creating new bureaucracies by sub-contracting the majority of the activities of government. The government can still be the massive tax collector, if that is how society wishes to allocate its resources to obtain greater forms of welfare for its population and redistribute income. But all activities would be set out on contract with private-enterprise companies. Contracts would be let for a sufficient period of time to make it economically attractive and feasible for the contractor, but they would then be terminated at the will of the government on the completion of the contract.

Nationalization is the opposite position, with the government claiming that (a) it could do a more effective job; (b) it would save the profit paid to private enterprise; or (c) private enterprise could not undertake the job because it was uneconomic. None of these reasons stands the scrutiny of close examination. There is little reason to think that government is more efficient than private enterprise, and the profit is a small price to pay for effective performance. If the job is uneconomical, then it must be questioned as to its validity to be performed at all.

Railways are nationalized in most of the countries of Europe, and they sustain massive losses. Why can government run railways better than private enterprise? If they are to be subsidized for losses, why not subsidize private enterprise? Another answer is that railways or telephones or airlines are natural monopolies and therefore must be run by the government. But the basic issue in the management of change is to ask whether government agencies are change responsive. It seems unlikely that the government of a Western democracy could be change responsive in its bureaucratic government agencies, where it resulted in massive shifts of resources or elimination of entire agencies.

The transition to total change responsiveness requires many years to phase out existing agencies and convert to sub-contracting. But without such reorganization government will become crisis-change oriented, with resulting resource waste and inflexibility.

5. **Redefinition of government goals and missions.** Modern governments have major problems of conflicting priorities, such as full employment and price stability. Such goals seem to be set independently, often on the basis of the general good for society, without consideration of resource availability or a priority ranking. Environmental scanning is an integral part of setting government goals and missions to determine what the environmental state will be for the society as a whole. This in turn could lead to a series of vector goals.

Vector goals could also be considered as overall guidelines which would determine goals and missions. They would be such things as freedom of entry for business firms, freedom of choice for individuals, and consumer protection. Such vector goals would be predominant over lesser goals, so that restriction of competition by large companies would not solely be judged on the basis that this was contrary to a set of sub-goals on concentration of financial resources and power in a few large companies. The vector goals would be predominant and if there were to be freedom of choice for individuals, etc., no action would be taken to break larger companies into smaller ones.

Rationalization of markets by merging of competitors may be best for society rather than being judged under the present laws of a country like the United States as lessening competition. Such industries as the steel industry might greatly benefit by some form of collusion among firms to eliminate obsolete plants, and share research and development. This could produce a major by-product of lower costs and lower prices.

The government should also have a major mission in effecting an orderly transition to change. The national planning commissions and the acceptance of longer time horizons should go a long way toward achieving such a mission.

A new internationalism

The interdependence of nation states will create a new internationalism and not a wave of nationalism. Trade requires that balance of payments not be piled up by one country to the disadvantage of its trading partners. Japan has learned that its drive to achieve major trade surpluses has created problems for it because it created trade deficits for its major trading partner, the United States. Even the maverick countries are beginning to mature their nationalism in favour of internationalism.

1. **EEC is pattern for the future.** Although the EEC has not yet reached either economic or political maturity, its pattern of free trade among its members is the pattern for the future. But trade restrictions, like any change-resistant factor, die hard. They have been heavily bargained for and seem to have major advantages. But just as the farm-subsidy and import-restriction programmes of the EEC have to be eliminated to allow the European consumer the advantages of free competition to lower food prices, so must all such trade restrictions be eliminated not only in the EEC but throughout the free world.

To make the EEC and other affected nations and groups receptive to freer trade and fewer restrictions, the effect of removing such restrictions must be recognized. This has been attempted in the EEC by means of farm subsidies and a multitude of new regulations. But subsidies must be for a transition period only, and be declining over that transition period. Furthermore, such subsidies may have to be paid to the country affected by the removal of the tariff or other trade restriction. For example, the textile industry in the United States and elsewhere has been greatly affected by the exporting of low-technology industries to high-labour countries like Singapore, Taiwan, and Hong Kong. This economic dislocation falls heavily on the textile industry in the United States and on the communities where such mills are located. It is only natural that political lobbying takes place to resist any change. But if a special tax were collected during a transition period on imports of foreign textiles to be used for a declining subsidy for the United States textile firms, a change-responsive model would be facilitated.

2. **Trade, not aid, for underdeveloped countries.** The have-not nations are getting poorer while the have nations become richer. Change-responsive strategies are difficult for underdeveloped countries (UDC's) because they are unable to break into the wheel of progress. Yet it is critical for the rest of the world that such nations are not left to rot in poverty and ignorance.

As labour costs increase in advanced industrial nations, low-technology industry exported to UDC's could benefit both the advanced nation and the UDC. Certain trade advantages have been granted UDC's both by Europe and the United States, but not on a systematic basis to use them to build industrial competence in UDC's. Government-to-government treaties, perhaps through the United Nations, could establish a common pattern for the export of such low technology to UDC's with the provision that no taxes be paid the host country but that the entire company be transferred intact as a going concern to the UDC at the end of 20 years.

3. **World dynamics—a general system model.** Interdependence of nation states means that extensive collaborative planning is required, extending from monetary systems to pollution control. International needs and priorities must necessarily impinge on national needs and priorities. This requires the same actions of environmental scanning, vector goals, and change-responsive institutions on a world-wide basis as are required on a national basis. The basic issue is to move toward change responsiveness among nations to develop international strategies for change. The issue is clear but the means are not. Although there seems considerable chance that individual nations, at least the advanced industrial ones, will move toward a change-responsive model, it seems unlikely that this will happen on any global scale for relations between nations.

References

Ackoff, Russell L. (1970) *A Concept of Corporate Planning*, Wiley, New York.

Ad Hoc Committee on the Triple Revolution (1964) 'Machines do it better than humans: an assessment of a workless society and proposals for action', *Advertising Age*, 6 April, 121–2+.

Alexander, Tom (1972) 'The packaging problem is a can of worms', *Fortune*, **85** (6), 104–7+.

Ansoff, H. Igor (1965) *Corporate Strategy: An Analytic Approach to Business Policy for Growth and Expansion*, McGraw-Hill, New York.

Ansoff, H. Igor (Ed.) (1969) *Business Strategy: Selected Readings*, Penguin Books, Harmondsworth, England.

Anthony, Robert N. (1965) *Planning and Control Systems: A Framework for Analysis*, Graduate School of Business Administration, Harvard University, Boston.

Argyris, Chris (1957) 'The individual and organization: some problems of mutual adjustment', *Administrative Science Quarterly*, **2** (1), 1–24.

Argyris, Chris (1960) *Understanding Organizational Behavior*, Dorsey Press, Homewood, Illinois.

Argyris, Chris (1962) *Interpersonal Competence and Organizational Effectiveness*, Irwin, Homewood, Illinois.

Argyris, Chris (1964) *Integrating the Individual and the Organization*, Wiley, New York.

Argyris, Chris (1970) *Intervention Theory and Method*, Addison-Wesley, Reading, Mass.

Assel, Henry (1959) 'Constructive role of interorganizational conflict', *Administrative Science Quarterly*, **14** (4), 573–82.

Badawy, M. K. (1971) 'Industrial scientists and engineers: motivational style differences', *California Management Review*, **14** (1), 11–16.

Baldwin, William L. and Gerald L. Childs (1969) 'The fast second and rivalry in research and development', *The Southern Economic Journal*, **36** (1), 18–24.

Bales, R. F., E. F. Borgatta, and A. S. Couch (1954) 'Some findings relevant to the great-man theory of leadership', *American Sociology Review*, **19** (6), 755–9.

Ball, Robert (1971) 'The Common Market is still good news', *Fortune*, **84** (6), 80–3, 129–35.

Ball, Robert (1972) 'Volkswagen gets a much-needed tune-up', *Fortune*, **85** (3), 82–5+.

Barnard, Chester I. (1938) *The Functions of the Executive*, Harvard University Press, Cambridge, Mass.

Basil, Douglas C. (1970) *Managerial Skills for Executive Action*, American Management Association, New York.

Basil, Douglas C. (1971) *Leadership Skills for Executive Action*, American Management Association, New York.

Basil, Douglas C. (1972) *Women in Management*, University of Cambridge Press, New York.

Basil, Douglas C. with Curtis W. Cook (1969) *Contemporary Management Develop-*

ment: A Research Study of Management Development and Training in the Super Market and Allied Industries, Super Market Institute, Chicago.

Basil, Douglas C. and Curtis W. Cook (1970) 'Managerial behavior and management styles in franchising', in Jim McCord (Ed.), *The Franchising Sourcebook*, Practicing Law Institute, New York, pp. 153–75.

Basil, Douglas C. and Curtis W. Cook (1973) *Developing Tomorrow's Managers*, University of Southern California, Los Angeles (mimeograph manuscript).

Bates, Marston (1969) 'The human ecosystem', in National Academy of Sciences, *Resources and Man*, Freeman, San Francisco, pp. 21–30.

Batten, J. D. (1966) *Beyond Management by Objectives*, American Management Association, New York.

Baumol, William J. (1967) 'Macroeconomics of unbalanced growth: the anatomy of the urban crisis', *American Economic Review*, **57** (3), 415–26.

Beckhard, Richard (1969) *Organization Development: Strategies and Models*, Addison-Wesley, Reading, Mass.

Ben-David, Joseph (1968) 'Fundamental research and the universities: some comments on international differences', Organization for Economic Cooperation and Development, Paris.

Bennis, Warren G. (1961) 'Revisionist theory of leadership', *Harvard Business Review*, **39** (1), 26–36, 146–50.

Bennis, Warren G. (1966) *Changing Organizations: Essays on the Development and Evolution of Human Organization*, McGraw-Hill, New York.

Bennis, Warren G. (1969) 'Theory and method in applying behavioural science to planned organizational change', in Frank Baker, Peter McEwan and Alan Sheldon (Eds.), *Industrial Organizations and Health* (Vol. 1), Tavistock Publications, London, pp. 626–47.

Bennis, Warren G. (1969) *Organization Development: Its Nature, Origins, and Prospects*, Addison-Wesley, Reading, Mass.

Berelson, B. and G. A. Steiner (1964) *Human Behavior: An Inventory of Scientific Findings*, Harcourt, Brace and World, New York.

'Better late than never', *Forbes*, 1 September 1972, p. 30.

Bivens, Karen K. and Helen S. Lambeth (1967) *A World-Wide Look at Business-Government Relations*, National Industrial Conference Board, New York.

Blake, Robert R. and Jane S. Mouton (1964) *The Managerial Grid*, Gulf Publishing, Houston, Texas.

Blake, Robert R. and Jane S. Mouton (1968) *Corporate Excellence Through Grid Organization Development*, Gulf Publishing, Houston, Texas.

Boettinger, Henry M. (1969) 'The impact of technology', in Peter F. Drucker (Ed.), *Preparing Tomorrow's Business Leaders Today*, Prentice-Hall, Englewood Cliffs, N.J., pp. 50–60.

Boulding, Kenneth E. (1956) 'General systems theory: the skeleton of science', *General Systems*, Yearbook of the Society for the Advancement of General System Theory (Vol. 1), pp. 11–17.

Boulding, Kenneth E. (1965) *The Meaning of the 20th Century: The Great Transition*, Harper Colophon Books, New York.

Boulding, Kenneth E. (1967) 'The price system and the price of the great society', in Myron H. Ross (Ed.), *The Future of Economic Policy*, Bureau of Business Research, University of Michigan, Ann Arbor, pp. 57–73.

Brand, David (1970) 'Electronic chips offer advances in computers and consumer goods', *The Wall Street Journal*, 22 June, 1.

Brandon, Henry (1973) 'The balance of mutual weakness', *The Atlantic Monthly*, **231** (1), 35–42.

222

Breckenfeld, Gurney (1972) 'Housing subsidies are a grand delusion', *Fortune*, **85** (2) 136–9+.

Brewer, Stanley H. (1966) *Air Cargo Comes of Age*, University of Washington, Seattle, Washington.

Brooks, Harvey (1972) 'What's happening to the U.S. lead in technology?' *Harvard Business Review*, **50** (3), 110–18.

Brown, W. (1960) *Exploration in Management*, Heinemann, London.

Bruner, Jerome S. (1960) *The Process of Education*, Vintage Books, New York.

Buckley, Walter (1967) *Sociology and Modern Systems Theory*, Prentice-Hall, Englewood Cliffs, N.J.

Burack, Elmer H. and Gopal C. Pati (1970) 'Technology and managerial obsolescence', *MSU Business Topics*, **18** (2), 49–56.

Burck, Charles G. (1972) 'A car that may reshape the industry's future', *Fortune*, **86** (1), 74–9+.

Burck, Charles G. (1972) 'While the big brewers quaff, the little ones thirst,' *Fortune*, **86** (5), 102–7+.

Burke, W. Warner and Warren H. Schmidt (1970) 'Primary target for change: the manager or the organization?' in Warren H. Schmidt, *Organizational Frontiers and Human Values*, Wadsworth, Belmont, Calif., pp. 151–69.

Burns, Tom and G. M. Stalker (1961) *The Management of Innovation*, Tavistock, London.

Bush, George (1972) 'Europe's new cities', *The Lamp*, **53** (1), 9–15.

Business International Corporation (1965) 'Organizing for worldwide operations: structuring and implementing the plan', Business International Research Report, New York.

Bylinsky, Gene (1972) 'Vincent Learson didn't plan it that way, but I.B.M.'s toughest competitor is—I.B.M.', *Fortune*, **85** (3), 54–61+.

Central Training Council (1969) *Training and Development of Managers: Further Proposals*, Report by the Management Training and Development Committee, Her Majesty's Stationery Office, London.

Chandler, Alfred D. (1962) *Strategy and Structure: Chapters in the History of the Industrial Enterprise*, Anchor, Garden City, New York (orig. M.I.T. Press).

Chandler, W. Porter, III (1972) 'A lot of learning is a dangerous thing', *Harvard Business Review*, **50** (2), 122–31.

Chapple, E. D. and Leonard R. Sayles (1961) *The Measurement of Management*, Macmillan, New York.

Child, John (1973) 'Predicting and understanding organization structure', *Administrative Science Quarterly*, **18** (2), 168–85.

Chorafas, D. N. (1970) *The Knowledge Revolution: An Analysis of the International Brain Market*, McGraw-Hill, New York.

Cole, K. C. (1973) 'Golden oldies: senior citizens go back to school', *Saturday Review of Education*, **1** (1), 41–4.

Congressional Record (1970) 91st U.S. Congress, Senate, 2nd Session, Vol. 116, pp. 19176–82.

Cook, Don (1973) 'The Common Market', *The Atlantic Monthly*, **231** (2) 18, 21, 22, 25.

Copithorne, W. L. (1971) 'Europe's energy revolution', *The Lamp*, **53** (1), 16–21.

Cordiner, Ralph (1956) *New Frontiers for Professional Managers*, McGraw-Hill, New York.

Cordtz, Dan (1972a) 'Pan Am's route across the sea of red ink', *Fortune*, **85** (1), 78–81+.

Cordtz, Dan (1972b) 'Corporate farming: a tough row to hoe', *Fortune*, **86** (2), 134–9+.

Cyert, Richard M. and James G. March (1963) *A Behavioral Theory of the Firm*, Prentice-Hall, Englewood Cliffs, N.J.

Dalton, Melville (1959) *Men Who Manage*, Wiley, New York.

Darling, Charles M. III and DuBois S. Morris, Jr. (1970) *Perspectives for the '70s and '80s: Tomorrow's Problems Confronting Today's Management*, National Industrial Conference Board, New York.

Darwin, Charles (1865) *On the Origin of Species by Means of Natural Selection* (rev. ed.), Appleton, New York.

Davidson, Glenn S., Robert S. Siegler, and Rita W. Poulos (1972) 'Television and aggression', in *Educational Psychology: Teaching and Resource Guide*, CMR Books, Del Mar, Calif., pp. 131–2.

Davis, Keith and Robert L. Blomstrom. (1971) *Business, Society, and Environment: Social Power and Social Response* (2nd ed.), McGraw-Hill, New York.

Davis, Kenneth N. (1971) 'The outlook for the United States and world trade', *Business Economics*, **6** (1), 48–50.

Davis, Louis E. (1971) 'Readying the unready: postindustrial jobs', *California Management Review*, **13** (4), 27–36.

Dawson, Leslie M. (1969) 'The human concept: new philosophy for business', *Business Horizons* **12** (6), 29–38.

Dearden, John (1972) 'How to make incentive plans work', *Harvard Business Review*, **50** (4), 117–24.

Demaree, Allan T. (1970) 'G.E.'s costly ventures into the future', *Fortune*, **82** (4), 88–93+.

Demaree, Allan T. (1972) 'RCA after the bath', *Fortune*, **86** (3) 122–32+.

Denison, Edward F. (1962) 'The sources of economic growth in the United States and the alternatives before us', Supplementary Paper No. 13, Committee for Economic Development.

Dennison, George (1969) *The Lives of Children*, Random House, New York.

Dickson, Paul (1971) *Think Tanks*, Atheneum, New York.

Diebold, John (1969) 'The information revolution', in Peter F. Drucker (Ed.), *Preparing Tomorrow's Business Leaders Today*, Prentice-Hall, Englewood Cliffs, N.J., pp. 61–73.

Dockson, Robert R. (1970) 'The winds of change', Graduate School of Business Administration, University of Southern California, Los Angeles, Report to Management No. 24.

Domhoff, G. William (1967) *Who Rules America?* Prentice-Hall, Englewood Cliffs, N.J.

Drew, Elizabeth (1973) 'Reports and comments: Washington', *The Atlantic Monthly*, **231** (1), 6, 7, 10, 12, 13, 16.

Driver, Michael J. and Siegfried Streufert (1969) 'Integrative complexity: an approach to individuals and groups as information-processing systems', *Administrative Science Quarterly*, **14** (2), 272–85.

Drucker, Peter F. (1963) 'Managing for business effectiveness', *Harvard Business Review*, **41** (3), 53–60.

Drucker, Peter F. (1969a) *The Age of Discontinuity*, Harper & Row, New York.

Drucker, Peter F. (1969b) 'Management's new role', *Harvard Business Review*, **47** (6), 49–54.

Drucker, Peter F. (Ed.) (1969c) *Preparing Tomorrow's Business Leaders Today*, Prentice-Hall, Englewood Cliffs, N.J.

224

Duhl, Leonard (1963) 'The human measure', in Lowdon Wingo, Jr. (Ed.), *Cities and Space*, John Hopkins Press, Baltimore, pp. 133–54.

Duncan, Otis Dudley (1967) 'Social organization and the ecosystem', in Robert E. L. Faris (Ed.), *Handbook of Modern Sociology*, Rand McNally, Chicago, pp. 36–82.

Easterbrook, W. T. (1957) 'Long-period comparative study: some historical cases', *Journal of Economic History*, 571–95.

Economic Report of the President (1970, 1972) United States Government Printing Office, Washington, D.C.

Eisner, Robert (1967) 'Fiscal and monetary policy for economic growth', in Myron H. Ross (Ed.), *The Future of Economic Policy*, Bureau of Business Research, University of Michigan, Ann Arbor, pp. 14–27.

Elden, James M., Raymond Goldstone, and Michael K. Brown (1970) 'The university as an organizational frontier', in Warren H. Schmidt, *Organizational Frontiers and Human Values*, Wadsworth Publishing, Belmont, Calif., pp. 87–101.

Emery, F. E. and E. L. Trist (1965) 'The causal texture of organizational environments, *Human Relations*, **18** (1), 21–32.

England, George W. (1967) 'Personal value systems of American managers', *Academy of Management Journal*, **10** (1), 53–68.

Etzioni, Amitai (1965) 'Dual leadership in complex organizations', *American Sociological Review*, **30**, 688–98.

Etzioni, Amitai (1967) 'Toward a theory of societal guidance', *The American Journal of Sociology*, **73** (2), 173–87.

Etzioni, Amitai (1968) *The Active Society: A Theory of Societal and Political Processes*, The Free Press, New York.

Etzioni, Amitai (1971) 'For more use of the private sector', *The Wall Street Journal*, 27 May, 12.

Ewing, David W. (1972) 'MNCs on trial', *Harvard Business Review*, **50** (3), 130–2, 134, 136, 138, 140, 142–3.

Farmer, Richard N. (1970) 'University management: future problems and their relevance to the teaching profession', *Economic and Business Bulletin*, **22** (3), 36–41.

Farmer, Richard N. (1969) 'Management of complex organizations', *Academy of Management Proceedings*, pp. 17–28.

Feldman, Arnold S. and Wilbert E. Moore (1969) 'Industrialization and industrialism: convergence and differentiation', in William A. Faunce and William H. Form (Eds.), *Comparative Perspectives on Industrial Society*, Little, Brown and Company, Boston, pp. 55–71.

Fiedler, Fred E. (1967) *A Theory of Leadership Effectiveness*, McGraw-Hill, New York.

Filley, Alan C. and Robert J. House (1969) *Managerial Process and Organizational Behavior*, Scott, Foresman, Glenview, Ill.

Fitzgerald, Thomas H. (1971) 'Why motivation theory doesn't work', *Harvard Business Review*, **49** (4), 37–44.

Fitzgerald, Thomas H. and Howard C. Carlson (1971) 'Management potential: early recognition and development', *California Management Review*, **14** (2), 18–23.

Flanigan, James (1972) 'Marx and management', *Forbes*, **109** (10), 49–51.

Fogarty, Michael (1967) 'British management: an uneasy legitimacy', *Columbia Journal of World Business*, **2** (4), 57–65.

Ford, Henry II (1970) *The Human Environment and Business*, Weybright & Talley, New York.

Forrester, Jay W. (1971) *World Dynamics*, Wright-Allen Press, Cambridge, Mass.

Frank, Lawrence K. (1968) 'The need for a new political theory', in Daniel Bell (Ed.), *Toward the Year 2000: Work in Progress*, Houghton Mifflin, Boston, pp. 177–84.

Freeman, Roger A. (1972) 'National priorities in the decade ahead', *The Intercollegiate Review*, **8** (1–2), 15–19.

French, Wendell (1969) 'Organization development objectives, assumptions and strategies', *California Management Review*, **12** (2), 23–34.

Friedlander, Frank (1966) 'Motivations to work and organizational performance', *Journal of Applied Psychology*, **50** (2), pp. 143–52.

Friedman, Milton (1962) *Capitalism and Freedom*, University of Chicago Press, Chicago.

Friedman, Milton (1970) 'Development fashions', *Newsweek*, 21 December, 82.

Friedman, Milton (1970, 1972) 'The social responsibility of business is to increase its profits', *The New York Times Magazine* (1970) 33, 122–6 and in George A. Steiner (Ed.), *Issues in Business and Society*, Random House, New York (1972), pp. 141–7.

Galbraith, Jay R. (1971) 'Matrix organizational designs: how to combine functional and project forms', *Business Horizons*, **14** (1), 29–40.

Galbraith, John Kenneth (1958) *The Affluent Society*, Houghton Mifflin, Boston.

Gardner, John W. (1965) *Self-Renewal: The Individual and the Innovative Society*, Harper Colophon Books, New York.

Gardner, John W. (1969) *No Easy Victories*, Harper Colophon, New York.

Glasser, William (1969) *Schools Without Failure*, Harper & Row, New York.

'Global companies: too big to handle?' *Newsweek*, 20 November 1972, pp. 96–104.

Gooding, Judson (1971) 'The engineers are redesigning their own profession', *Fortune*, **83** (6), 72–5+.

Gooding, Judson (1972) *The Job Revolution*, Walker & Company, New York.

Gorz, André (1968) *Strategy for Labor: A Radical Proposal*, Beacon Press, Boston.

Gouldner, Alvin (1960) 'The norm of reciprocity: a preliminary statement,' *American Sociological Review*, **25** (2), 161–78.

Grayson, C. Jackson, Jr. (1972) 'Controlling prices is an educational experience', *Fortune*, **86** (4), 76–9+.

Greiner, Larry E. (1970) 'Patterns of organization change', in Gene W. Dalton and Paul R. Lawrence, *Organization Change and Development*, Irwin, Homewood, Ill., pp. 213–29.

Greiner, Larry E. (1972a) 'Red flags in organization development', *Business Horizons*, **15** (3), 17–24.

Greiner, Larry E. (1972b) 'Evolution and revolution as organizations grow', *Harvard Business Review*, **50** (4), 37–46.

Gross, Bertram M. (1968) 'An overview of change in America' (unpublished progress report), Twentieth Century Fund, New York.

Guetzkow, Harold (1965) 'The creative person in organizations', in Gary A. Steiner (Ed.), *The Creative Organization*, University of Chicago Press, Chicago, pp. 35–45.

Hage, Jerald and Michael Aiken (1970) *Social Change in Complex Organizations*, Random House, New York.

Hall, D. T. and K. E. Nougaim (1968) 'An examination of Maslow's need hierarchy in an organizational setting', *Organizational Behavior and Human Performance*, **5** (1), 12–35.

Hall, Jay (1971) 'Decisions, decisions, decisions', *Psychology Today*, **5** (6), 51–4, 86–8.

Hardbeck, George W. (1965, 1971) 'Unionism again at the crossroads', *Labor Law Journal* (1965) **16** (2), reprinted in John G. Hutchinson (Ed.), *Readings in Management Strategy and Tactics*, Holt, Rinehart and Winston, New York (1971), pp. 504–13.

Harrison, Roger (1972) 'Understanding your organization's character', *Harvard Business Review*, **50** (3), 119–28.

Hauptfuhrer, Robert P. (1968) 'The challenge of managing change', *Business Today*, Autumn, 48–54.

Hauser, Ernest O. (1973) 'Long live the book!', *Reader's Digest*, **102** (609), 27–32.

Hayes, Douglas A. (1970) 'Management goals in a crisis society', *Michigan Business Review*, **22**, 7–11.

Hedberg, Haakan (1969) *Den Japanska Utmaningen* (*The Japanese Challenge*), Albert Bonner Publishing, Stockholm.

Heller, Walter W. (1972) 'Cooling off Japan's trade surplus', *The Wall Street Journal*, 12 December, 18.

Herzberg, Frederick (1966) *Work and the Nature of Man*, World Publishing, New York.

Herzberg, Frederick, B. Mausner, and B. Snyderman (1959) *The Motivation to Work*, Wiley, New York.

Holden, Paul E., Carlton A. Pederson, and Gayton E. Germane (1968) *Top Management: A Research Study of the Management Policies and Practices of Fifteen Leading Industrial Corporations*, McGraw-Hill, New York.

Holmes, Thomas H. and Richard H. Rahe (1967) 'The social readjustment rating scale', *Journal of Psychosomatic Research*, **11** (2), 213–18.

Holt, John (1964) *How Children Fail*, Dell, New York.

Holt, John (1969) *The Underachieving School*, Dell, New York.

Homans, George C. (1950) *The Human Group*, Harcourt, Brace & Co., New York.

House, Robert F. (1968) 'Leadership training: some dysfunctional consequences', *Administrative Science Quarterly*, **12** (4), 556–71.

Houston, Bryan (1972) 'Let's put more esprit in de corporation', *Harvard Business Review*, **50** (6), 55–61.

Howe, Martyn (1967) 'Multinational corporations in a nationalistic world', in John K. Ryans and James C. Baker (Eds.), *World Marketing: A Multinational Approach*, Wiley, New York, pp. 98–105.

Jacoby, Neil H. (1972) 'What is a social problem?', in George A. Steiner, *Issues in Business and Society*, Random House, New York, pp. 70–81.

Janis, Irving L. (1971) 'Groupthink', *Psychology Today*, **5** (6), 43–6+.

'Japan, Inc.: winning the most important battle', *Time*, 10 May 1971, pp. 84–9.

Jaques, Elliot (1951) *The Changing Culture of a Factory*, Tavistock, London.

Jasinski, Frank J. (1956) 'Technological delimitation of reciprocal relationships: a study of interaction patterns in industry', *Human Organization*, **15** (2), 24–28.

Johnson, Harry G. (1965) *The World Economy at the Crossroads*, Oxford University Press, New York.

Kahn, Herman and B. Bruce-Briggs (1972) *Things to Come: Thinking About the Seventies and Eighties*, Macmillan, New York.

Kahn, Herman and Anthony J. Wiener (1967) *The Year 2000: A Framework for Speculation on the Next Thirty-three Years*, Macmillan, New York.

Katona, George, Burkhard Strumpel, and Ernest Zahn (1971) *Aspirations and Affluence*, McGraw-Hill, New York.

Katz, Daniel (1964) 'Approaches to managing conflict', in Robert L. Kahn and Elise Boulding (Eds.), *Power and Conflict in Organizations*, Basic Books, New York.

227

Katz, Daniel and Robert L. Kahn (1966) *The Social Psychology of Organizations*, Wiley, New York.

Keatley, Robert (1972) 'Soviet faces woes in paying for U.S. grain, hurting Russian consumer, West's exports', *The Wall Street Journal*, 8 December, 30.

Keith, Robert J. (1960) 'The marketing revolution', *Journal of Marketing*, 24 (1), 35–8.

Knight, Andrew (1972) 'What the EEC is not', *The Economist*, 1 January, 10–13.

Knowles, Henry P. and Borje O. Saxberg (1971) *Personality and Leadership Behavior*, Addison-Wesley, Reading, Mass.

Knudsen, John W. (1971) 'Productivity changes', *Monthly Review* (Federal Reserve Bank of Kansas City), April, 3–9.

Kohlberg, Lawrence with Phillip Whitten (1972) 'Understanding the hidden curriculum', *Learning*, 1 (2), 10–14.

Kraar, Louis (1972) 'A Japanese champion fights to stay on top', *Fortune*, 86 (6), 94–103.

Kroos, Herman E. and Peter F. Drucker (1969) 'How we got there: fifty years of structural changes in the business system and the business school, 1918–1968', in Peter F. Drucker (Ed.), *Preparing Tomorrow's Business Leaders Today*, Prentice Hall, Englewood Cliffs, N.J., pp. 1–23.

Kuhlmeijer, H. J. (1971) 'The European Common Market: a new system of production and distribution in the making', *Michigan Business Review*, 13 (2), 16–22.

Lawrence, Paul R. and Jay W. Lorsch (1969) *Organization and Environment: Managing Differentiation and Integration*, Irwin, Homewood, Ill.

Lawrence, Paul R. and John A. Seiler (1965) *Organizational Behavior and Administration: Cases, Concepts, and Research Findings*, Irwin, Homewood, Ill.

Leavitt, Harold J. (1964) 'Applied organizational change in industry: structural, technical, and human approaches', in William W. Cooper, Harold J. Leavitt, and Maynard W. Shelly II (Eds.), *New Perspectives in Organization Research*, Wiley, New York, pp. 53–71.

Leavitt, Harold J. and Thomas L. Whisler (1958) 'Management in the 1980's', *Harvard Business Review*, 36 (6), 41–8.

Levitt, Theodore (1960) 'Marketing myopia', *Harvard Business Review*, 38 (4), 24–35.

Levitt, Theodore (1968) 'Why business always loses', *Harvard Business Review*, 46 (2), 81–9.

Lessing, Lawrence (1972) 'Why the U.S. lags in technology', *Fortune*, 85 (4), 69–73+.

Levine, Sol and Norman A. Scotch (Eds.). (1970) *Social Stress*, Aldine, Chicago.

Levinson, Charles (1969) 'Collective bargaining in perspective', Report 1B, *Trade Union Seminar on New Perspectives in Collective Bargaining*, Office of Economic Cooperation and Development, Manpower and Social Affairs Directorate, Paris.

Levinson, Harry (1968) *The Exceptional Executive: A Psychological Conception*, Harvard University Press, Cambridge, Mass.

Liebert, Robert M. and Rita W. Poulos (1972) 'TV for kiddies: truth, goodness, beauty—and a little bit of brainwash', *Psychology Today*, 6 (6), 122–4, 126, 128.

Likert, Rensis (1967) *The Human Organization*, McGraw-Hill, New York.

Livingstone, J. Sterling (1971) 'Myth of the well-educated manager', *Harvard Business Review*, 49 (1), 79–89.

Locke, Lawrence (1971) 'A million guests a year', *The Lamp*, 53 (1), 43–7.

Long, John D. (1972) 'The protestant ethic reexamined', *Business Horizons*, 15 (1), 75–82.

Loving, Rush, Jr. (1972) 'How a hotelman got the red out of United Air Lines', *Fortune*, **85** (3), 72–7.

McClelland, David C. (1965) 'Achievement motivation can be developed', *Harvard Business Review*, **43** (6), 6–8+.

McGregor, Douglas (1957) 'An uneasy look at performance appraisal', *Harvard Business Review*, **35** (3), 89–94.

McGregor, Douglas (1960) *The Human Side of Enterprise*, McGraw-Hill, New York.

McGregor, Douglas (1966) 'The manager, human nature, and human sciences', in Warren G. Bennis and Edgar H. Schein (Eds.), *Leadership and Motivation: Essays of Douglas McGregor*, M.I.T. Press, Cambridge, pp. 201–38.

McGregor, Douglas (1967) *The Professional Manager*, McGraw-Hill, New York.

McGuire, Joseph, W. (1964) *Theories of Business Behavior*, Prentice-Hall, Englewood Cliffs, N.J.

Macrae, Norman (1971) 'Building the New Europe', *The Lamp*, **53** (1), 2–7.

Maddox, John (1972) *The Doomsday Syndrome*, McGraw-Hill, New York.

Mager, Robert F. (1968) *Developing Attitude Toward Learning*, Fearon Publishers, Palo Alto, Calif.

Markham, Jesse W. (1967) 'Antitrust policy after a decade of vigor', in Myron H. Ross (Ed.), *The Future of Economic Policy*, Bureau of Business Research, University of Michigan, Ann Arbor, pp. 46–56.

Martyn, Howe (1967) 'Multinational corporations in a nationalistic world', in John K. Ryans, Jr. and James C. Baker (Eds.), *World Marketing: A Multinational Approach*, Wiley, New York, pp. 98–105.

Maslow, Abraham (1954) *Motivation and Personality*, Harper & Row, New York.

Mechanic, David (1964) 'Sources of power in lower participants in complex organizations', in William W. Cooper, Harold J. Leavitt, and Maynard W. Shelly II, *New Perspectives in Organization Research*, Wiley, New York, pp. 136–49.

Mecklin, John M. (1970) 'Asia's great leap in textiles', *Fortune*, **82** (4), 77–83+.

Mee, John F. (1969) 'Management challenges of the 1970's', *S.A.M. Advanced Management Journal*, **34** (4), 39–47.

Mee, John F. (1971) 'Speculation about human organization in the 21st century', *Business Horizons*, **14** (1), 5–16.

Meyers, Harold B. (1971) 'The salvage of the Lockheed 1011', *Fortune*, **83** (6), 66–71.

Miller, Andrew, Charles Tillinghast III, James Garrison, and Cecil H. Bell (1972) 'Boise Cascade's organization renewal project', *Proceedings of the Academy of Management* (1971 meeting), Academy of Management, Seattle, Washington, 185–94.

Miller, David W. and Martin K. Starr (1969) *Executive Decisions and Operations Research* (2nd ed.), Prentice-Hall, Englewood Cliffs, N.J.

Miller, James G. (1955) 'Toward a general theory for the behavioral sciences', *American Psychologist*, **10** (9), 513–31.

Mills, C. Wright (1959) *The Power Élite*. Oxford University Press, New York.

'Miracle, maybe' *The Economist*, 19 November 1968, 54, 55.

Mishan, E. J. (1969) *Technology and Growth: The Price We Pay*, Praeger Publishers, New York.

Morris, Jack H. (1972) 'Steelmakers' spending to clear up the air stirs up more wrath', *The Wall Street Journal*, 30 November, 1, 15.

Mossberg, Walter (1972) 'Gene Cafiero labors to enhance the quality of assembly-line life', *The Wall Street Journal*, 7 December, 1, 23.

Naylor, Margot (Ed.) (1970) *Financial Times Yearbook Business Information*, St. Martin's Press, New York.

'Netherlands', *Quarterly Economic Reviews*, No. 3, The Economist Intelligence Unit, London (1972).

'New anti-hijack rules promise to make flying a complicated affair', *The Wall Street Journal*, 5 January 1973, 4.

Newhouse, John (1967) *Collision in Brussels*, Norton, New York.

Nixon, Richard M. (1971) 'State of the Union', an address by the President of the United States to Congress, 22 January.

Norman, Geoffrey (1972) 'Blue-collar saboteurs', *Playboy*, **19** (9), 96–8, 104, 250–3.

Normann, Richard (1971) 'Organizational innovativeness: product variation and reorientation', *Administrative Science Quarterly*, **16** (2), 203–15.

O'Donnell, Laurence G. (1972) 'General Motors' plan to increase efficiency draws ire of unions', *The Wall Street Journal*, 6 December, 1, 39.

O'Donnell, Laurence and Walter Mossberg (1972) 'UAW will emphasize escape from "the job" in 1973 contract talks', *The Wall Street Journal*, 8 December, 1, 16.

Olken, Hyman (1969) 'Technological growth and the evolution of new industries', *Economic and Business Bulletin*, **22** (1), 15–24.

Olsen, Marvin E. (1968) *The Process of Social Organization*, Holt, Rinehart & Winston, New York.

Organization for Economic Co-operation and Development (1970) *The Outlook for Economic Growth: A Summary Report on Experience, Prospects and Problems of Policy 1960–1980*, OECD, Paris.

Packard, Vance (1972) *A Nation of Strangers*, McKay, New York.

Patton, Arch. (1972) 'Why incentive plans fail', *Harvard Business Review*, **50** (3), 58–66.

Peter, Lawrence J. and Raymond Hull (1969) *The Peter Principle: Why Things Always Go Wrong*, Bantam Book, New York.

Phillips, A. W. (1958) 'The relation between unemployment and the rate of change of money wage rates in the United Kingdom, 1861–1957', *Economica*, New Series, **25**, pp. 283–99.

Phillips, Leslie (1968) *Human Adaptation and its Failures*, Academic Press, New York.

Phillips, Warren H. (1972) 'The paradox of the Maoist man', *The Wall Street Journal*, 31 October, 7.

Piaget, J. (1952) *The Origins of Intelligence in Children*, International Universities Press, New York.

Polanyi, Karl (1944) *The Great Transformation*, Holt, Rinehart and Winston, New York.

Pond, Elizabeth (1972) 'Japan', *The Atlantic Monthly*, **230** (4), 22–28.

Porter, Lyman W. (1962) 'Job attitudes in management: perceived deficiencies in need fulfillment as a function of job level', *Journal of Applied Psychology*, **46** (4), 375–84.

Porter, Lyman W. (1963) 'Job attitudes in management: perceived importance of needs as a function of job level', *Journal of Applied Psychology*, **47** (2), 141–8.

Prestbo, John A. (1972) 'Computer terminals replace cash registers at more retail stores', *The Wall Street Journal*, 20 November, 1, 13.

Price, Charlton R. (1970) 'Between cultures: the current crisis of transition', in Warren H. Schmidt (Ed.), *Organizational Frontiers and Human Values*, Wadsworth, Belmont, Calif., pp. 27–45.

Prince, George M. (1972) 'Creative meetings through power sharing', *Harvard Business Review*, **50** (4), 47–54.

Pugh, D. S., D. J. Hickson, C. R. Hinings, and C. Turner (1969) 'The context of organization structures', *Administrative Science Quarterly*, **14** (1), 91–114.

Rahe, Richard H., Joseph D. McKean, Jr. and Ramsom J. Arthur (1967) 'A longitudinal study of life-change and illness patterns', *Journal of Psychomatic Research*, **10** (4), 355–66.

Raia, Anthony P. (1972) 'Organizational development—some issues and challenges', *California Management Review*, **14** (4), 13–20.

Raskin, A. H. (1963) 'AFL-CIO: a confederation or federation?', *The Annals of the American Academy of Political and Social Science*, 36–45.

Reich, Charles A. (1970) *The Greening of America*, Random House, New York.

Reid, Graham L. and Kevin Allen (1970) *Nationalized Industries*, Penguin Books, Harmondsworth, England.

Rhodes, John B. (1969) 'The American challenge challenged', *Harvard Business Review*, **47** (5) 45–57.

Rice, George H, Jr. and Dean W. Bishoprick (1971) *Conceptual Models of Organization*, Appleton-Century-Crofts, New York.

'Rich, poor nations collide on SDRs, Chilean seizures at IMF meeting', *The Wall Street Journal*, 29 September 1972, 3.

Riesman, David, with Nathan Glazer and Reuel Denney (1950) *The Lonely Crowd: A Study of the Changing American Character*, Doubleday Anchor Books, Garden City, N.Y.

Rogers, Carl (1961) *On Becoming a Person*, Houghton Mifflin, Boston.

Rogers, Kenn. (1973) 'The mid-career crisis', *Saturday Review of the Society*, **1** (1), 37–8.

Rose, Stanford (1972) 'The going may get tougher for Caterpillar', *Fortune*, **85** (5), 161–6+.

Rostow, Walt W. (1959) ' "The Stages of Growth" as a Key to Policy', *Fortune*, **60** (6), 135–6, 201–9.

Rubenstein, Morton K. (1972) 'The outdated U.S. doctor', *Los Angeles Times*, Opinion Section J, 3 December.

Sampson, Anthony (1968) *Anatomy of Europe*, Harper & Row, New York.

Savage, Jay M. (1969) *Evolution* (2nd ed.), Holt, Rinehart and Winston, New York.

Sayles, Leonard R. and Margaret K. Chandler (1971) *Managing Large Systems: Organizations for the Future*, Harper & Row, New York.

Schacht, Richard (1970) *Alienation*, Doubleday, New York.

Schiff, Michael (1969) 'Ends and means in business education', in Peter F. Drucker (Ed.), *Preparing Tomorrow's Business Leaders Today*, Prentice-Hall, Englewood Cliffs, N.J., pp. 261–8.

Schirra, Walter M., Jr. (1970) Introductory comments to Sherwood Harris, 'A raw December day at Kitty Hawk', *Smithsonian*, **1** (3), 28–31.

Schmidt, Warren H. (1970) *Organizational Frontiers and Human Values*, Wadsworth Publishing, Belmont, Calif.

Schollhammer, Hans (1969) 'National economic planning and business decision-making: the French experience', *California Management Review*, **12** (2), 74–88.

Schon, Donald A. (1967) *Technology and Change: The New Heraclitus*, Dell Publishing, New York.

Schriever, B. A. and W. W. Seifert (1968) *Air Transportation 1975 and Beyond*, MIT Press, Cambridge, Mass.

Schroder, H., M. Driver, and S. Streufert (1967) *Human Information Processing*, Holt, Rinehart & Winston, New York.

Schultz, Theodore W. (1967) 'Public approaches to minimize poverty', in Myron H. Ross (Ed.), *The Future of Economic Policy*, Bureau of Business Research, University of Michigan, Ann Arbor, pp. 28–46.

Q

Seeman, Melvin (1967) 'On the personal consequences of alienation in work', *American Sociological Review*, **32** (2), 273–85.

Seitz, Frederick (1968) 'Can we afford not to support good research?' *Business Today*, Autumn, 43–6.

Servan-Schreiber, J.-J. (1969) *The American Challenge*, Atheneum, New York.

Sethi, S. Prakash (1971) *Up Against the Corporate Wall: Modern Corporations and Social Issues of the Seventies*, Prentice-Hall, Englewood Cliffs, N.J.

Shank, John K., Edward G. Niblock, and William T. Sandalls, Jr. (1973) 'Balance "creativity" and "practicality" in formal planning', *Harvard Business Review*, **51** (1), 87–95.

Simon, Herbert A. (1957) *Administrative Behaviour: A Study of Decision-Making Processes in Administrative Organization* (2nd ed.), The Free Press, New York.

Simon, Herbert A. (1965) *The Shape of Automation for Men and Management*, Harper & Row, New York.

'Sinking feelings in the Land of the Rising Sun', *Forbes*, 1 October 1972, pp. 30–2.

Skertchly, Allan R. B. (1968) *Tomorrow's Managers*, Staples, London.

Skinner, B. F. (1968) *The Technology of Teaching*, Appleton-Century-Crofts, New York.

Skinner, B. F. (1971) *Beyond Freedom and Dignity*, Alfred A. Knopf, New York.

'Small Japanese cars score big success in American markets', *The Wall Street Journal*, 6 May 1971, p. 1.

Smelser, Neil J. (1969) 'Mechanisms of change and adjustment to change', in William A. Faunce and William H. Form (Eds.), *Comparative Perspectives on Industrial Society*, Little, Brown and Company, Boston, pp. 33–54.

Smith, 'Adam' (1972) 'The last days of cowboy capitalism', *The Atlantic Monthly*, **230** (3), 43–55.

Smith, Richard A. (1963) *Corporations in Crisis*, Doubleday, Garden City, N.Y.

Snow, C. P. (1959) *The Two Cultures and the Scientific Revolution*, Cambridge Univ. Press, Cambridge.

Sombart, W. (1913) *The Jews and Modern Capitalism*, Unwin, London, 1913.

Sorokin, Pitrim (1937) *Social and Cultural Dynamics*. American Book, New York.

Steiner, George A. (1969) *Top Management Planning*, Macmillan, New York.

Stolk, William C. (1968) 'Beyond profitability: a proposal for managing the corporation's public business', *The Conference Board Record*, December, 52–4+

Stratford, Alan H. (1967) *Air Transport Economics in the Supersonic Era*, Macmillan, London.

Sullivan, Harry Stack (1953) *The Interpersonal Theory of Psychiatry*, Norton, New York.

Swanson, Theodor (1971) 'Europe cleans house', *The Lamp*, **53** (1), 36–41.

Swingle, Paul (Ed.) (1970) *The Structure of Conflict*, Academic Press, New York.

Thompson, James D. and Donald R. Van Houten (1970) *The Behavioral Sciences: An Interpretation*, Addison-Wesley, Reading, Mass.

Toffler, Alvin (1971) *Future Shock*, Bantam Books, New York.

Triffin, Robert (1967) 'International monetary reform', in Myron H. Ross (Ed.), *The Future of Economic Policy*, Bureau of Business Research, University of Michigan, Ann Arbor, pp. 74–95.

Trippett, Frank (1972) 'The shape of things as they really are', *Intellectual Digest*, **3** (4), 25–28.

Trist, Eric L. (1970) 'Urban North America: the challenge of the next thirty years', in Warren H. Schmidt, *Organizational Frontiers and Human Values*, Wadsworth, Belmont, Calif., pp. 77–85.

232

'U.S. plan to revise world money system emphasizes need for warnings of trouble', *The Wall Street Journal*, 14 November 1972, 8.

Vance, Stanley C. (1969) 'The management of multi-industry corporations', *Academy of Management Proceedings*, August, pp. 29–42.

Vanderwicken, Peter (1972a) 'G.M.: the price of being "responsible" ', *Fortune*, **85** (1), 99–101+.

Vanderwicken, Peter (1972b) 'USM's hard life as an ex-monopoly', *Fortune*, **86** (4), 124–30.

Veiga, John F. (1973) 'The mobile manager at mid-career', *Harvard Business Review*, **51** (1), 115–19.

Vicker, Ray (1970) 'British railway system makes money stressing its passenger service', *The Wall Street Journal*, 17 July, 1, 19.

'Volume, not profits,' *Forbes*, 1 May 1972, 26–8, 30–1.

Wallbank, T. Walter and Alastair M. Taylor (1954) *Civilization Past and Present*, Vol. 1 (3rd ed.), Scott, Foresman & Co., Chicago.

Walsh, A. E. and John Paxton (1969) *The Structure and Development of the Common Market*, Taplinger, New York.

Walton, Richard E. (1972) 'How to counter alienation in the plant', *Harvard Business Review*, **50** (6), 70–81.

Waters, William R. (1970) 'Technological growth and evolution', *Economic and Business Bulletin*, **22** (3), 42–4.

Ways, Max (1966, 1971) 'Tomorrow's management', *Fortune*, reprinted in John G. Hutchinson, *Readings in Management Strategy and Tactics*, Holt, Rinehart and Winston, New York (1971) pp. 539–51.

Webb, James W. (1969) *Space Age Management: The Large Scale Approach*, McGraw-Hill, New York.

Weber, Max (1904, 1930) *The Protestant Ethic and the Spirit of Capitalism* (trans. by Talcott Parsons), Scribner, New York (orig. publ. 1904).

'Weeding out auto plants', *Business Week*, 22 May 1971, 36.

Weiner, Bernard (1972) *Theories of Motivation: From Mechanism to Cognition*, Markham Publishing, Chicago.

Weinstein, Gerald and Mario D. Fantini (1970) *Toward Humanistic Education: A Curriculum of Affect*, Praeger, New York.

Weissbourd, Barnard (1964) 'Segregation, subsidies, and megalopolis', Center for the Study of Democratic Institutions, Santa Barbara, Calif., Occasional Paper No. 1 on The City, 1–12.

White, Ralph K. (1971) 'Selective inattention', *Psychology Today*, **5** (6), 47–50+.

Wohlking, Wallace (1970) 'Attitude change, behavior change: the role of the training department', *California Management Review*, **13** (2), 45–50.

Wyatt, S. and R. Marriott (1956) *A Study of Attitudes to Factory Work*, Medical Research Council, London.

Zand, Dale E. (1969) 'Managing the knowledge organization', in Peter F. Drucker (Ed.), *Preparing Tomorrow's Business Leaders Today*, Prentice-Hall, Englewood Cliffs, N.J., pp. 112–36.

Zehr, Leonard (1972) 'Many in Canada say their socialized medicine plan treats the ill but also treats too many of the well', *The Wall Street Journal*, 6 November, 28.

Index

235

236

Middle East, 11
Mission-control centres, 190-192
Missions, organizational, 64, 95-96, 136, 139, 145, 187, 189-191, 196, 218-219
Models, change responsive, 168-170, 189-193, 210-212, 220
Modular organization, 189-195
Monetary crises, 2, 10
Monetary policy, 116
Monopolies, 11, 47
Monte Carlo strategy, 14
Motivation, 100-104, 177-179, 183
    assumptions, 60-65, 160-161, 201
    change in, 7, 52, 164, 183, 193, 200
    institutional dismotivation, 15-18, 48
Motor car (see Automobile)
Multinational corporations:
    concept of, 6-7, 24
    national bias, 7, 153
    size by sales, 21

NASA, 41-42, 45
National Health Scheme (UK), 16, 27
National Training Laboratories, 198
Nationalism, 7, 10
Nationalization of industry, 6, 8, 12, 14, 148, 218
1984 (Orwell, G.), 72
Nissan Motor (Datsun), 62, 143, 155
Normative organizations, 100
Norms, 48, 51, 68

Obsolescence, 25, 33, 38, 44-45, 47, 52, 109, 160, 165-166, 181, 213
OECD, 22, 68
One world era, 56-58
Operations research, 89, 94
Opportunity, 49-50, 170
Organic organizations, 96
Organization:
    adaptive, 82, 127, 199-200
    bureaucratic, 46, 61-65, 90, 96, 136, 185, 202, 217
    centralization of, 91-95, 187, 195
    change responsive, 82-83, 87-88, 94-95, 123-124, 180-181
    characteristics, 53, 81-82, 96, 181
    climate, 132, 182-185, 196-197, 203
    decentralization of, 91-95, 187, 195
    democratic, 97-99
    development, 89, 125-126, 197-200
    differentiation, 89-90
    flexible, 47, 50, 89, 95, 188-197, 203, 210-211, 214
    free-form, 97, 189, 214
    hierarchy, 90, 96, 99, 117, 184, 197
    integration, 89-90, 95
    matrix, 181, 189

modular, 189-195
rigidity, 63, 88, 117, 144-147, 188
sclerosis, 90-91
slack, 91
stability, 95
structure, 183, 185, 189-195, 199, 202-203
temporary, 97, 188-189, 202
theory, 60-65
Orwell, G., 72
Ostpolitik, The, 10

Packaging industry, 144, 150
Pan American World Airways, 147-148
Panama Canal, 26, 39
Percy, Senator C., 39-40
Petroleum industry, 150-151
Pharmaceutical industry, 48-49, 151
Philippines, 34
Planning:
    central, 216
        in France, 69, 216
    national, 69
    long-range, 89, 138-140, 149, 180, 188, 207-208
Polarization of perception, 52-53, 81
Pollution:
    atmospheric, 39-40
    second-order effect, 39
    social cost, 49
    water, 26
Pompidou, G., 75
Population changes, 20, 26, 59
Post-industrial society, 56-60, 63-64, 70, 72, 77, 96, 127
Power:
    centrality of, 95, 185
    forms of, 54, 104
    industrial concentration, 23-24
    national, 41, 54
    shifts in, 40, 86-87, 199
Poverty, 10, 15-16, 105
Prediction, 29, 38-40, 55
    astigmatism, 45-48
Pre-industrial stage, 56-59, 66
Price changes, 54, 68, 84, 105
Proactive strategies, 82-83, 98
Pro-change, 111-112
Production, 90
    capacity, 84, 148-150
    input factors, 35, 44
Productivity:
    increases, 34-37, 84, 150
    resource needs, 44-45, 203
    (*See also* Economies of Scale)
Profile of Organizational Characteristics, 184, 198
Profit, 218
    centres, 93, 173, 181

Vietnamese war, 52
Volkswagenwerk, 21, 62, 85, 153, 155-156

Wales, 7
Wankel, F., 143
   engine, 143, 155
Watson, T. J., Jr., 147
Weber, M., 57, 61
Welfare economists, 17
Welfare state, 2, 7, 15-18

Westinghouse, 21, 46
Wilson, F. P., 84
Wohlking, W., 199

Xerography, 118

Youth, 3, 60, 68, 102, 127, 165

Zeitgeist, 56
Zero-sum game, 67, 84